THE DEBT SHALL DIE WITH THE DEBTOR

The Story of CUNA Mutual Insurance Society

We must dare to think "unthinkable" thoughts. We must learn to explore all the options and possibilities that confront us in a complex and rapidly changing world. We must learn to welcome and not to fear the voices of dissent. We must dare to think about "unthinkable things" because when things become unthinkable, thinking stops and action becomes mindless.

—*J. William Fulbright*

THE DEBT SHALL DIE WITH THE DEBTOR

The Story of CUNA Mutual Insurance Society

ISBN 0–9630549–0–2

Manufactured in the United States of America.

**Research, writing, design and production by
Hakala Associates Inc., St. Paul, Minnesota**
Project director: William Hakala
Writer: Philip Strand
Designers: Victoria Hakala, Brent Kastler
Production coordinator: Colleen Riley
Copy editor: Ellen Green

Contents

Acknowledgments and Sources

Millions of dedicated people built the credit union movement. The list of those who contributed to this project is somewhat smaller, but their commitment is no less evident. *The Debt Shall Die With The Debtor* could not have been completed without the cooperation and assistance of numerous credit union people who shared with us their recollections, opinions, and, most importantly, their love for the movement.

We are especially grateful to the CUNA Mutual Board of Directors history committee: Chairman Franklin Miroff, Robert Curry, Paul Deaton, Clyde Dwyer, Richard Heins, Robert Kratt, Gerald Ring, and Donald Roby. The committee provided useful perspective without attempting to color the ultimate direction of the story. Their trust made our work easier, and their enthusiasm made our job a pleasure.

Thanks also to the staff assistants to the history committee: Charles Eikel III, Martha Ann Robbins, and Richard Radtke, who, as CUNA Mutual's senior public relations officer, deftly coordinated the project and was a valuable liaison between us and the company.

Special thanks are also due the more than forty credit union leaders we interviewed in 1989 and 1990. These interviewees, some of whom gave us several hours worth of memories, especially aided our understanding of the last thirty years of the credit union movement and CUNA Mutual. The interview participants are named on page viii.

Researching in the CUNA Mutual Archives made us feel at times like children in a toy store. Almost everything we wanted was there: personal correspondence, office memos, diaries, biographies, political propaganda, court documents, company publications, annual reports, press releases, and photographs. CUNA Mutual has also collected newspaper and magazine articles and books written about the movement. Because of this historical diligence, most of the research material used to write and produce *The Debt Shall Die With The Debtor* came from the CUNA Mutual Archives.

We are deeply indebted to CUNA Mutual's archivist, Menzi Behrnd-Klodt, who, with her assistants, built the society's archives from nothing during this project, transforming the chaotic contents of scores of boxes into an orderly and comprehensive collection. Menzi contributed immensely to our research as an archival guide, diligently made thousands of copies, and was a prompt and reliable verifier of facts.

We also relied greatly on verbatim minutes from CUNA meetings and conventions of the 1940s and 1950s. Besides increasing our understanding of political issues, the minutes gave us the chance to enliven the story with dialogue. We are grateful to Gabriel Kirkpatrick, CUNA and Affiliates' archival librarian, for making hundreds of pages of minutes available, as well as many photographs.

Acknowledgment is also due the late CUNA leader R. C. Morgan, who entrusted us with one of two existing verbatim copies of the CUNA Mutual-CUNA-CUMIS insurance committee studies of the early 1960s.

In the mid-1960s, CUNA Mutual's Howard Custer conducted interviews with numerous CUNA Mutual and CUNA pioneers, many of whom, like Charles Hyland and Dora Maxwell, were present at the creation of the organizations. These intimate, candid, and sometimes opinionated conversations provided indispensable detail and analysis.

Custer's interviews with Hyland, Maxwell, Cliff Skorstad, Louise McCarren, Willard King,

Herbert Evans, M. A. Pottiger, Roy Bergengren, Jr., Louis Bonderefsky, R. A. "Doc" West, Claude Orchard and Moses Davis helped us understand the early years of the movement and the characters of its leaders. His conversations with Tom Benson, John Colby, E. K. Watkins, Charles F. Eikel, Jr., William Tenney, and Marion Gregory traced postwar events, such as the Truman visit, and provided many valuable details of events leading to the political split between CUNA Mutual and CUNA. Custer's talks with Carlos Matos and Stan Arneil aided our study of international development, and his discussions with George Berquist, C. Gordon Smith, Donald Smith, and J. D. Nelson MacDonald bolstered our description of the Canadian credit union movement.

Several books contributed to our research. Foremost was *Crusade*, Roy Bergengren's inspiring account of the birth of the credit union movement. Other Bergengren books, *CUNA Emerges* and *I Speak for Joe Doakes*, also were helpful. *Liberal's Progress*, an entertaining, comprehensive analysis of Edward Filene by Gerald W. Johnson, helped us round out Filene's enigmatic character and philosophy. Charles Hyland's *I Rode With the Captains* captured the spirit and humor of his experiences on the road organizing credit unions and the early CUNA Mutual office. *10 to 10: Canadian Credit Unions from 10 Cents to 10 Billion Dollars in 75 Years,* by Fred McGuiness, aided our understanding of the roots of the credit union movement in Canada. *A Century of Commitment: Lutheran Mutual Life 1879-1979* detailed the history of Century Life. Special recognition must be given *The Credit Union Movement: Origins and Development 1850 to 1980,* by J. Carroll Moody and Gilbert C. Fite, which served as our primer of the major developments of the movement and was an impor-

tant corroborating source.

Other valuable sources included Edward Filene's diary of his trip to India and his lengthy obituary in the *New York Times* on September 26, 1937. Articles in the *Journal of Commerce* on April 25 and May 6, 1957, described the tension between cooperative leaders and CUNA Mutual supporters. "When Change and Continuity Collide: Capitalizing on Strategic Gridlock in Financial Service," an article by Erich W. Sipple in the Spring 1989 issue of the *California Management Review* contributed to our study of conditions that led to the CUNA Mutual-Century Life affiliation.

Finally, a word on style. Because we approached the project both as storyteller and historian, we selected not only the elements and events essential to an understanding of CUNA Mutual's development, but those that best moved the narrative forward. In our telling, we occasionally edited quotes for grammatical purposes or space requirements, but only when it did not affect meaning or context. We also reconstructed scenes and dialogue, carefully relying on written accounts, recollections of people involved in the incidents, and, in many cases, verbatim minutes.

The result, we believe, is an instructive and informative history, and a candid, compelling, and human story as well.

—W.H.

Interview Participants

The following individuals were interviewed
for *The Debt Shall Die With The Debtor:*

A. A. (Paddy) Bailey

James C. Barbre, Jr.

George W. Berquist

John Brady

W.F. Broxterman

Irving R. Burling

Jerry K. Burns

G. A. (Al) Charbonneau

James R. Cooper

Fred L. Crump

Robert L. Curry

Howard C. Custer

Paul D. Deaton

Clara DiLoreto

Clyde P. Dwyer

Charles F. Eikel III

Eunice Eikel

Julian E. Geiger

Samuel B. Harper, M.D.

Richard M. Heins

Robert Hood

A. W. (Al) Jordan

Michael J. Judge

Robert A. Kratt

J. L. Herve Lanctot

Harry E. Manzer

Carlos M. Matos

Mary Jean McGrath

Jack McLanahan

Franklin D. Miroff

R. C. Morgan

Humio Okimoto

William E. Phillips

John R. Prindle

Elaine Richgels

Gerald J. Ring

Martha Ann Robbins

R. C. Robertson

Marion M. Sachtjen

Rosemarie M. Shultz

Henry L. Timme

Richard J. Uphoff

John M. Waggoner

Leon A. Wagner

Robert L. Wermuth

James J. Yates

Foreword

Two years ago, when the CUNA Mutual board of directors was considering commissioning a history of our company, several questions were asked about the reasons for the project. The most important was "Why?"

Urgency was a primary consideration. Many significant records and documents had been lost, and many of the people who had participated in the building of CUNA Mutual had died. Some company pioneers had been interviewed, but nowhere had their memories been integrated into an overall story. An important by-product of the research leading to *The Debt Shall Die With The Debtor* is the collection of documents and recollections vital to our past; through our new archives, CUNA Mutual will preserve these records indefinitely into the future.

Another important reason for a corporate history is cultural. In the rush of everyday business, it is easy to overlook the contributions of the past that have made us what we are today. What we seek in recalling and analyzing the issues, events, and developments of the distant and recent past is a cultural memory. This memory is critical for us as an organization to understand what we are to be in the future.

A cultural memory should also be inspirational, motivating future leaders in the credit union movement and at CUNA Mutual to carry out their dreams and aspirations for meeting the needs of credit unions and credit union members. Readers of *The Debt Shall Die With The Debtor* may be instructed by the struggles and disappointments of our past and encouraged by the victories that were finally won. Who knows what benefits these enlightening lessons may confer on future generations of credit union members?

Enlightenment can also be entertaining.

The Debt Shall Die With The Debtor is an intriguing and compelling story, with colorful and dedicated characters, conflict in the pursuit of idealism, and moving examples of dedication, sacrifice, and faith. It is a tale of human beings, with all their strengths and shortcomings, doing their best to serve other human beings.

It has often been said that "those who fail to learn from history will inevitably be forced to repeat and relive the mistakes of the past." It is our hope that *The Debt Shall Die With The Debtor* will help us all learn from our history, as we search for new ways and strategies to fulfill our unchanging mission: serving the credit union movement.

—History Committee
Board of Directors

In 1933, millionaire Edward A. Filene toured nine midwestern cities, speaking about credit unions and economic issues. Among his stops was St. Louis, Missouri, where he visited the St. Andrew Junior Credit Union on January 27. Filene is at the center of the front row.

CHAPTER ONE

For the People

Progress is not the mere correction of evils. Progress is the constant replacing of the best there is with something still better.

—Edward A. Filene

Outside the city of Jaipur an ancient fortress rested upon a plateau rising almost five hundred feet above the plains of northwestern India. Ruins of temples and palaces stood inside its seven gates, along with a tower covered with ornate carvings.

Edward A. Filene scrutinized the tower, his keen eyes moving from carving to carving with a thoroughness rare among travelers. Filene had not come to India—part of his trip around the world in 1907—simply to peruse and enjoy, but to inspect, analyze, and question. Travel was one of the few luxuries the frugal Boston millionaire allowed himself. Constantly seeking information on social, economic, and political conditions around the world, he used his trips less as vacations than as fact-finding missions.

Outlined against the setting sun, hundreds of wild peacocks suddenly circled the tower. Feathers of blue and green collided with rays of reddish gold, and the resulting explosion of color and form seemed to bring the carvings to life. Sacred monkeys danced, mighty warriors clashed, and ancient gods tossed thunderbolts at each other. The colors fused in a brilliant stream of light, then disappeared. The tower was still.

Startled, Filene reached for his pencil and notebook, tried to write what he had just seen, then gave up. Writing while riding an elephant was not easy; he likened the experience to that of a drunk on an angry ocean.

Darkness had fallen when Filene and his guide started back to Jaipur. The elephant plodded slowly through poor villages at the base of the plateau, passing natives who came out of the night, some silent as shadows, others singing strange songs. The rhythmic lurch of the elephant, the stars and stillness, and the memory of the majestic tower overwhelmed the American traveler.

Filene had eschewed traditional—and safer—forms of tourist travel because he wanted to see the real India. The approach brought him face to face with stunning beauty but also exposed him to terrible poverty. "The average income in India is said to be not over two rupees or 66 cents a month per person," he wrote, "and that means a life deprived of everything but the scantest necessities and housing in herds like pigs in dirt. The average person can save nothing and if the harvest fails, famine kills more than a million."

Though touched by the love and peacefulness of the people, Filene, also devoted to facts and rationality, was frustrated by their seeming acceptance of fate. Asked by a native about being Filene's guide, Filene said he had already hired someone else: "You might have gotten the job if you had asked me earlier."

"No," the man replied. "If it were destined that I should have you, I would have you. Who shall fight destiny?"

In Calcutta Filene did meet a man who was fighting destiny. William Gourlay, a British official working for the Indian Civil Service, had voluntarily reduced his own rank and salary to work with a system of cooperative agricultural banks. Filene was intrigued: here was an idea that might help lift people out of poverty. He persuaded Gourlay to take him on a tour of rural villages to see how these cooperative associations worked. They hired a car and driver and set off across the Indian subcontinent.

The journey was arduous. The party often had to create its own roads and sometimes visited villages where the people had never seen an automobile. Some regarded the machine as a god, a belief Gourlay put to practical use when the car got stuck crossing a sandy riverbed. He took out a rope, attached it to the front axle, and announced that anyone wishing to receive heavenly favor should help Filene and him pull the car out. The extraction of the mired automobile was the first true miracle he had ever seen, Filene wryly recalled.

Filene learned that the poverty of the rural villages had little to do with acceptance of fate. The problem was usury. Many families had been for generations in debt, often born of money borrowed for a lavish wedding or funeral. "It is the custom and custom is supreme," Filene wrote. "The peasants are abstemious to a degree inconceivable to an American. They live almost entirely on rice and a few vegetables and very little milk. I have been unable to find that they indulge in a single pastime or amusement that costs anything. But no matter how poor he is, a man will not disgrace his family by omitting a celebration."

The moneylenders took advantage of this tradition, charging interest as high as 120 percent. Defaults were common, and many peasants lost their land. Forced to sell crops to the moneylenders at low prices and to buy seed and supplies at high prices, the villagers became, in effect, slaves.

When British agents investigated, they found most defaults due not to dishonesty but to unavoidable occurrences like death, crop failure, and loss of livestock. They persuaded villagers to become jointly responsible for their collective debts by pooling their funds in cooperative credit associations. The government helped by lending them sums equal to those they raised, at no or low interest.

Through the agricultural banks, the villagers could borrow money from each other at reasonable rates, about 12 percent per year, allowing them to pay off debts. Steadily the villagers worked their way out of poverty. This uncommon idea of common people helping each other fascinated Filene. When he returned to the United States, he wrote to President Theodore Roosevelt, urging him to consider adopting the idea in the Philippines. While Roosevelt was interested, nothing further developed. Filene turned his attention to other matters but main-

Though he wanted to be a lawyer, Edward A. Filene was forced as a young man to take over the family business when his father's health failed. He transformed it into one of the most successful and innovative retailing operations in the country.

tained a strong interest in credit associations.

The idea of cooperative credit appealed to Filene not only as a social solution but also as a business idea, for his beliefs were grounded less in altruism than in logic. He thought even the most selfish persons must be liberal, not only out of a desire to do good but also because it was in their interests.

He knew that usury flourished in America in part because banks rarely provided personal loans to working people. A student of mass production and distribution, Filene was convinced the country's economy would never reach its full potential if businesspeople continued their obsession with short-term profits through low wages and long hours. By contrast, Filene preached higher wages, lower prices, shorter hours, and low-interest credit, convinced that greater prosperity for the masses would increase their spending, leading to higher profits for business.

His introduction to credit associations strengthened those beliefs. The real wealth of the Indian moneylenders was not in their own money but in the prosperity of the villages from which they drew their incomes. Reducing that

prosperity through usurious interest rates made everyone poor. Whatever they could do to make the villages prosper would in the long run increase their profits. The same lessons applied to American business, Filene believed. The most valuable assets of a business were in the pockets of its customers.

That kind of thinking made Filene a paradox, and sometimes an outcast, in the atmosphere of economic Darwinism then prevalent in American business. But though they scorned some of his ideas, his peers could not ignore him. Filene was too successful. His store, Filene's, became one of the country's great retailing operations, and he was one of its richest businessmen.

He also became one of the world's leading thinkers. He would advise Woodrow Wilson and Franklin Delano Roosevelt, consult with Neville Chamberlain and Georges Clemenceau, and argue with Vladimir Lenin. He would champion pursuits as diverse as the League of Nations, the U.S. Chamber of Commerce, and the cooperative movement.

Filene always looked for a better way of doing things. Long before the system was first used by the United Nations, he conceived the idea of simultaneous translation, allowing people of different tongues to listen to the same speech at once. At a time when only the rich traveled abroad, he saw the economic possibilities of lower-priced fares. He recommended that companies develop special products for people with particular health problems like diabetes. He tried to bring water-skiing to America years before it was popular.

Filene was an enigma even to his admirers. He believed it a crime to pay more than something was worth, but he donated millions to numerous social causes. He could be petty and selfish in personal matters, but he was generous in projects involving many people. An autocratic employer, he nonetheless tried to turn his store over to employees. He loved children but was unable to get along with most adults.

Born in 1860 to Jewish immigrants, at age five he took a serious fall that kept him from participating in exercise or sports. He spent much of his childhood alone, reading and thinking. Young Edward also suffered from severe facial eczema, which flared when he was tense or nervous, limiting his contact with the opposite sex. By the time the condition cleared he was in his twenties and irreversibly attached to business and other pursuits. A lukewarm romance during his mid-thirties fell by the wayside when one night Filene interrupted a date to conduct business.

Though Filene was not religious, he practiced a kind of moral austerity, for he felt guilty about his wealth and was determined to use it to improve the world. He had little use for philosophy; his goals were more practical. He was anxious to effect social change, and even after he became financially secure, his moral ambitions led him to write: "I cannot think fast enough or logically enough to satisfy myself and allow myself to rest."

Filene at first satisfied his hunger for social change by applying his theories to business. Though he had wanted to be a lawyer and was set to enter Harvard, at age nineteen he was forced to take over the family business when his father's health began to fail. When Edward took charge, the Filenes had two clothing stores, the most successful a twenty-four-foot-square room in Boston.

Despite his lack of formal schooling, Filene became one of the most ingenious retailing minds in the country. He understood that the best merchants do not sell products but serve human needs. Good will expressed through high quality, low prices, and fair play was the best way to attract business; customers passed other stores by to shop at Filene's because of it. When Filene's ran out of an item, salespeople were instructed to tell customers where else they could find it.

Filene created the automatic bargain basement to fulfill many of the same principles. Thus his store could move goods that had not sold earlier, and his customers were assured goods priced to sell quickly. Items that did not sell in twelve days were reduced by 25 percent, then by 25 percent more every six days thereafter. Items not sold in thirty days were given to charity. The automatic bargain basement kept Filene's Boston store profitable during the depression of the 1930s, even when the eight floors above it lost money.

Though Filene paid high wages and provided many benefits, he was difficult to work for. He rarely explained the reasons for his actions and was unable to give praise for work well done. Because he saw through problems so quickly, Filene was disappointed when others did not reach the same conclusions. After years of study, he became convinced that cooperatives were the most efficient means of mass distribution, and he tried to turn his store into a cooperative by selling stock to the employees. To his surprise and dismay, they were not interested.

Filene also was disappointed by his brothers, who were part owners in the store. They tolerated experiments like the automatic bargain basement because they worked, but they worried about his preoccupation with new theories. Eventually his brothers, along with several top managers whom Filene had allowed to purchase stock, wrested control of the store from him. The defeat, though it left him very wealthy, ended his use of the store as a laboratory for distribution experiments.

With time on his hands, Filene turned his attention to social experiments. He gave to charity but viewed it as patching up rather than preventing damage. He preferred to fund organizations that sought solutions to social problems, and he donated millions to various community experiments.

Filene also renewed his interest in credit associations. In 1908, Pierre Jay, commissioner of banks in Massachusetts, became interested in cooperative credit as an alternative for poor people being preyed upon by loan sharks. He invited Alphonse Desjardins, a Canadian journalist who had promoted a form of credit association in Quebec called *caisses populaires* (people's banks), to speak to a group of Boston leaders about spreading the idea in America. Filene was among them.

Desjardins had learned about credit associations from leaders in England, France, and Italy; they had learned about them from Germany, as

had the British agent who introduced the idea to Filene in India. The first to develop practical credit associations or credit unions was Hermann Schulze-Delitzsch, a German legislator. His cooperative credit societies, founded in 1850, were democratic, providing loans based more on the character of the borrower than on collateral. All loans had to be approved by two other members, and the lending period could not exceed three months.

About the same time, Friedrich Raiffeisen, mayor of a small town in Germany, started an-

Edward A. Filene possessed both unquenchable curiosity and keen intelligence, a combination that always led him to seek a better way of doing things. He advised world leaders like Woodrow Wilson and championed pursuits as diverse as the League of Nations and the credit union movement.

MILESTONES

1909 First credit union in the United States chartered April 6 at Manchester, New Hampshire.

On May 21, Massachusetts enacted first credit union law in the United States.

1921 Credit Union National Extension Bureau organized July 1 in Boston, Massachusetts.

1934 United States Federal Credit Union Law enacted June 26.

Credit Union National Association (CUNA) founded August 10 at Estes Park, Colorado.

First federally chartered credit union formed October 1 in Texarkana, Texas.

other form of credit association to help farmers struggling from the effects of famine. Raiffeisen's initial credit experiments were essentially charitable associations underwritten by wealthy merchants and citizens. They were neither cooperative nor democratic; the merchants decided who could join and who could get a loan.

Raiffeisen's credit associations worked well only to the extent that they were supported by beneficent merchants, and he began to see that member control was critical to success. He looked to Schulze-Delitzsch's methods and introduced new regulations: Any farmer judged to be of good character by his fellow members could join. All members voted at the annual meeting, electing a committee to approve loans and ensure that borrowers used the money for productive purposes.

Unlike Schulze-Delitzsch, who viewed cooperative credit strictly as an economic tool, Raiffeisen viewed credit societies as a way of building community, of teaching and encouraging brotherly love. His emphasis on credit societies as means of social reform was important at a time when Europe was torn between capitalism and communism. Karl Marx was born the same year as Raiffeisen, and he completed *The Communist Manifesto* not long before Raiffeisen organized his first credit association.

Raiffeisen saw the same problems Marx saw: an immobile class structure in which the poor were dominated by exploitive capitalists. But Raiffeisen viewed self-help, education, and cooperation—not violent revolution—as the solution.

Filene agreed, arguing with Lenin over this same point. No matter how noble its goals, change could not be forced. People must come to see its benefits for themselves, through experience and education. "If I had a son who was not a socialist before he was twenty, I would disown him," Filene explained. "But if he remained a socialist after he turned twenty, I would also disown him."

Filene believed credit unions could be important educational tools. In a credit union operated by its members, everyone would be compelled to learn something about banking, the value of regular saving, and the wise use of credit.

Despite Filene's financial support, the American credit union movement grew slowly. By 1921, twelve years after the first credit union law was passed in Massachusetts, fewer than two hundred credit unions existed in the country, most of them in New York and Massachusetts. The credit union movement had stalled before it had begun, embroiled in internal disputes about how to proceed.

Filene was determined to activate the movement, but he had little time personally to devote to the effort. He needed someone to devote full time to the crusade. Filene found him when Roy F. Bergengren, a forty-year-old lawyer, visited his office to inquire about an opening for managing director of the Massachusetts Credit Union Association (MCUA). Something about Bergengren—an ability for colorful speech, perhaps a touch of the evangelist—impressed Filene. He offered the job to Bergengren, who accepted enthusiastically and went home wondering what a credit union was.

Tall and courtly in bearing, Bergengren was the son of Swedish immigrants who had settled in Gloucester, Massachusetts. He attended Dartmouth College, where he was named "Class Member Most Likely to Succeed—in an Argument." He became a lawyer, primarily serving the poor. Though he had not heard of credit unions, he was familiar with loan sharks. Many of his clients were unable to pay their legal fees because of 25 percent interest payments per month to other creditors. One man he knew had borrowed thirty dollars, paid more than a thousand dollars in interest, and then been sued for the thirty.

Bergengren made little money from law and decided to find other work after his discharge from World War I. He opened a candy business with a military buddy and was on his way to success when the cost of sugar unexpectedly jumped to a higher price than they were getting for their candy. The business failed. Heavily in debt, Bergengren sought out Filene.

Bergengren's career with the Massachusetts Credit Union Association, however, was nearly as unlucky as his candy business. Bergengren soon discovered that the association had been funded for several months by a bank overdraft that increased weekly, and the MCUA owed several thousand dollars. During the next eight

Roy F. Bergengren tried his hand at practicing law and making candy before he was hired by Edward Filene to promote credit unions. Bergengren is pictured in his World War I uniform with wife Gladys and their children.

weeks, he visited credit union supporters throughout the state, raising funds to eliminate the debt. Still, the MCUA had no prospects for future income, and its board decided to close it. Bergengren was ready to look for another job when Filene, impressed with the lawyer's ability to persuade, called him to discuss extending the credit union movement on a national scale.

"I am prepared to take one more chance," Filene said, "and will fund the effort as the field enlarges, if you will head up the effort."

Filene and Bergengren then entered into an agreement with four objectives: (1) to get the laws, (2) to organize several credit unions in each state as soon as legislation was complete, (3) to bring the number of credit unions to the point where it would be possible to organize self-sustaining credit union leagues, and (4) to establish a national association of credit unions.

As Bergengren left Filene's office, he

tripped over a typewriter on the floor.

"What's that doing there?" he asked Filene's secretary.

"I'm sorry," she said. "That thing is so old we're throwing it away."

Bergengren asked for the typewriter; he would need it to draft bills, write bylaws and text-books, and prepare information and correspondence. The typewriter became one of the first and only items of equipment, along with an old chair and desk, at the austere office of the new Credit Union National Extension Bureau (CUNEB).

In CUNEB's early years, Bergengren spent little time at the office. He was usually on the road, trying to convince state legislators to support laws enabling the organization of credit unions. In 1921, only fourteen states had such laws. In three years, Bergengren got credit union laws passed in six more states, laying the groundwork for future laws in a dozen more.

Despite these accomplishments, Bergengren realized that ensuing legislative success depended on showing rather than telling people that credit unions worked. With his wife, Gladys, he began to tour several eastern and southern states to organize credit unions. The experience was trying. For every meeting he could arrange with a group of workers at a store or factory, Bergengren was ushered out twenty times trying to organize others. One early organizational meeting was held in the corner of a work area while nearby ma-

Courtesy CUNA Mutual Archives

Destined for the trash, this old typewriter was rescued by Roy F. Bergengren, who typed on it most of the important early legislative bills, books, and correspondence of the credit union movement.

chinery operated at full speed. Bergengren had to shout at the top of his lungs, finishing just as his voice gave out.

Possessing a puritanical streak, Bergengren was often harder on himself than were the most skeptical prospects. After failing to organize a credit union one day, he punished himself on the train home by refusing a berth in the sleeper car and sitting up all night in the day coach.

Bergengren encountered two basic arguments against credit unions, the first being a general mistrust of new ideas. There had to be a catch; why would Filene and Bergengren do this work simply to help people? The second objection was cultural. "The plan you're describing is the same as banking," people would say. "Banking is for bankers. Ordinary people cannot manage money."

Many companies had employee stock purchase plans that in owners' minds made credit unions unnecessary. One personnel director told Bergengren that the company made regular deductions from employees' paychecks, putting the money into company operations. "That's the way our employees save," he said. "At the end of the year, as an expression of good will, we add 5-percent interest to what the employees have saved." But Bergengren discovered the company was paying its shareholders 10 percent! Such plans left the employees doubly vulnerable, for if the company went out of business, they lost their jobs and their savings. Other owners and managers, already lending employees money at usurious rates, naturally opposed credit unions.

Where an owner was interested in a credit union, indecision sometimes doomed its establishment. After making six presentations at one plant, Bergengren received an appreciative letter from the personnel director: "We are not ready to organize a credit union and may never be, but do not think that we are not interested."

Outside opponents slowed progress too. Bergengren once visited a small Iowa town at the invitation of a local priest determined to start a credit union in his parish. Plowing through high snowdrifts, they contacted sixteen people who promised to attend an organizational meeting that night. They didn't know the town's banker was following them, notifying those who owed the bank that he wouldn't look

Edward A. Filene, left, and Roy F. Bergengren.

Many early credit unions developed in urban areas. Among them was the Industrial Credit Union in Boston. By 1923, when this photograph was taken, it was the oldest credit union in Massachusetts. The sign on the treasurer's desk reads: "Be pleasant every morning until 10 o'clock. The rest of the day will take care of itself."

favorably on their attendance at the meeting.

That night, Bergengren and the priest sat waiting by a pot-bellied stove, but no one came. The priest, who died a few months later, was devastated. "I have seen men at moments of great discouragement," Bergengren wrote in his book, *Crusade,* "but I never saw a man take a reverse so hard."

But an idea as sound as the credit union could not be denied forever. The need for affordable credit was obvious to most companies and factories. On paydays, their offices were often crowded with sheriffs, installment officers, loan sharks, and process servers, all waiting for a

piece of the worker's paycheck. Enlightened owners and managers realized that employees deep in debt would have a hard time thinking about their jobs. A credit union might help.

Bergengren set up credit unions along the lines of Raiffeisen's credit societies. Members had some common bond of association, work, or neighborhood; current laws required at least seven people to sign an application for a charter. Loans could be granted only to members, at reasonable rates of interest (usually 12 percent) and only for "provident or productive purposes," such as medical bills or to build a house or garage, pay for education, or repay creditors. All earnings after deduction of administrative expenses and surplus were to be returned to members as dividends on savings. Each member had one vote no matter the number of shares.

Although some well-intentioned employers wanted to help by financially supporting or running the credit union, Bergengren made it clear that the money must come solely from members and be managed through their own elected officers and board of directors. Their common interest and control encouraged involvement, and involvement was critical to success.

Most employers granted credit unions space in factories or plants. Louis Bonderefsky, who worked for the Grand Central Railroad Station in New York, operated a credit union out of a corner where janitors kept their supplies. The credit union worked so well that his supervisor said he could take time off during work hours for credit union business, as long as this created no hardship for his department. Bonderefsky declined because he did not want the credit union to appear to take special favors. He put in long hours at the credit union before and after work, for little or no pay.

Teaching thrift was one of the credit union's most important goals. All members were encouraged to save regularly, if only a quarter or a few cents a week. Yet the credit union was careful not to become too conservative, denying loans simply out of fear. C. M. Harrell, the first treasurer of the Atlanta Postal Credit Union, had difficulty convincing members to apply for credit until an old employee who had broken his dentures decided he could do without no longer. He got a loan and repaid it promptly. Several loan applications soon followed.

Many early credit unions developed in urban areas, especially among railroad and postal workers, civil servants, and teachers. From these groups Bergengren cultivated an ever-widening band of disciples, who spread the word about credit unions in their industries and neighborhoods. Bergengren hired some of them as field workers, but others were volunteers. A few large companies, recognizing the value of credit unions, gave these people paid leave to accompany Bergengren and others to organize credit unions at other company sites.

"What we're trying to do," Bergengren told early credit union volunteers, "is like a man trying to move a heavy packing box. First, you've got to get the box up on one of its edges. When you can do that, the box sort of moves itself. It moves with you."

Because the credit union movement was "moving," Bergengren began to assume a supervisory and inspirational role, leaving the organization of credit unions to others, among them Claude R. Orchard, personnel director for a meat-packing company in Omaha; Dora Maxwell, an idealistic church worker from New York City; Joseph S. DeRamus, editor of an employee publication for the Chicago, Rock Island & Pacific Railroad; Angus B. MacDonald, a Canadian cooperative leader; and Hubert M. Rhodes, a postal clerk from North Carolina.

And there was Thomas W. Doig, a postal worker from Minneapolis. Doig answered a credit union advertisement in 1923, corresponding with Bergengren. He served as treasurer for the first credit union in Minnesota, the Minneapolis Post Office Employees Credit Union, and helped to organize many more in the state.

Short and thin, with a handsome face and sad, expressive eyes, Doig was energetic and ambitious. For several years, he worked all day at the post office, managed its credit union after work, then drove around town selling life insurance policies after supper. Much of his energy was born of necessity. Doig's mother died when he was fifteen, and his father, a stonemason, died eighteen months later. The Doigs were not poor, but Tom's older sister had to quit her job to care for her four brothers and sisters. Tom helped by selling subscriptions to the *Saturday Evening Post*. He worked his way through business school, studying by day and cleaning the school by night. After serving in World War I, he joined the post office.

Doig's energy was matched by his idealism. He was not much of a churchgoer and friends described him as "a devil on wheels," but he applied the Bible's lessons to his life with consistency and dedication. He had a fundamental urge to help people and was remarkably free of the cynicism expected from someone so familiar with life's hard knocks.

One winter Doig was walking with a minister he had helped to organize a credit union. The

Early CUNEB field organizers like Thomas W. Doig, center, spread the credit union message across the United States during the 1920s and early 1930s. During his career, Doig organized more than a thousand credit unions. Pictured with Doig in Alma, Georgia are, from left, George M. Gentry, president of the Georgia Credit Union League, and M. E. Jones, treasurer of the Alma Credit Union.

man had only a light jacket, and Doig removed his own heavy coat for him. "I've got another," Doig said. He didn't. Such incidents were typical of Doig. While some friends viewed him as naive, they nevertheless admired him.

Doig saw in the credit union a practical way to help people help themselves. His passion for the movement led Bergengren to offer him a job as a full-time credit union organizer. Doig wanted the job but realized it would take time away from his family.

"It's your decision," his wife, Beulah, said. But Doig sensed her reluctance and turned Bergengren down. For the next several weeks, Doig was unusually quiet, even morose.

"Take the job," his wife said.

"I made my decision. I'm going to stick by it."

A few weeks later, Bergengren wrote Doig: "I cannot understand how you can turn down such a great opportunity. I guess you're not really the man I thought you were."

Angry, Doig wrote back: "I want the job." In January 1930 he set up an office in Minneapolis and began traveling in the Midwest. He became one of the most prolific credit union organizers

in history, organizing more than a thousand during his career.

Doig did not rely on literature or statistics. He was successful because of his ability to bring a human side to his presentations. Pressure was unnecessary; the people had to convince themselves. Thus he sold with enthusiasm, with a zeal bordering on religious fervor. His message was simple: Credit unions offer a way to make life a little better. Doig's message might have seemed ingenuous except that the country had just entered the depression of the 1930s. People wanted a message of hope as well as practicality, and Doig gave it to them.

As Bergengren had found Doig, so Doig found other disciples for the movement. In 1930 he visited La Crosse, Wisconsin, to convince the fire department to organize a credit union. One of the firemen, Charles G. Hyland, believed a credit union was a great idea, but he did not trust Doig. After Doig's presentation, Hyland asked him for references. Doig rattled off the names of several banks, inviting Hyland to write them. Satisfied, Hyland signed the incorporation papers. Had he checked with the banks, he would have learned that most of them did not exist.

Doig told the firemen he would be back shortly to help them get started, but after a month Hyland became impatient and set up the credit union himself. By the time Doig returned, the credit union had $4,200, all out on loan. Impressed, Doig asked Hyland to take a job promoting credit unions.

"I can't," Hyland said. "I've put in twelve years with the department, and I don't want to lose my seniority and pension. Besides, I'm no good at talking to people."

"Well," Doig said, remembering a letter he had once received, "I guess I misjudged you. I thought I was a good judge of human character. I was sure you were sincere about credit unions, about helping other people. I guess you're just like other people, committed only on the surface."

Hyland was ready to take a swing at Doig. He was also hooked. After Doig convinced the Wisconsin Banking Department of the benefits of credit unions, the department hired Hyland as a credit union organizer, the only such position in the country. Over the next seven years, Hyland went through nine cars while organizing four hundred Wisconsin credit unions.

Unlike most organizers, who acted as if the group or company letting them start a credit union were doing them a favor, Hyland considered that he was the one offering the gift. He became particularly skilled at working his way past tough receptionists, sometimes using other salesmen's cards to get in, then relying on his gift of gab as well as his story to keep the managers from throwing him out.

Despite an initial reticence about public speaking, Hyland became an effective communicator. One of his stories concerned a young man seeking to borrow a hundred dollars from a banker.

"What do you have as collateral?" the banker said.

"I don't have any."

"I'm sorry I can't help you, but I am a sporting man and I'm willing to make you a proposition. I happen to have one glass eye. If you can tell me which one it is, I'll make you the loan."

"It's your left eye, sir."

The banker was amazed. "How did you know?"

"Well, sir," the young man said. "I thought I saw a glint of human kindness in your left eye, so I knew it had to be made of glass." The harder the crowd laughed, the faster Hyland took out the incorporation papers.

Hyland, Doig, and sometimes Orchard traveled together during the depression. Life on the road was often wearisome, full of long days, uncomfortable hotel beds, and endless driving. The three men often gave presentations in rural buildings so cold they had to wear heavy coats and gloves.

On one trip to northern Wisconsin, Hyland and Doig happened upon two men standing by the side of the road. The temperature was well below zero, and the men showed signs of hypothermia. Hyland and Doig helped them into their car and started to push the other auto into a nearby town. The bumpers did not match well so Doig, who was not adequately dressed, sat on the hood to get them aligned. By the time they reached town, Doig was in bad shape.

"If I get pneumonia and start to act out of my head, don't call my family," he told Hyland. "I'll come out of this all right. I've been sick on

Courtesy CUNA Mutual Archives

Though crippled with polio, Ralph G. Long, right, of Decatur, Illinois, was one of the most energetic of the early credit union pioneers. Long and several members of the Decatur Fire Fighters Credit Union traveled to Oklahoma in the 1930s for the International Fire Chiefs' Convention in Oklahoma City. With Long is Edward Bretz.

the road lots of times." Doig ran a high fever for several days. Then the two men moved on.

Ironically, the credit union movement made its greatest strides during the depression, primarily because it impressed upon working people the importance of thrift and inexpensive credit. The speculators and financiers, the banks failing by the thousands, would not help them; only they could help themselves. The hard times helped convince legislators, too. Several states passed credit union laws in the early 1930s, and the number of credit unions rose to nearly three thousand.

Bergengren was the credit union movement's cheerleader, constantly reminding the movement that better times were ahead. Credit union members had to be more careful with their money when there was less of it. Any amount a member could save was encouraged. Pennies and nickels helped keep the credit unions afloat, and even Bergengren was surprised to learn how resilient credit unions could be. While banks were failing left and right, few credit unions closed. When they did fail, it was usually because they had placed reserves in banks that failed or invested too heavily in bonds or real estate.

Credit unions survived the tough times because they invested in people. One credit union had assets of ten thousand dollars and more than eight thousand in loans outstanding when the plant in which it was located closed for seventeen months. When the plant reopened, the credit union members, few of whom had found new jobs, had reduced their loan debt to eight hundred dollars.

Edward Filene watched all these developments with quiet satisfaction. He had done little actual work with the credit union movement, but he continued to fund the effort. By 1933 Bergengren, a master of promotion, decided it was time to put Filene to work. The New Deal was getting started, and Filene was one of the few businesspeople who had given their full support to President Franklin D. Roosevelt. Filene's ideas made news, and it was time for some free publicity.

In January 1933, Filene toured nine cities in five midwestern states in twenty days, making thirty-six speeches to various credit union and business groups. As earlier, his opinions created a stir. During an address in Indianapolis he chastised bankers for their myopia. "In their minds," Filene said later, "a working man who had broken his leg should not ask for a loan, although a manufacturer who had a broken-down plant might be expected to do so. A good leg was not looked upon as a problem for banks to worry about. Banks were organized to serve business needs; the fact that businesses must have people with good legs was somehow overlooked." Filene got more than a few boos from the bankers in the audience.

But Filene also criticized "emotional" charity: "The three greatest enemies of modern progress are poverty, ignorance, and charity," he said. "The greatest of these is charity. Even in worthy cases, it is often difficult to give help without wounding the self-respect of those who are helped. Mere relief of suffering is never enough. Cooperation with the sufferers to prevent suffering is of the greatest humane use. The credit unions of America would be worthwhile even if they had done nothing more than to foster this kind of Americanism.

Thomas W. Doig's appointment book shows scheduled stops in Illinois, Iowa, and Minnesota.

They have shown the way of self-help to thousands."

The Filene tour made big news. Lillian Schoedler, Filene's assistant, calculated that the tour received eighty thousand lines of free newspaper publicity, worth about forty thousand dollars at the going advertising rate. Filene, who had spent over three thousand dollars to fund the tour, figured he got his money's worth. But his reward was more than financial. The tour showed Filene his faith in credit unions was well founded. He appreciated credit union members, many of them poor and some poorly educated, people with whom he had little in common. His peers in business and industry had turned a deaf ear to many of his ideas, but credit union people believed in him.

A reporter later wrote of one meeting: "I have seen a good many demonstrations but nothing that quite equalled that given the founder of the credit union movement . . . It was not the volume of the cheering or the duration that impressed. It was the spontaneous love of disciples for a master . . . Filene was visibly touched by these demonstrations by the plain people to whom he had given only an idea."

The tour demonstrated the unity of the movement, but Filene and Bergengren were often privately divided over its direction. While they were committed to the same goals and shared a mutual respect, both men were strong-willed and stubborn. Each was sensitive about receiving recognition for his contributions. Once when Bergengren was introduced at a meeting

The board of directors and credit committee of the Marathon Paper Mills Employees' Credit Union in Rothschild, Wisconsin. Pictured, from left, front row: H. Holt, R. Sanders, J. Rucinski. Second row: R. Oatman, G. Till, J. Pflieger, and N.J. Dumdei. Back row: T. Norton, N. Cota, J. Majeski, J. Cress, and F. C. Wendorf.

as Filene's employee, he whittled a new pencil into a short stump, a typical sign he was upset. Later, the speaker was emphatically informed that Filene and Bergengren were "partners."

If so, Filene was the partner with the money. His most loyal assistants acknowledged he was difficult to work for. A bachelor, he often worked evenings as well as days, and he expected Bergengren, who had a family, to do the same. Though Filene often told others what a good job Bergengren was doing, he rarely said so to the CUNEB director.

The two leaders argued often and vigorously over strategy, Bergengren's salary, CUNEB's annual appropriation, Filene's reluctance to hire new field organizers, and Bergengren's penchant for ignoring instructions. Bergengren was regularly fired, only to be instantly rehired. Their battles drove Bergengren to describe Filene as the epitome of the human condition: part God and part devil.

There were good times. Filene never forgot Bergengren's children on their birthdays, a practice that continued until their late teens.

When they traveled together, Filene always enjoyed himself when Bergengren talked him into attending a movie or play, though he fought the idea they should relax at night. In Louisville, Kentucky, after a hard day at the legislature in Frankfurt, the two men saw a staging of *Macbeth*. When the lead, an aging Shakespearean actor with a wooden leg, struggled but completed the duel scene, Filene became so excited he stood up and shouted, "Bravo!"

Filene and Bergengren's biggest arguments centered on credit union legislation. Filene believed the best way to proceed was state by state—educating, organizing credit unions, and building grass-roots support. Bergengren had agreed, but by 1933 he believed the state-by-state approach had reached its limit. Forty states already had credit union laws, and small but powerful groups of hostile legislators prevented favorable legislation in the rest of the states. Bergengren thought it futile to fight these opponents when the passage of a federal law would instantly override their opposition.

Bergengren urged Filene to use his influence with the new Roosevelt administration to help pass a federal credit union law. Although Filene refused, firing Bergengren for a few hours, Bergengren went ahead. He typed the original

Courtesy CUNA Mutual Archives

Help for the Little Man

Few "people" have made such a large contribution to the credit union movement as the Little Man Under the Umbrella. The cartoon was created in the late 1920s by Joe Stern, editorial cartoonist of the *Boston Herald*, at the request of Roy Bergengren, head of the Credit Union National Extension Bureau. Bergengren wanted a symbol to represent the common people of the credit union movement.

The Little Man appeared in various poses over the years, sometimes carrying an account book or insurance policy; he also went to the beach, to war, and to Christmas parties. The Little Man Under the Umbrella was the most popular and recognizable symbol of CUNA, affiliated organizations like CUNA Mutual, and the credit union movement. Copyrighted in 1936, the Little Man Under the Umbrella continued as the official CUNA trademark until the 1960s.

Among the Ohio delegates to the Estes Park convention in 1934 were Louise McCarren, a member of the personnel department at the Kroger Company in Cincinnati, and Claude E. Clarke, an attorney from Cleveland.

bill on the old typewriter he had stumbled over outside Filene's office.

Congress, occupied with New Deal legislation, did not get to the bill for several months. In the meantime, Bergengren cultivated several supporters of the bill, especially Senator Morris Sheppard and Congressman Wright Patman, both of Texas. After a whirlwind campaign session, Congress passed the bill.

Filene had no part in the legislative effort but wrote to President Roosevelt after the bill passed, encouraging him to support it. Roosevelt signed the Federal Credit Union Act into law on June 26, 1934.

By then, three thousand credit unions were operating in almost forty states with almost half a million members. Bergengren decided it was time to move toward the last of the four goals he and Filene had agreed upon thirteen years earlier: a national association of credit unions. But

Filene opposed the move. Only five states had effective credit union leagues (though several more had loose organizations), and only that of Massachusetts was self-supporting. It was too early for a national organization, Filene insisted. He threatened to eliminate Bergengren's funding should he try to organize a national association on his own.

Bergengren feared he might lose the funding anyway. He sent all the credit unions questionnaires, asking whether they were willing to join state leagues and pay dues. He also asked for suggestions about how a national organization should be organized, managed, and financed. Most credit unions favored a national association. In April 1934 Bergengren invited seventy credit union leaders from states across the country to attend an organizational meeting in August. Fifty accepted.

The meeting convened at a YMCA camp in Estes Park, Colorado, nestled in the Rocky Mountains. Credit union leaders figured that if they had to give up their summer vacations to attend the meeting, it might as well take place in a vacation spot. Bergengren made the arrangements, then learned that only a few rooms had baths. He wrote the camp director to cancel.

"You owe $1,800 to cover loss of business," the director wired back.

Bergengren called the director: "We're coming."

Most of the delegates met in Chicago, traveling west to the Rockies by train. Among them was Louise McCarren, a representative of the Kroger Grocery and Baking Company in Cincinnati, who had organized several Ohio credit unions. News of her work had reached Bergengren, and he was anxious to meet her.

A few hours after the train left Chicago, McCarren, who had been deeply absorbed in a book since boarding, decided to cool off in the air-conditioned observation car. There she saw a woman with gray hair arguing loudly with a tall, distinguished-looking man.

"I know she missed the train!" the woman said, frustrated. "I have walked through this entire train and asked every woman if she was Louise McCarren, and the only one I missed was some kid reading a book."

"I am positive she's on this train!" the man

CREDIT UNION NATIO

insisted. "She said she would be!"

McCarren interrupted. "You must be talking about me," she said. "I'm Louise McCarren."

The man's jaw dropped. Though in her early twenties, McCarren looked like a teenager, barely five feet tall with a close-cropped, boyish haircut.

"I...uh...I'm Roy Bergengren," he stammered. "This is my assistant, Agnes Gartland."

Suddenly Bergengren scowled. "Here we are going to an important conference like this, and the Kroger Company sends me a young brat," he muttered and walked away in a huff.

Bergengren, recognizing the young woman's abilities, quickly got over his anger. He and McCarren, who would become managing director of the Ohio Credit Union League, eventually became close friends. After weeks of arguing

EXTENTION BUREAU-ESTES PARK, COLO. AUG. 7-10, 1934

about the meeting and the future of the movement, Bergengren also patched up his differences with Filene, and Filene decided to accompany the delegates, bedecked in a ten-gallon hat. A reporter from the *Christian Science Monitor* rode along, too.

The delegates and their families enjoyed horseback riding, softball, singing, plays, and hiking in the Rockies. They also worked hard.

Bergengren had anticipated disagreements over how the national association was to be financed. He believed it must be supported entirely by dues, proposing that each credit union member pay ten cents a year. Others wanted to subsidize the association at least partially through "hidden taxes," profits derived from ancillary activities like insurance and accounting supplies.

Fifty-two delegates signed the constitution and bylaws establishing the Credit Union National Association at Estes Park, Colorado, on August 10, 1934. The first to sign was Harold P. Winchester of Albany, New York. The last to sign was Leo Kaminsky of Indianapolis.

Before the meeting, Bergengren had written a supporter: "Personally, I think this business of financial support is going to be a good deal like the process to which my mother used to submit me in the spring, which involved a copious amount of sulphur and molasses—difficult to

In witness of our acceptance and subscription to this Constitution and these By-laws we hereunto set our hand at Estes Park, Colorado this tenth day of August, 1934.

tackle but doubtless good for the recipient."

He was right. A group led by Tim O'Shaughnessy, head of the Illinois Credit Union League, adamantly opposed Bergengren's dues proposal. Delegates from the largest states also disagreed strongly when Bergengren proposed that the national association's board of directors consist of one person from each affiliated state league.

"We have the majority of members and will be paying the majority of dues," they argued. "We won't be getting representation equal to our level of financial support."

When discussion overheated, delegates went outside and cooled off. The mountains surrounding the cabin where they met seemed to have a calming effect. Within four days, the delegates agreed to a constitution and bylaws that called for the national association to be supported by dues, leaving the amount to the national directors. O'Shaughnessy's group won a provision permitting each state one additional director, to a maximum of five, for each hundred credit unions in the state.

Bergengren decided the agreement should be signed on parchment, as were many historic documents. He and his wife searched several mountain towns for parchment with no success. Finally, they went to a small printing office to ask the aged proprietor whether he had any.

"I sure do," he said, "and I have been waiting twenty years for some damn fool to come along and buy it."

Fifty-two delegates signed the document, and the Credit Union National Association (CUNA) was born.

Having organized a national association, Bergengren and Doig turned their attention to creating its membership. Only thirteen states had formal leagues; unless several more were organized, CUNA would be little more than a paper organization. In four months, the two held meetings across the country, convincing credit union representatives to organize and support state leagues. By January 1935, thirty-three state leagues had ratified the national constitution and voted to apply for admission to CUNA.

Filene would die in Paris two years later at age seventy-seven. He was in Europe, attending an international cooperative conference, when he contracted pneumonia. He had almost died

Courtesy CUNA and Affiliates Archives

Edward A. Filene, Roy F. Bergengren and Claude R. Orchard of Nebraska paused for a picture during meetings at Estes Park in 1934. A special button, lower right, was created for the delegates.

the year before in the Soviet Union, and his doctors had warned him to slow down. Shortly before his death, on his way to Paris, Filene decided he must bag a chamois. He hired a guide and went hunting in the Alps. A picture of Filene and a dead chamois eventually found its way to Bergengren.

Filene's death made headlines. By 1937 he was less famous for his wealth and business success than for his economic and political insights. He was one of the first to denounce Hitler, warning that the world would regret its tolerance of his dictatorial ways. Filene later gave a large sum to a study of propaganda so people would recog-

nize and not be fooled by it.

While most of Filene's obituaries were admiring, some were not. Like most people ahead of their time, Filene often walked alone. Few people agreed on who he was. Charles Hyland once watched a poorly dressed newsboy shiver in subzero weather while Filene, one of the country's richest men, dug in his pockets until he found exactly six pennies for two newspapers. He said it was wrong to give the boy the impression he should be overpaid. Minutes later, Filene generously tipped a waiter, maintaining that tips were a vital addition to his salary.

Few of Filene's industrial peers understood

Shortly before his death in 1937, Edward A. Filene, age seventy-seven, was traveling near the Alps when he decided he must "bag a chamois." He hired a guide, got his chamois, and had a picture taken. The photo eventually found its way to Roy F. Bergengren and appeared on the May 1938 cover of *The Bridge*.

his economic thinking, which concentrated less on profits than on the happiness and prosperity of customers, which would guarantee profits. They scoffed when he proposed old-age and unemployment insurance, shorter work weeks, and higher wages. They derided him when he said: "I am for capitalism but not capitalism of the present order. Things will improve when businessmen get over their traditional 'age of scarcity' thinking and adapt themselves to the 'age of plenty.'"

If Filene did not always please his contemporaries, he almost never pleased himself. Despite his overwhelming success, most of what Filene considered his best ideas were failures. Some ideas failed even when people were interested or sympathetic because he lacked the patience and diplomacy to see them through. Filene was not prone to compromise, and he gave up on some projects when miracles did not occur. Shortly before his death, Filene said any biography written about him should be titled, "The Life of an Unsuccessful Millionaire."

But Filene never felt like a failure around credit union people. He had a great time at CUNA's first national meeting in 1935, putting on a lavish party for the national directors, even hiring a singer. When the singer's act became interminable, Filene turned to Ruth Davis, wife of national director Moses Davis, and said he would pay her ten dollars to tell the entertainer to shut up. Several minutes later, his secretary told him it was past his bedtime.

"I've got to go to bed now—she's making me—but you enjoy yourself," Filene told Ruth Davis. "Keep the party going as long as you can."

Filene kept the the credit union movement going at a critical point in its development. He never organized a credit union, and he was involved in the organization of the national association in only a broad way. But he was the movement's spiritual leader. He gave it life through his money and his reputation, and he gave it inspiration.

Edward Filene made millions, traveled the world, and advised presidents and kings. But his greatest moment may have occurred in 1933, during his credit union speaking tour. A thousand credit union members, along with a band, chorus, streamers, and banners, filled a Chicago

A Presidential Tribute to Edward A. Filene

He was a prophet who perceived the true meaning of these changing times. He was an analyst who was able, by mathematical calculation, to make it plain to us that our modern mechanism of abundance cannot be kept in operation unless the masses of our people are enabled to live abundantly. His democracy was, therefore, more than tradition. His liberalism was more than a formula. His faith was more than a mere assent to the principles which have proved to be tried and true. He did not repudiate the past, after the fashion of some reformers; nor did he repudiate the future, after the fashion of those who fear reform. He believed in learning, and in searching out the way of human progress.

—Franklin Delano Roosevelt

hotel ballroom. When Filene was introduced, several people began to march around the room. Soon the crowd was in motion, stamping and cheering and, as Bergengren recalled, "acting about as sensibly as do the delegates at a national political convention when the favorite son has been nominated."

Filene began to cry, probably for the first time since he was a child. As tears poured down his face, he turned to his longtime associate: "Bergengren, you didn't tell me it was like this!"

Staff and board members gathered in the first CUNA offices in 1935. Pictured, from left, are: Clifford O. Skorstad, Roy F. Bergengren, Jr., Earl Rentfro, Roy F. Bergengren, Percy Brown, Dora Maxwell (back to camera), Joseph S. DeRamus, Edward L. Shanney, Garfield Seibert, P. D. Holmes, Ben F. Hillebrandt, Charles G. Hyland, Thomas W. Doig, unidentified, Louise McCarren, Claude E. Clarke, Hubert M. Rhodes, Claude R. Orchard, unidentified, unidentified, Helen Logue, and unidentified.

CHAPTER TWO

Building the Foundation

Earl Rentfro: "Chief, do you realize we are an insurance company?"

Roy F. Bergengren: "Yes, and I am just as scared as you are."

George Feller hung up the phone. He shook his head slowly and took a deep breath. His face was ashen.

"What's the matter?" asked a clerk.

Feller, an accountant for the City of St. Paul and treasurer of the City and County Employees Credit Union, shook his head again.

"Remember that policeman who joined the credit union last month?" he said.

The clerk nodded.

"He was on patrol last night," Feller said. "Saw two guys getting in a car near city hall. Something didn't seem quite right, so he decided to see if they were okay. He didn't know they were escaped convicts. One of them shot him. He died this morning."

Feller opened his credit union ledger. The policeman had taken out a loan of five hundred dollars the week before.

"At least he didn't have a wife and kids," the clerk said.

"Yeah," Feller said. "But he had two cosigners. They are legally responsible, and they have families."

"Nobody forced them to sign."

"Maybe so," Feller said. "But it sure doesn't feel right."

Feller closed the ledger. He had gone into credit union work because it seemed a way to help others, but he hated this part of the job. It happened all the time. A credit union member took out a loan, then died suddenly or was disabled, leaving family members or cosigners responsible. If they couldn't pay, the credit union absorbed the loss.

"It doesn't make sense," Feller said. "We insure buildings, cars, houses. Why can't we insure credit union borrowers?"

By the early 1930s, credit union treasurers across the country were asking themselves the same question. They found few satisfactory answers. Some companies insured the lives of borrowers but only at extremely high rates. Small credit unions were treated differently from large ones, and some occupational groups, like police and firefighters, paid higher premiums. To gain new business, commercial companies sometimes paid to credit unions fees based on the amount of premiums collected; the fee often went directly into the pocket of the treasurer.

Roy Bergengren and other credit union leaders began to see that insurance was as fundamental to the movement as savings and credit, and they believed the movement should supply its own insurance. Most delegates at Estes Park had strongly agreed, though Edward Filene was initially opposed, for he thought the movement "was getting too far out of its field."

The Estes Park delegates, occupied with other matters, came to no agreement on an insurance program. But insurance was prominent on the agenda at the first meeting of the Credit Union National Association (CUNA) in Kansas City in January 1935. Several national directors, including Feller, testified about the overwhelming need for group credit life insurance. Earl Rentfro, director of the Missouri Credit Union League, said insurance policies carried by the league had paid over five thousand dollars on thirty-one claims in 1934.

"The credit unions do their best not to burden the families," he said. "But I know of cases where a credit union's reserve was too small to absorb the loss, and the treasurer had to collect from cosigners who couldn't buy shoes for their children."

There was little disagreement. The board voted to establish an insurance program and in-

structed the executive committee (a small group of national directors who ran the association between national meetings) to draw up a plan in six months.

The directors voted at the meeting to establish CUNA headquarters in Madison, Wisconsin, for a trial period of three years. The decision did not come until after long argument. Several preferred Chicago. Some thought Madison too small, too cold in the winter. Several cities and states made site offers to the association; a company in Kansas City even offered free rent for a year as an incentive.

But Filene and Bergengren liked Madison.

It was home to a prestigious university that might be helpful in research projects. The president of the University of Wisconsin, Glenn Frank, had once been Filene's personal secretary. The area had a reputation for encouraging liberal thought, and the government seemed friendly to cooperative endeavors. The Wisconsin Banking Department also had the only employee, Charles Hyland, devoted to organizing credit unions.

Madison was also centrally located. The credit union movement in the western United States was beginning to develop, as was credit union growth in Canada. Despite opposition,

The CUNA executive committee was appointed as the first board of CUNA Mutual. Charles G. Hyland was added to the insurance board and his picture cut and pasted onto a photo of the CUNA executive committee to create CUNA Mutual's board portrait. Front row, from left: Hubert M. Rhodes, Roy F. Bergengren, Edward A. Filene, and Earl Rentfro. Back row: Thomas W. Doig, Claude R. Orchard, Edward L. Shanney, Claude E. Clarke, John L. Moore, and Hyland.

Bergengren and Filene won out. But because the vote to make Madison the national headquarters was temporary, Bergengren was instructed to rent, not buy, property. He gave the assignment to Hyland, who found what seemed an ideal spot for seventy-five dollars a month. But an insurance company bought the building first.

Hyland located an old home renting for one hundred dollars a month. But after Bergengren okayed the agreement, the landlord doubled the price. Bergengren was livid.

"Maybe Madison doesn't want to be the site of the national headquarters!"

Hyland managed to talk the company into increasing its rent to only $125 a month. The property was in a residential neighborhood, next door to the governor's mansion.

CUNA Mutual was incorporated on May 20, 1935, at a meeting in Madison. The nine executive directors of CUNA were named to its board: Filene, Bergengren, Doig, Earl Rentfro of Missouri, Claude E. Clarke of Ohio, John L. Moore of California, Hubert M. Rhodes of North Carolina, Edward L. Shanney of Massachusetts, and Claude R. Orchard, who had just moved from Nebraska to Washington, D.C., to head the Federal Credit Union Bureau, recently created to regulate and organize credit unions. Hyland was

also elected to the first CUNA Mutual board. Despite his initial reticence about the insurance company, Filene had changed his mind, and he was named president. Bergengren was elected managing director, and Rentfro was named general manager.

Because the company was headquartered in Madison, operation under a Wisconsin charter seemed logical. The state was a leader in insurance legislation and regulation and had never had a major insurance scandal. The directors discussed incorporating elsewhere after learning that the state required mutual insurance companies to have at least twenty-five thousand dollars in original capital. But they settled on Wisconsin, deciding that a mutual company, owned by its policyowners, was most consistent with credit union philosophy.

Some directors proposed that credit union leagues pledge the start-up funding, but Bergengren, mindful that some wanted to subsidize the national association through activities like insurance, spoke against the measure. He also downplayed the suggestion that fifty or more members each borrow five hundred dollars from their credit unions towards the total. Throughout the meeting, Bergengren glanced at Filene, hoping he would offer to lend CUNA Mutual the money. But Filene said nothing. The matter was put on hold, and so was the company.

Sometime between May and August, Bergengren talked to Filene about a loan. Filene suggested CUNA Mutual borrow the money from the Twentieth Century Fund, which often invested money in cooperative causes. But the fund turned Bergengren down.

Filene was angry at hearing the loan had been denied, especially since he had endowed the Twentieth Century Fund with the bulk of his fortune. He lent CUNA Mutual twenty-five thousand dollars of his own money at 4 percent interest, a rate he jokingly called "usurious" because of his conviction that the insurance company was a wise investment.

Filene resigned as president in October, a few months after his election, thinking it un-

Courtesy CUNA Mutual Archives

Raiffeisen House, first offices of CUNA, CUNA Mutual and CUNA Supply Cooperative, 142 E. Gilman Street 1935-1940.

Raiffeisen House, first headquarters of CUNA, CUNA Mutual, and CUNA Supply, was located at 142 East Gilman Street in Madison, Wisconsin.

ethical to head a company to which he had provided a loan. He was replaced by Claude Clarke.

CUNA Mutual opened for business August 6, 1935, in an old house on the shore of Lake Mendota in Madison. Doig, Bergengren, his teenage son, Roy, Jr., and one of Roy's friends had come to Madison the week before to clean the place, which had formerly housed university students and fallen into disrepair. They scrubbed for days. Bergengren also hired plumbers, painters, and carpenters.

The house was christened Raiffeisen House in honor of the credit union pioneer. The national association occupied the first floor; CUNA Mutual took a couple of rooms on the second. CUNA Supply, an affiliate established to supply credit unions with bookkeeping and promotional materials, would be set up in the basement a year later. Two secretaries who had come from Boston to work for the national association lived in two other rooms. Rent for the building was $125 per month, of which $50 was charged to CUNA Mutual, $50 to CUNA Supply and $40 to the secretaries, leaving a $15 subsidy for CUNA.

Though Filene's loan made it possible for the insurance company to incorporate, it did not provide a plan. Shortly after CUNA Mutual's charter was issued, Bergengren, Doig, and Rentfro sat around a table, looking at the twenty-five-thousand-dollar note.

"Chief, do you realize we are an insurance company?" Rentfro said.

"Yes. And I am just as scared as you are."

The first job was to determine a premium rate. Other companies were charging from eight to twelve cents per hundred dollars of insurance per month. Rentfro suggested CUNA Mutual charge five cents per hundred. Doig said four. They split the difference and the company started at four-and-one-half cents per hundred dollars of insurance per month.

The first month's receipts totaled $145.22. CUNA Mutual received its first claim, for $40.00, three months later. Unsure of how to pay the claim, Bergengren went to the Wisconsin insurance commissioner and asked whether the company could pay claims out of its original capital. The commissioner emphatically said no, so Filene lent CUNA Mutual another $10,000.00.

Initially CUNA Mutual sold only individual credit life insurance. Policies were issued only to individual credit union members, who paid for the policies themselves. No real underwriting requirements existed: Any credit union member physically able to work or to resume work

This 1943 brochure advertised Loan Protection insurance from CUNA Mutual.

CUNA Mutual Insurance Society and the credit union movement had a symbiotic relationship. CUNA Mutual's Loan Protection insurance was a convincing incentive to join credit unions, and credit union volunteers and league personnel played a significant role in promoting and selling CUNA Mutual insurance. Hundreds of credit union members attended an Illinois Credit Union League banquet at Hotel Sherman in Chicago on March 18, 1939.

within a reasonable period was eligible.

The company's low rates had an immediate effect on the competition. Bergengren reported to the board that the organization of CUNA Mutual "caused the other companies writing individual credit life insurance to halve their rates, and we have already broken up the racket which the CUNA Mutual Society was organized to eliminate."

The company grew quickly. By September 1935 it wrote $193,000 worth of insurance on 1,669 loans made by 205 credit unions. By the end of 1936, CUNA Mutual's total coverage was more than $11,000,000, and it had paid 98 death claims totaling nearly $11,000. Although its assets totaled about $50,000 and the company was steadily paying off Filene, frugality was a priority: CUNA Mutual's first annual report was typed on a single sheet of paper.

Despite the company's explosive growth, Bergengren was dissatisfied with its individual credit life insurance. In his opinion, making individual borrowers pay for their own coverage was contrary to the credit union philosophy of equal service for all members, borrowers as well as savers.

SERVING THE MOVEMENT

CUNA Mutual's low rates had an immediate effect on the competition. Bergengren reported that the organization of CUNA Mutual caused commercial companies writing credit life insurance to cut their rates by half.

"The principle of putting the burden on the weak and protecting at all hazards the strong is the basic principle which has caused most of the industrial misery which has now encompassed the world," he argued. "If we adopt this principle . . . and if out of that cost we take support for our state leagues and our national association, we have gone on record as saying that we are in favor of the non-borrower, and we are going to make it as easy as we can for him, at the expense of the fellow who is paying all the bills."

Selling only to individuals also created a legal dilemma for some credit unions. Both the Wisconsin and federal credit union laws stipulated that interest and insurance charges could not exceed 1 percent per month on the unpaid balance of the loan. The cost of individual credit life insurance often pushed the cost of loans above that limit. Keeping track of individual payments was difficult, and some borrowers mistakenly paid their premiums twice.

To solve these problems and help credit unions better serve their members, CUNA Mutual introduced group credit life insurance in December 1935. The product, an industry first, was called Loan Protection insurance. The credit union paid the entire premium, providing coverage free to borrowing members. CUNA Mutual initially charged credit unions eighty-five cents per thousand dollars per month for Loan Protection coverage, but within months it lowered that to sixty-five cents per thousand. The latter rate remained in effect for many years.

(Why CUNA Mutual began expressing its insurance premium rates in thousands of dollars, rather than hundreds, is not known. Some speculate that the former method was used for the society's individual credit life contracts because nearly all individual credit union loans were for less than a thousand dollars. But with the introduction of group coverage and Loan Protection insurance, most credit union contracts were for a thousand dollars or more.)

Like everyone else, credit unions were caught in a money squeeze. The suggestion that they absorb the additional expense of insurance premiums met with little enthusiasm, especially when the demand for loans was already high. But one year after Loan Protection was introduced, CUNA and CUNA Mutual could show that credit unions offering the product grew much faster than credit unions that did not. Loan Protection quickly became one of the most persuasive selling points of credit unions.

"If you want a bank loan, you'll have to pay extra to protect it," credit union treasurers told potential members. "But with Loan Protection, you're covered—for free!"

Besides playing a vital role in the growth of

the credit union movement, Loan Protection became so popular that CUNA Mutual's individual credit life policy became virtually obsolete.

CUNA Mutual introduced another industry first in 1936: Loan Protection against total and permanent disability. For younger borrowers, the odds of disability were much higher than the odds of death, and disability prevented credit union members from repaying loans almost as effectively as death. CUNA Mutual offered Loan Protection with disability coverage for seventy-five cents per thousand dollars per month.

In 1938, having helped the credit union borrower, CUNA Mutual turned its attention to the saver. Credit unions were founded on the principle of thrift as well as credit. Yet studies showed that almost 75 percent of credit union members had only about five dollars in their savings accounts. Credit unions would not grow if this trend continued, and neither would CUNA Mutual.

To encourage regular savings, the company introduced Life Savings insurance. The first such product in the industry, the Life Savings contract insured the life of the borrower, for an amount depending on the size of savings at the time of death, up to a thousand dollars. (There were a few restrictions on savings received from members in higher age brackets). Credit unions paid for the service out of earnings; members paid nothing. Only 519 credit unions took advantage of Life Savings insurance during its first three years, but the product eventually became a critical factor in credit union growth.

The credit union movement also played a vital role in the growth of CUNA Mutual. By June 1941, just five years after receiving its charter, the society was providing a hundred million dollars in coverage, a remarkable feat considering it sold only by mail and had no sales force. The society's explosive growth was due almost entirely to local credit union members and state league personnel who spread the word about the benefits of its services. These "salespeople," who received no pay for their work, saw CUNA Mutual as their company, part of their movement. CUNA's Organization and Contact Department, whose main job was to organize credit unions, also encouraged credit unions to use the society's services. CUNA Mutual sent litera-

ture to credit unions promoting its services and advertised in *The Bridge*, the magazine of the credit union movement started by Bergengren.

When credit unions grew, so did CUNA Mutual, and vice versa. Between 1936 and 1941, when CUNA Mutual was growing so rapidly, credit union membership tripled, from 1,100,000 to 3,300,000.

Despite the success of selling by mail, Rentfro believed it essential that the company become legally qualified in every state. Some insurance departments warned CUNA Mutual not to do business in their states without a license. Claude Clarke, the company's legal counsel, emphasized that unlicensed companies often lacked even basic legal rights, making lawsuits difficult to defend.

Rentfro spent much of his time in the late 1930s on the road, talking to insurance commissioners, trying to get the company qualified. In 1940, the Indiana insurance department approved CUNA Mutual after the society added "insurance" to its name. But most states had surplus and reserve requirements that would take at least a few years to fulfill in the face of a demand for high dividends. In the meantime, Rentfro was usually able to work out agreements allowing the company to sell by mail until it could become licensed.

An Iowa native, Rentfro had worked as a rancher and railroad clerk before joining the credit union movement. He played a critical role in passing several state credit union laws and was Bergengren's right hand during the passage of the federal credit union law. Rentfro's ability to lobby legislators led Bergengren, whose persuasive talents were also prodigious, to offer Rentfro his highest praise: "Earl, you could walk through a snowdrift four feet high and never leave a footprint."

Bald and bespectacled, with a twinkle in his eye that belied his seriousness, Rentfro was an alert and clever manager. In 1936 CUNA Mutual had just one other office worker (though Rentfro's wife, Bess, had served as an unpaid stenographer during the company's first few months). Bergengren admitted Rentfro needed more secretaries but could not add any because the company lacked the funds.

When Rentfro told Bergengren he had to be

During the 1930s and 1940s, when smokers were plentiful, umbrella ashtrays were present at many credit union meetings.

Courtesy CUNA Mutual Archives

Earl Rentfro, Roy F. Bergengren, and Charles G. Hyland in the late 1930s.

out of the office for a week, Bergengren asked Hyland, who was still organizing credit unions for the Wisconsin Banking Department, to run the office in his absence. After a hectic week of opening mail, writing letters, and figuring pre-

miums, the weary Hyland recommended that Bergengren hire more staff for the insurance company. Hyland later learned Rentfro had no particular place to go that week. He had taken the trip, confident that Hyland would recognize

the need for more help and certain Bergengren would listen to him.

With Rentfro on the road often and sales expanding, the CUNA Mutual home office staff grew quickly through the late 1930s. A few secretaries in their teens needed child labor permits to work for the company. Most of the other staff members were under thirty, having just come out of high school, vocational school, or college. Besides Bergengren, the only employee over fifty was Rentfro, whom his young charges called "Pops" in his absence.

Among the CUNA Mutual employees hired in the late 1930s was Orville H. Edgerton, an accountant from Beaver Dam, Wisconsin. Edgerton, a talented drummer, was better known as "Orch," a derivative of his first two names. Other early employees were Jack Fortnum, the chief accountant who ran the office in Rentfro's absence; Ralph T. Peterson, who had worked as an accountant for CUNA Supply since 1935; and Thomas B. Benson, a recent college graduate whose knowledge of credit unions, gleaned from a banking exam, won him an accountant's job.

Most of the early office work involved accounting procedures. Ledgers were posted by hand. There were no actuaries and little underwriting, though staff members spent a lot of time discussing the placement of commas and language in contracts. There were no job descriptions; employees did what was needed.

The company had no public relations department, but Harvey Williams, the building's janitor and jack-of-all-trades, more than fulfilled the role. Williams had come to Madison from Kansas City as Rentfro's chauffeur, which Joe DeRamus discovered as Rentfro and he were preparing to go to lunch after an early board meeting.

DeRamus, who replaced Filene as a CUNA Mutual director after his death, tried to open the car door.

"Stand back!" Rentfro commanded. "Harvey will do that."

When Bergengren heard about the chauffeur, Rentfro was told to do his own driving and Williams was hired to keep the Raiffeisen House heating system in order. He also delivered the company receipts to the bank. An uncommonly cheerful man, Williams constantly promoted credit unions and CUNA Mutual during his deliveries, and he helped create greater awareness of the movement at a time when the average person in Madison knew nothing about credit unions.

Bergengren and Williams became close friends. The managing director treated Williams' family to a complete turkey dinner every Thanksgiving. When Bergengren learned the family had not been able to buy the house they wanted because they were black, he helped them buy another house.

Charles Hyland joined the CUNA Mutual staff in 1938, splitting his time as treasurer and

Among CUNA Mutual's early accountants were, from left, Thomas B. Benson, Orville H. "Orch" Edgerton, and Ralph T. Peterson.

CUNA and CUNA Mutual employees wished Edward Filene a Merry Christmas in December 1935. Front row, from left: Harvey Williams, Julian Grinde, Mrs. Grinde, Ruth Ryan, and Ralph Peterson. Back row: Printer Collum, Thomas W. Doig, Helen Logue, Roy F. Bergengren, Janet Bubier, and Jack Fortnum.

comptroller between the insurance society and CUNA and CUNA Supply. He was in charge of CUNA Mutual's investments and bank accounts, and he prepared statistics on death claims, the nature of death, and other topics.

Hyland often worked on the road. Among his responsibilities was signing checks for payment of CUNA Mutual claims. He was instructed to examine each death claim before signing the check. Rentfro, a cautious man, decided to check on whether Hyland was reading the claims. On his next trip, Hyland found a death claim with his own name on it, made out with a check.

The generally serious Rentfro and Hyland, a

fun-loving sort, tangled occasionally. After Hyland came to work for CUNA Mutual, Rentfro announced he had installed a buzzer system.

"Your call is five buzzes," Rentfro told Hyland.

The comptroller saw little use for a buzzer system in such a small place, and he decided not to answer it.

"Why aren't you answering your buzzer?" Rentfro asked.

"It's hard for me to count to five when I'm excited by such terrible noises."

Rentfro frowned. "I expect you to answer the next time I buzz you."

Upset, Hyland went outside to calm down. He discovered a small pail, got an idea, and filled the pail with rocks. He went back to the office and hung the pail and rocks between his chair and, unbeknownst to his secretary, her chair. He waited for quiet, then yanked on the chain. The secretary, a proper and efficient young woman named Ruth Mueller, nearly jumped out of her chair at the racket.

Rentfro dashed out of his office.

"What's going on out here?"

"I've installed my own buzzer system," Hyland said proudly.

Rentfro stopped using his buzzer system.

The CUNA Mutual office was otherwise quiet, for the employees were expected to work hard once they walked in the door. Women were to wear hats and gloves to work, and men were to wear coats and ties. Salaries were modest. Managerial employees averaged a hundred dollars per month in the late 1930s; clerical and secretarial workers averaged about half that.

Office hours were from 8:00 A.M. to noon and 1:00 to 5:00 P.M. with two ten-minute rest periods. For a time in 1940, the company dispensed with the rest periods and closed the office at 4:30 P.M. Many employees also worked Saturday mornings.

No matter how much it snowed, the office remained open and employees were expected to be at work on time, even if they had to walk. On November 29, 1940, Edgerton received this terse message from Rentfro: "Please explain your absence from the office this morning at 8:00 A.M."

Edgerton responded that he had left his house at 7:35 A.M. and driven his car half a block before it stalled. He ran his keys back to the house and tried to catch a ride but was passed by two cabs and a bus. He walked several blocks as four more cabs passed, hitched a ride, then caught a cab, and was at work by 8:15 A.M. Rentfro let him off with a warning.

Though the office was crowded, staff members enjoyed working at Raiffeisen House, which was fronted by a beautiful lawn stretching onto a high bank off the lake. The property had its own pier, and employees often ate there in the summer, then swam or played ball.

Because Raiffeisen House was very old, all male employees of the national association and its insurance and supply companies were expected to paint the porch before the national directors came to town for annual meetings. They also washed windows.

Raiffeisen House almost went up in flames in March 1938. A neighbor noticed smoke coming from the rear of the house. The fire department extinguished a fire, which apparently had originated from a defective flue in the ceiling above Bergengren's desk.

The CUNA Mutual office was scorched from one end to the other. Every desk had heat damage, and a large hole had burned in the floor. None of the records stored in the safe was damaged, but several others had to be reconstructed. All the doors and windows had been closed, keeping the fire from spreading. Rentfro later reported the whole building might have gone up had the firefighters not arrived when they did.

CUNA, CUNA Mutual, and CUNA Supply moved out of Raiffeisen House in November 1939. Their staffs had outgrown the space, and

Courtesy CUNA Mutual Archives

In November 1939, CUNA, CUNA Mutual, and CUNA Supply moved to new headquarters at 1342 East Washington Avenue in Madison. A two-story brick building, the structure's only claim to elegance was the gold-lettered spelling of "CUNA" over the entrance.

the rent had been raised to $250 per month. The executive committee of CUNA voted to move into a two-story brick building on East Washington Avenue. The building, used by the city to house transients, needed repair, and rats and mice ran freely through the dirty basement, which had served as a soup kitchen. After a thorough cleaning by employees, a cafeteria was built in the basement.

CUNA Mutual shared the second floor of the building with CUNA; CUNA Supply and the staff of *The Bridge* were on the first floor. The building served its purpose, but its only claim to elegance was in the four gold letters spelling out CUNA over the door. A CUNA Mutual employee would later observe that the effect of the letters "was like putting a Brooks Brothers suit on Gabby Hayes."

A Question of Control

A few years after CUNA Mutual opened, Bergengren hired an outside auditor to review the society's operations. After the auditor received his instructions, Bergengren asked him to come to his office later and detail ways to steal money from CUNA Mutual. Though the request bothered him, the auditor complied with the managing director's wishes.

"I know thirteen ways you can steal money from this company," the auditor said. "What are your intentions?"

"My intentions," Bergengren said, "are to have you show me how to lock up all thirteen leaks."

Bergengren knew there were other problems too. CUNA Mutual had been founded by people who knew much about the need for insurance but little about the business. Because its mission was unique and its products often without precedent, the company often operated by trial and error. Some of its decisions, like the first premium rate, worked out well. Others did not. Bergengren and Rentfro knew these problems might threaten the company's financial stability.

In 1940, CUNA Mutual hired E. F. Caldwell, an actuary, to study its insurance policies. Caldwell reported that CUNA Mutual's policies were ambiguous and imprecise. For example, the Loan Protection contract granting coverage to

"a person who is able to perform or within a reasonable time to resume the usual duties of his livelihood" was too open to interpretation. Coverage was often issued to people who had been disabled for years and sometimes to people on their deathbeds.

Caldwell believed the company, in its eagerness to serve credit unions, was too liberal in its payment of claims. CUNA Mutual sometimes received claims based on the deaths of cosigners or claims made after the loan had been paid off. Of the thousands of claims filed each year, only a few were challenged and fewer were denied. In 1940, the company paid 5,489 claims, denying only 10.

The actuary also cautioned CUNA Mutual against setting its rates too low by charging credit union members of all ages the same rate—sixty-five cents per thousand dollars. The rate was sufficient for young members, Caldwell said, but it was only a fraction of the charge needed to cover people over sixty five. As the average age of members and thus their odds of death increased, premium income would fall short of claims payments. Without making changes in its policies and practices, CUNA Mutual might go out of business.

"It is your purpose, as I see it, to provide liberal protection at low cost," the actuary wrote. "But liberality does not mean every claim presented should be paid. I do not believe it to be equitable to the large proportion of your credit unions, which are fair and reasonable in their presentation of claims, to have to cover the cost of claims originating in other credit unions where it is apparent the loans were made in anticipation of death."

"In the case of such a young and rapidly growing institution and one which holds such great promise for future development and service," the actuary continued, "it is essential that nothing be done to endanger its solvency either now or in the years to come. Anything which will impair the welfare of the society will reduce its usefulness to the members of the credit unions it is designed to serve."

Caldwell's report echoed what the Wisconsin Insurance Department had been saying about the company. The department was especially critical of CUNA Mutual's relationship with the national association that had created, promoted, and initially funded it. CUNA Mutual had been created as a legally independent entity, the department said, yet "the interlocking directorates of the two organizations have placed the company under the domination of the association."

Some overlap was unavoidable. The original board of CUNA Mutual had been comprised of the CUNA executive committee and Hyland. During the next few years, almost every insurance society director was also a national director of CUNA. By 1939, five CUNA Mutual directors, including CUNA president William Reid and vice president John L. Moore, also served on the CUNA executive committee.

The credit union movement saw this relationship as natural and synergistic. CUNA helped CUNA Mutual by promoting its services when it organized credit unions. By selling only to credit unions affiliated with CUNA, the insurance society's products helped CUNA build and maintain a strong membership.

Though the state insurance department recognized the benefits of the relationship, it saw dangers. "The desire of the association for abnormally low rates has manifested itself on more than one occasion," a department examiner said. "There may develop a disposition to encroach on the funds of the company to subsidize the association."

Although these charges were true, many credit union leaders did not view them as evidence of danger. How could low rates possibly hurt credit union members? Why should CUNA Mutual not support the national association? Bergengren devoted some of his time to the insurance company; it was only fair that the company pay part of his salary. CUNA Mutual was expected to cover a portion of the Organization and Contact Department's budget as well.

Politics was an issue in the subsidization argument too. Bergengren's belief that CUNA should be supported entirely by dues had prevailed at Estes Park but remained a volatile political topic since then. Some credit unions had left CUNA over the question. Mindful of growing unrest among state leagues who wanted their dues lowered, some CUNA and CUNA Mutual directors were beginning to believe unity within the movement depended on upping the insur-

ance society's level of support for the national association.

The Wisconsin Insurance Department was unmoved by these considerations. CUNA Mutual had been organized as a mutual insurance company. It belonged to its policyowners, not to the national association. That the company had the same goals as CUNA was fine, the department said. But it must "adopt its own policies free from the dominating influence" of the association. Most important, the state said, CUNA Mutual's managers were responsible for setting rates that would ensure the solvency of the society.

Aware that the insurance department might invoke tighter regulation over the society, some CUNA and CUNA Mutual directors began to fear CUNA Mutual might eventually escape the control of the national association altogether. At a meeting of the CUNA national directors in 1939, George Jacobson, a cooperative manager from Minnesota, said he had seen other mutual companies drift away from the organizations that had created them.

"CUNA Mutual has become so valuable to the credit union movement that we must take every precaution to safeguard its ownership and democratic control," Jacobson said. He moved that CUNA and CUNA Mutual enter a contract turning management of the insurance operations over to CUNA. The matter was referred to a special committee for study.

The desire for greater control of CUNA Mutual by the national association was based primarily on fear of the Wisconsin Insurance Department. However, disagreement between CUNA Mutual's managers and several directors of CUNA and CUNA Mutual also was a contributing factor. On the advice of the consulting actuary and the Wisconsin Insurance Department, Bergengren and Rentfro had tightened CUNA Mutual's contracts, restricted claims payments, and refused to decrease rates. It was bad enough that the insurance department was unfavorable to their vision of CUNA Mutual, several directors felt, and worse that Bergengren and Rentfro seemed too willing to do everything the state insurance department wanted.

Opposition to Bergengren had been growing among some CUNA executive committee members for several months. Because of his as-

MILESTONES

1937 In June, first **CUNA Mutual** contract written for a Canadian credit union: Dalhousie Industrial Credit Union Society, Ltd., in Dalhousie, New Brunswick.

CUNA Mutual became leading provider of credit life insurance in the United States.

1938 Life Savings coverage first offered by **CUNA Mutual**, an industry first.

1939 CUNA Mutual began offering individual life insurance to credit union members.

CUNA, CUNA Mutual, and **CUNA Supply** moved into new quarters at 1342 East Washington Avenue.

1940 CUNA Mutual Society renamed CUNA Mutual Insurance Society January 10.

CUNA Mutual paid first World War II claim on member serving on Royal Canadian Navy ship sunk by Germans.

sociation with Filene and his pioneering efforts, Bergengren's opinions had seldom been questioned. But Filene had died. The credit union movement was no longer a tiny clan held together by a few patriarchs. It was a national association, complex and diffuse, with new leaders. Despite their respect for Bergengren, they had plans and opinions of their own.

As CUNA grew, Bergengren's deficiencies as an administrator became more obvious. An outside consultant, hired to examine the business practices of the national association, described the managing director as "a secretariat, that is, one who could act as a promoter, whip up enthusiasm, but who could not manage well."

Bergengren was also criticized as autocratic. Used to following his private inclinations, he often ignored the directives of the executive committee or failed to consult with them.

His handling of *The Bridge* was typical, critics said. It was his creation and major interest, a publication he felt would one day be the credit union movement's great asset. He spent many hours at his old typewriter, pounding out articles at the last minute, expounding as only he could on the goals and philosophy of the movement. By the spring of 1938, despite a circulation of

SERVING THE MOVEMENT

A year after Loan Protection insurance was introduced, CUNA and CUNA Mutual could show that credit unions offering the product grew much faster than those that did not. Loan Protection thus became one of the most persuasive arguments for joining a credit union.

114,000, the magazine was thirty thousand dollars in debt. Hyland was so disgusted he said he would not sign another check for *The Bridge* unless something was done. But in a meeting with the executive committee, Bergengren appealed for patience and faith. *The Bridge*, he promised,

would soon be in the black.

Six months later, the magazine was forty-five thousand dollars in debt, accounting for almost all of CUNA's debt. Convinced Bergengren did not have the managerial ability to pull *The Bridge* out of the red, the CUNA executive committee in November 1938 removed Bergengren as editor, replaced him with DeRamus, and put Hyland in charge of finances.

That same year, after the national association had started to seek donations for a new headquarters, Bergengren took an option on property in Madison without the executive committee's knowledge. Though the national association had decided to stay in Madison permanently, many directors were livid, and they decided to limit Bergengren's authority to sign checks.

By January 1939, most members of the executive committee believed Bergengren must resign or be fired. They approached him cautiously with their criticisms; the managing director was still the most important person in the movement. To the committee's surprise, Bergengren acknowledged his managerial shortcomings and said he was willing to resign.

"I don't want to create a split in the movement," he said. "I have been thinking about doing some credit union organizing in Canada. But before I leave, I'd like to be given the title of managing director emeritus." The committee agreed.

But Bergengren, the most politically astute leader in an extremely political organization, did not intend to resign. He knew that if he could hold out for a few months and present his side to the entire national board, he could defeat his critics on the executive committee. He eventually admitted his real intentions.

The mood of the national meeting in May was tense. Bergengren exchanged charges and insults with some executive committee members for three days before the other national directors arrived.

"You've been sitting around here doing nothing!" Reid told the managing director.

But Bergengren had the last word. After the executive committee had presented its grievances, he rose slowly and looked into the eyes of those who would judge him.

"I recall the Estes Park meeting and review all that has happened since, mistakes and all, and do not read failure in it," he said, his voice cracking with emotion. "I look into the hearts of all of you, who love the credit union as I do, who give it the same sort of service I have tried to give you. There was a first day when I first met almost every one of you. When the credit union first came into your life, it was a day to remember and a day to celebrate."

In a few minutes, Bergengren had turned the directors around. Some were standing and shouting in his defense: "As long as I'm around here, nobody is going to take your job away!" The showdown ended in a draw. Bergengren was unanimously reelected managing director, while the executive committee was granted the power to suspend or remove the managing director only after specific charges were made and a formal hearing was held.

Though Bergengren's past had saved him, his future would be carefully watched. Angry over the managing director's tactics, some CUNA executive committee members and their allies on the CUNA Mutual board turned on the pressure, aiming their criticism at Bergengren and Rentfro's handling of CUNA Mutual.

In October 1939, CUNA Mutual director Joe DeRamus of Illinois reported that a commercial insurance company had offered an Illinois credit union a rate of fifty-eight cents per thousand dollars of insurance, well below the sixty-five-cent rate CUNA Mutual charged. DeRamus had argued for a rate reduction at a recent CUNA Mutual meeting, but the insurance department had balked at the reduction, for it had the potential for huge losses. Bergengren had complied.

Other companies could offer a lower rate temporarily, the department said, because they

As CUNA Mutual's coverage grew, so did the size of its office at 1432 E. Washington Avenue, shown here in the mid-1940s. In the background at left, Charles Eikel, Orch Edgerton, and Thomas Doig discuss business, while Ralph Peterson is seated nearby. At right center, in front of the supporting beam, Thomas Benson talks with Hazel Moe. At far right, standing by the calendar, are Elaine Richgels and Marcella Sturgis.

had sizable reserves, built over many years, to cover losses. CUNA Mutual was a young company with small reserves. If its rates were too low to cover claims, its tiny surplus was threatened.

"Other companies are lowering rates to put you out of business," the insurance commissioner said. "Leave your rates alone; they are already lower than almost any other company. First build your surplus, then lower your rates. You are a mutual company. If your rates are too high, you can return the excess to members through dividends."

These arguments did not placate the fiery and populistic DeRamus.

"Ever since I have been a member of the board, there have been certain forces at work attempting to subvert or otherwise restrict and tighten up the policies," he told Bergengren. "Personally, I would much rather see the CUNA Mutual Insurance Society go absolutely broke performing a service for credit union people in keeping with credit union philosophy than to see it follow its present tendency and build up an institution with a billion dollars in assets."

DeRamus was so upset that he and others began investigating whether the Illinois Credit Union league could start its own insurance company. Bergengren was alarmed. Not only did CUNA Mutual stand to lose the major portion of its business (the Illinois league was one of the nation's largest) but the league also might be tempted to withdraw from the national association—sending a signal to other leagues to do the same.

"The inevitable result would be," Bergengren said, "that within five or six years we would have a group of contending life insurance companies all fighting for credit union business with a resulting complete disruption of the national association."

Bergengren foresaw the same scenario should CUNA become too dependent on CUNA Mutual. If the national association began to rely on insurance activities for income, he believed, it might adopt policies that made money but hindered unity. For example, several large credit unions had lobbied for lower premium rates. Large organizations typically paid less for insurance because their sizable memberships decreased the risk of excessive claims. Smaller organizations, subject to greater actuarial volatility, paid more.

CUNA's Organization and Education Department played an important role in promoting CUNA Mutual services. Members of the department in 1941 were, front row, from left: Hubert M. Rhodes, William B. Tenney, Dora Maxwell, and John A. Colby. Back row: Clifford O. Skorstad, Thomas W. Doig, Charles F. Eikel, Jr., unidentified, and J. Orrin Shipe.

But Bergengren insisted that all credit unions, big or small, pay the same rate. Unity was at stake. Different rates, based solely on size of membership, would, in his opinion, encourage selfishness. The movement might eventually split. Though he believed, as did almost everyone in the credit union movement, that CUNA Mutual should be controlled by CUNA, Bergengren felt the society could best serve the movement by operating financially apart from CUNA.

Rentfro agreed. CUNA Mutual's proper role was to serve the credit union movement's insurance needs but not to contribute to its funding. While he believed strongly in the need for credit insurance, Rentfro a few years before had questioned the wisdom of CUNA forming an insurance company. Such a company, he felt, "would eventually become a source of conflict should it display aggressive activity."

"I think that a very simple plan could be worked out which would require only the appointment of a department head for administration, but which would be quite opposed to the setting up of an expensive insurance company subject to all sorts of regulations and whatnot," he said.

But CUNA Mutual had been organized and Rentfro, having seen the potential pitfalls of CUNA control, had changed his tune.

"We have benefitted repeatedly by friendly relationships with the Wisconsin insurance department and warnings against our own youthful enthusiasm," he said. "It seems to me we should accept gracefully the 'strict supervision' and do everything in our powers to build up a good reputation with this department and at the same time accomplish all the good purposes we have in mind."

"Sometimes I wonder if our attitude toward the Wisconsin department is not something like that of a spoiled child toward a parent when discipline is applied," he continued. "We, like the child, have been pampered and possibly coddled, but now we must conform with the laws that govern every life insurance company."

Rentfro's opinion did not endear him to those directors who viewed the state insurance department as an interloper. DeRamus became particularly upset with Rentfro. In Madison for a board meeting, DeRamus noticed the general manager had placed a "Private" sign on his office door. The sign struck him as imperious, and he made a motion at the board meeting that Rentfro be required to remove it. The motion passed.

Neither did Rentfro's attitude about Bergengren's political problems make him popular. "After witnessing the various campaigns that have been carried on over the country against Mr. Bergengren," he said, "I feel that the question in regard to the control of the society is a manufactured issue."

The tension between Rentfro and some members of the CUNA Mutual board became so pronounced that in 1939 the general manager received a raise only after a bitter argument. Five directors voted for the raise, including Bergengren, Edward Shanney, Claude Clarke, Gurden P. Farr, a new board member from Michigan, and Moses Davis, managing director of the Georgia league. Four directors opposed the raise.

The ruckus over Rentfro's raise prompted one anonymous pundit—DeRamus, a gifted poet, was a prime suspect—to send a song to Bergengren's office. It was sung to the tune of "She'll be Coming Round the Mountain When She Comes."

Oh, 'twas Shanney, Davis, Bergie, Clarke and Farr
Yes, 'twas Shanney, Davis, Bergie, Clarke and Farr
At a CUNA Mutual meeting
All our people took a beating
Cause of Shanney, Davis, Bergie, Clarke and Farr.

Oh, 'twas Shanney, Davis, Bergie, Clarke and Farr
Yes, 'twas Shanney, Davis, Bergie, Clarke and Farr
It was "Yes" these five men voted
When Earl Rentfro they promoted
Oh, 'twas Shanney, Davis, Bergie, Clarke and Farr.

When old Bergie cast his vote for Rentfro's raise
When old Bergie cast his vote for Rentfro's raise
'Twas our Birthright that he traded
And our Treasury he raided
When old Bergie cast his vote for Rentfro's raise.

Oh, these five men we'll remember by and by
Oh, these five men we'll remember by and by
They betrayed the CUNA Mutual
At a moment that was crucial
Oh, these five men we'll remember by and by.

In such an atmosphere the move to implement tighter control of CUNA Mutual by CUNA picked up momentum. In 1940, a CUNA committee headed by Nat C. Helman, a New York lawyer, determined that the most effective way to control CUNA Mutual was to reorganize it as a stock company with all the stock owned by the national association through its state leagues.

The biggest reason for its decision, the committee said, was that CUNA Mutual had started selling individual life insurance policies in 1939. Bergengren, for one, had viewed individual life insurance as potentially CUNA Mutual's most important service. The primary need for Loan Protection, he said, had been because so few credit union members had individual life insurance and because those who did have it paid exhorbitant rates.

The only drawback to increasing individual life insurance sales was that individual policyowners might take over the company someday. At the time, fewer than a thousand of CUNA Mutual's 5,330 policyowners owned individual contracts; the remainder had group Loan Protection or Life Savings contracts. Since the company sold only to credit unions affiliated with CUNA and withdrew group coverage from credit unions leaving the national association, there was no danger of CUNA Mutual getting out of the control of the organized credit union movement.

But some noted that individual policyowners could leave their credit unions while continuing their CUNA Mutual policies. If individual policyowners not affiliated with the national association ever outnumbered the group policyowners, Helman warned, they might unite and take over the company. And just like that, CUNA Mutual would have no connection with CUNA.

In Rentfro's opinion, the scenario was "a bogeyman," and reorganizing CUNA Mutual into a stock company was comparable to curing a minor illness with strychnine. "It is best to restrict ourselves to actual conditions and evidence, rather than along lines of extreme thinking," he said. "Otherwise the credit union movement may easily bog down in contemplation of terrible things."

Bergengren admitted that the organizational relationship between CUNA Mutual and CUNA was not perfect, but he said it was the best possible arrangement. The company's directors all were active members of CUNA, and CUNA Mutual limited services to credit unions affiliated with state leagues and CUNA.

"The CUNA Mutual Insurance Society belongs naturally to those credit unions and those credit union members who participate in it," he said. "It seems to me they should control it. I can't for the life of me see how any system could be devised to get any more widespread and completely democratic and representative management."

Rentfro noted that a stock company controlled by CUNA was less democratic than a mutual company because some CUNA national directors belonged to credit unions that had insurance with companies other than CUNA Mutual. Credit unions had the right to get insurance from any company they liked, Rentfro said: "On the other hand, it would be a mistake to have their representatives in a position to dictate the policies of the society, which would inevitably result if leagues owned the stock."

Ultimately, Bergengren said, "There is no possibility of CUNA Mutual getting out of control of the credit union movement, not any more than there is of the moon dropping to the earth."

If the stock advocates were not influenced by these arguments, they were forced to consider the legal barriers. Helman found that under Wisconsin law a mutual insurance company could not be reorganized into a stock company unless the policyowners were given the same rights they had before. Neither could CUNA Mutual be liquidated without forfeiting some of its reserves to the state school fund. The movement could not afford that.

On Helman's counsel, the national association decided to organize its own stock company to sell individual life insurance while CUNA Mutual sold only group Loan Protection and Life Savings insurance. The move would prevent anyone outside the credit union movement from gaining control of CUNA Mutual and also allow the two organizations to eventually merge. Nearly all credit union leaders, including Bergengren, backed the plan.

When committees from CUNA and CUNA

The CUNA Calendar Bank helped credit union members make savings a regular habit in the early 1940s. The date display advanced only when a coin was inserted.

Mutual met in November 1941 to discuss the plan, however, even the CUNA directors were having second thoughts. Starting a stock company was expensive, requiring up to $250,000 in original capital, and it might take several months, even years. George Jacobson, who had made the resolution calling for increased CUNA control, said that preventing CUNA Mutual from selling individual life insurance while the stock company was being organized might do irreparable harm to the credit union movement.

"My objection to the present CUNA Mutual setup is not that I am afraid the company is going to be grabbed off by somebody," Jacobson said. "My objection is that the setup is a cumbersome one and not the best democratic way." He preferred reforming CUNA Mutual through its existing structure and allowing it to continue selling individual life insurance.

On December 6, 1941, when the CUNA Mutual directors met in Chicago to talk about the stock plan and about limiting individual life insurance sales, Ed Shanney and Gurden Farr reported that several state leagues opposed the reorganization of CUNA Mutual into a stock company without previous approval of the society's policyowners. Attorney Horace Hansen pointed out that if a minority of the policyowners objected to the stock reorganization, the process would be legally difficult. The directors might even be liable for the potential loss of policyowner assets through reorganization.

A long and fiery philosophical discussion ensued.

"We in Michigan are not afraid of the control of this company getting away from the credit union people," Farr said. "We believe very firmly that the control is where it belongs, rightfully with the policyowners, and we don't think they will run away from this company any more than they would with our own credit unions."

Farr drew a sharp rebuttal from Joe DeRamus.

"I have always said and contended that our structure is not democratic, and we are just kidding ourselves into believing it is," DeRamus said. "Now we have had a request from the CUNA national board for action, and you do not wish to concur."

When George Feller moved that the board

defer approval of the plan until CUNA Mutual's policyowners had been consulted, Hugh Stout of Oregon challenged him.

"I come on your board new, of course," he said, "and all this time I have been thinking of credit unions and credit union folks, and now I hear them being referred to as policyowners."

"Who built the CUNA Mutual?" Feller asked.

"It was built through the credit unions," Stout replied.

"It was the policyowners."

"The policyowners were members of the national association."

"I disagree with Mr. Feller," DeRamus said. "The CUNA Mutual Insurance Society up to now has been built chiefly by the Organization and Contact Department, the national association, your state leagues and chapters. All the machinery of the credit union movement has built up the CUNA Mutual Society and without it would fall apart."

"Don't forget that CUNA Mutual requires affiliation through the leagues in the national association," John Moore said. "That has been a very strong stabilizing influence in holding together your leagues in the national association.

SERVING THE MOVEMENT

Studies showed that 75 percent of credit union members had five dollars or less in their savings accounts. Life Savings insurance, insuring the life of the borrower for an amount equal to his or her savings up to a thousand dollars, was a critical factor in boosting credit union savings.

So it works both ways."

William Pratt of Pennsylvania, who favored the reorganization plan, tried another tack.

"The control of the CUNA Mutual Insurance Society does not rest with the policyowners and never will," he said. "It rests with the directors. We can do that which is beneficial to the

policyowners, and we can do a lot of things that are not beneficial. The whole idea of the stock company is an attempt to retain control in the hands of the credit unions instead of in the hands of the thousands of policyowners who could never express their opinion except on a piece of paper prepared in such a way that the answers would be received in the manner desired. That is not healthy."

"There has also been criticism about the power of the executive committee and criticism on the part of the national association operating in various states," Farr responded. "If this thing is allowed to become a stock company, some state leagues might pull out of the national association. I don't see why we have to be a stock company. We are set up as a mutual company and doing a good business. There has been no criticism on the part of the policyowners at large. The criticism has been from a few delegates at a national meeting. I think the great majority feel we are doing them a great service. We are at a point where we have accomplished something, and now we have gotten to the point where we can return bigger dividends to our policyowners."

But Pratt was concerned that the CUNA executive committee, scheduled to meet the next week, would view CUNA Mutual as uncooperative: "I think some of the boys might feel we want to keep the business to ourselves."

"Why is it that they have that opinion that we want to keep this thing to ourselves?" Farr asked. "Why is that?"

"Because human nature has never changed in all mutual companies to the best of my knowledge, and they have always ended up that way," Pratt said.

"That is a direct reflection against the members of this board," Farr said.

"Yes," Pratt responded, "and against me, too."

"I want to say for the record I am just as interested in the national association and perhaps have done as much for it as anyone," Farr said.

Pratt shook his head. "You forget that you and I won't be sitting here forever."

"But there will be others like us," Farr said. "Credit union people are loyal to this thing and believe in it."

The CUNA Mutual board voted seven to zero not to consider the reorganization plan until the policyowners had been consulted. Reid, who had favored the stock reorganization, was absent. Pratt and DeRamus abstained from voting.

The next day the Japanese bombed Pearl Harbor.

A Common Chore

Philip Eldred heard the planes but did not realize at first what was happening. When he did, he ran toward the large U.S. Army Air Corps hangars at Hickam Field, where he served as a clerk. The Hawaiian Air Depot Federal Credit Union was located in the corner of one of the large hangars. The Japanese bombers were approaching fast, and Eldred knew they would hit the hangars. He had to get the credit union records.

Eldred was cut down by machine-gun fire. A few minutes later, the hangar was destroyed by hundred-pound bombs. Ninety percent of the credit union records were lost. CUNA Mutual paid six claims, including Eldred's, after the Pearl Harbor attack. America was at war.

By January 1942 twelve men who worked at national headquarters had joined the military or would soon be on their way. Thomas Benson, an accountant with CUNA Mutual, had already left. His draft number had been the first drawn—the first time, Benson said, he had ever won anything. In a few months he was in California, training and guarding trucks against possible attack. Private Ralph Peterson was cooking and cleaning hundreds of chickens in Missouri, and Arthur Sanborn was getting ready to report. Bergengren's son and two of Hyland's sons were in the service.

The credit union movement felt the effects of the war in other ways. Strict rationing of iron, gas, and rubber had gone into effect. All credit unions had been designated by the Department of the Treasury as agents for the sale of war bonds, and all credit unions were urged to invest at least 10 percent of their incomes in war bonds.

"We are all in the army now and should govern ourselves accordingly," Rentfro wrote Peterson. "The sooner we quit quibbling about gas, tires, and other rationing and settle down to the

business of doing without them, our presence in the war effort will be more distinctly felt."

The government had imposed Regulation W on financial institutions. Intended to reduce consumer demand for wartime goods and to dampen inflation, Regulation W placed a ceiling on loan amounts and restricted the types of loans and repayment periods. Almost immediately loans dropped off sharply, by more than half in some credit unions. CUNA Mutual's loan coverage, which had been as high as $106 mil-

lion in the fall of 1941, plummeted to $72 million by 1943.

Bergengren realized his most important job was to keep spirits high among credit union members.

"A war affects every citizen and every organization of citizens," he said in the 1942 CUNA Mutual annual report. "It may be felt in the home pantry; it is felt in the loan balances of credit unions. War is an abnormal interruption in the usual life of the people. It is the common

Claire Onsgard, treasurer of the Dane County Farmers Equity Union Coop Credit Union in Cottage Grove, Wisconsin, showed member Fritz Swenson where to sign his loan application on February 5, 1941.

chore of all the people, to be won by unity of action on the battle front and on the home front."

Although Regulation W would curtail credit union loans, Bergengren admitted, it did not have to eliminate them.

"A great bulk of loans is not affected by Regulation W," he said. "Yet I find a few credit unions have so paralyzed their loan service that their money is piling up while their members resume their weary visits to the high-rate lenders. This must stop. On the other hand, I find more treasurers who, for the first time, are making a study of their potential loan service and keeping every penny at work. They find that there are loans to be made they had never appreciated before."

CUNA Mutual also was seeking new areas of service. Of 10,000 credit unions, only 3,796 were CUNA Mutual policyowners. Only 519 had Life Savings insurance, and as the movement began to emphasize the importance of thrift, Life Savings coverage increased steadily.

CUNA Mutual did not forget the credit union members in uniform. Other companies had begun issuing "war" policies, raising premiums, or limiting or canceling coverage for those who might die in action. Bergengren decided against that option.

"The serviceman is going to risk his life for those of us who stay home. Has he a monopoly on courage? His credit union should match his will to take chances. We should make loans to him. We should make loans to the family when the need exists," he wrote.

Throughout World War II, CUNA Mutual did not alter or withdraw coverage for servicemen, and it paid all claims for those killed or missing in action. Moreover, it devised a plan to increase the coverage of servicemen. Credit unions were encouraged to waive loan payments for those in the military provided they deposited an equal amount in their share accounts, thus increasing their Life Savings coverage.

While Americans fought in Europe and the Pacific, the CUNA Mutual staff worked hard in Madison. Rentfro, Fortnum, and Edgerton were the only men on the company's staff, which numbered nineteen employees most of the war. They worked extra hours to keep up with the loss of employees like Benson and Peterson;

they needed a few extra minutes for processing on April 29, 1942, when the company paid a claim to the Board of Water Supply Federal Credit Union of Honolulu for member David Iini Kaliokalaniolapakauiwelakuikahekekilika-makaokaopua.

With coverage and premiums down, the managers took a pay cut in 1944. Rentfro's salary was decreased from $6,000 to $5,500 and Fortnum's from $4,500 to $4,100. Bergengren took the largest cut: $1,000.

Though his salary was diminished, Rentfro's morale was not. Despite a heart problem that sometimes forced him to miss work, he was an active, energetic cheerleader at the office. In addition to his regular duties, he corresponded weekly with servicemen from CUNA Mutual, CUNA, and CUNA Supply, putting them in touch with credit union members near their bases. With others at national headquarters, he sent Christmas cards and packages; a grateful Peterson reported to Rentfro that he had smoked so many cigarettes after receiving the gift that he had "a slight headache that night."

The spirit of cooperation extended to the negotiations over control of CUNA Mutual. The issue had laid dormant for more than a year; even proponents of the stock plan had felt it inappropriate to organize one company and liquidate another when credit union members were so strapped for money. Rentfro had held down sales of individual life insurance to placate opponents, but nearly everyone believed it was time to revive sales efforts.

The president of the national association, R. A. "Doc" West, told Rentfro in October 1943 that he was confident CUNA and CUNA Mutual could resolve the issue.

"This will be an easy matter as long as we have real credit union-minded men on both boards," West said. "Our problems are never so serious they cannot be worked out, providing we really want to. Factions always retard the progress of any movement, and if I am able to keep down factional arguments, I think I will have accomplished a great deal."

Working through the Wisconsin Credit Union League, CUNA and CUNA Mutual sponsored a bill in the 1943 Wisconsin legislature to allow CUNA Mutual to hold area meetings for its policyowners. The intent was to let policy-owners vote for delegates to the CUNA Mutual biennial meeting in much the same way they elected CUNA delegates. Mail ballots were eliminated. Policyowners were bound by the actions of the area meetings unless they wanted to attend the biennial meeting in person. CUNA Mutual was permitted to require its delegates to be national directors of CUNA.

The legislation passed easily. In 1944, policyowner meetings held in 117 locations in the United States and Canada helped CUNA Mutual put "more mutuality and democracy" in the society, Bergengren said. The area meetings were beneficial because rationing and restrictions on travel made a large, nationwide meeting almost impossible.

CUNA Mutual opened an office in Canada in 1944. The Canadian credit union movement had preceded its American counterpart, spurred primarily by Alphonse Desjardins, the journalist who had rekindled the idea for Filene. But while the movement started by Desjardins had spread throughout Quebec, it had not reached the rest of Canada.

In 1931, the Rev. J. J. Tompkins, better known to his parishioners in Nova Scotia as "Father Jimmy," burst into Bergengren's office in Boston and asked him to help organize credit unions in Canada. Bergengren was about to go on vacation, but the priest convinced him to spend part of it in Nova Scotia.

This was neither the first nor last time Tompkins got his way. A nun once called him "God's greatest nuisance," for he usually accomplished his goals by nagging people until they gave in. With a derby hat on his head and ever-present cigar between his lips, he looked more like a circus barker than a priest. His mink-lined overcoat had been made for industrialist Andrew Carnegie and sent to the priest by Carnegie's widow.

His flamboyant exterior masked a caring soul dedicated to eliminating the poverty of his parishioners. In his first parish, a poor fishing village, he had been called to anoint a child who seemed close to death. Tompkins examined the child and realized he was undernourished.

"Do you have any milk?" Tompkins asked the mother.

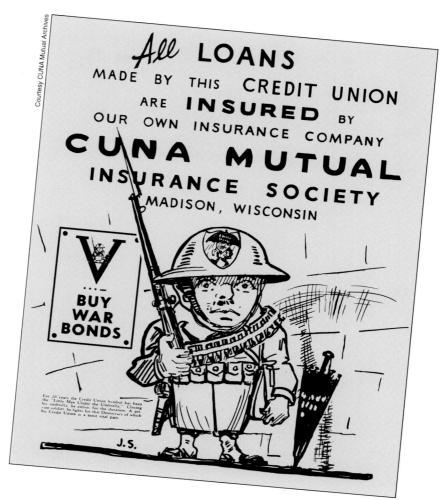

When the United States entered World War II in December 1941, the Little Man exchanged his umbrella for a rifle, helmet, and uniform.

"There are no cows in this village."

Instead of anointing the child, he obtained some condensed milk and nourished the boy back to health. Then he convinced the government to provide several goats, which he distributed among the villagers. It was the first milk, besides that of their mothers, that the children of the village ever tasted.

Tompkins was convinced credit unions could help these people pull themselves out of poverty and, while in Nova Scotia, he introduced Bergengren to others who felt the same, including the Rev. Moses M. Coady and Angus B. MacDonald. The men were connected with the Antigonish movement, which started at St. Francis Xavier University in Antigonish, Nova Scotia.

Born of the hardships of the Great Depression, the movement was dedicated to the principle, as coined by Coady, that "the people can do ten times what they think they can." Poverty could not be solved by outside agencies. Government grants and donations were not permanent answers. Instead, the people must be educated through study groups and trained to create their own economic tools.

Though started by Catholics, the Antigonish movement cut across religious lines. Among its eventual leaders was a rough-hewn Episcopal priest, the Rev. John Donald Nelson Mac-Donald, who started his social experiments in Baddeck, Nova Scotia, where Alexander Graham Bell had conducted his own experiments with the telephone.

MacDonald, who believed that the gospel of Christ demanded social action as well as the saving of souls, often stirred controversy.

"If a few people don't walk out of church when you are giving a sermon," he often said, "then you are not really preaching."

Many rich merchants and bankers in his congregation began walking out after he began organizing credit unions. One parishioner wrote: "It is wrong for a man of the cloth to be engaged in work you are doing. I cannot think of anyone in the whole range of scripture who can be compared to you unless it would be Judas Iscariot."

Such opposition did not stop MacDonald. No one would help the poor unless

they helped themselves, and the credit union seemed the most empowering way to do it. He watched as credit union members, who started with little more than the twenty-five cents required as an entrance fee, deposited their pennies and nickels every week, using ten-dollar loans to build their farms and their lives. Mac-Donald was later named to the CUNA Mutual board, and he served as its first president from Canada.

Because of the work of men like Mac-Donald, Tompkins, and Coady, Canadian credit unions grew steadily in the early 1930s. Bergengren, who spent a lot of time in Canada during that period, was a proponent of developing a united North American movement. In 1939, CUNA amended its charter to allow provincial leagues to affiliate with the national association. By 1940, there were 1,167 credit unions in Cana-

CUNA Mutual began serving Canadian credit unions in 1937. These were 1940 claim checks from CUNA Mutual to Canadian members through the Bank of Montreal.

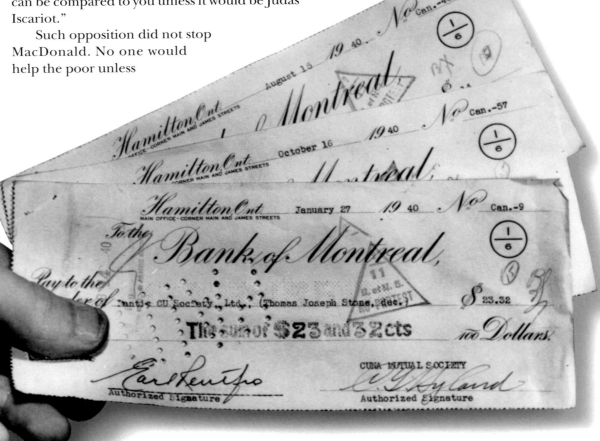

Courtesy CUNA Mutual Archives

da, with assets of twenty-five million dollars and more than two hundred thousand members.

CUNA Mutual entered Canada in 1937, selling a Loan Protection contract to the Dalhousie Industrial Credit Union, which served papermill workers in New Brunswick. The Dalhousie credit union paid a first-year premium of $4.43. Three years later, CUNA Mutual paid its first war claim on the life of Joseph Blanchard, a Dalhousie member who served on H.M.S. *Jervis Day,* a Royal Canadian ship torpedoed by the Germans.

As CUNA Mutual's Canadian business increased, the company ran into the same problem it had encountered in the United States: the lack of a license. In 1940, the Canadian superintendent of insurance told CUNA Mutual it was operating illegally and he would deny the company use of the mail until it qualified with a deposit of a hundred thousand dollars.

There was no way CUNA Mutual could raise the deposit quickly, and for a time it considered trying to qualify as a fraternal society. Rentfro continued to correspond with the superintendent, primarily as a stalling tactic. The society continued to operate until it raised the full deposit in 1942.

The license required that CUNA Mutual employ an agent in Canada. Rentfro offered the job to C. Gordon Smith, an employee for the City of Hamilton and the president of the Ontario Credit Union League. CUNA Mutual's first Canadian office was located in Smith's kitchen. Tired of the clutter, Smith soon asked Rentfro to allow him to rent an office and a desk. In 1946, the company opened an office that rented for ten dollars a month in downtown Hamilton. Smith was eventually named manager of the Canadian operations of both CUNA Mutual and CUNA.

A Spiritual Force

In 1934, Roy Bergengren said he was organizing the Credit Union National Association to work himself out of a job. His prediction came true eleven years later.

Bergengren was still an inspiring speaker and writer. His cheerleading efforts had been critical during the war, and few forgot his pioneering efforts. He had survived attempts to retire him in 1939 because he still retained the

admiration of most of the national directors. But as Bergengren neared age sixty-five and the national association grew larger, he played a smaller role in administering its affairs. He had become an elder statesman, and many members of the CUNA executive committee wanted him to hand the reins of managing director to someone else.

Though Bergengren's friends agreed he was ill-suited as a manager, some felt the political opposition had more to do with his views on cooperation. He often argued with credit union leaders, especially De-Ramus, about the credit union's connection with the cooperative movement. Many of these leaders had worked for large private corporations; Bergengren believed they viewed credit unions more as a "beneficial personnel activity" than as a separate and unique economic system.

Bergengren saw credit unions as just one of many segments of the cooperative movement and saw cooperation as the logical heir to capitalism. "In the long run," he once said, "I believe that cooperation will be found to be more consistent with what the forefathers had in mind for America than capitalism." That opinion did not endear him to the executive committee members who feared such opinions might alienate industrial credit unions.

But others believed Bergengren's poor relationship with the CUNA executive committee had more to do with his penchant for ignoring their direction.

"Management pays no attention whatsoever, if it can avoid it, to those motions adopted by the board if it doesn't like such motions and pays attention only to those they do like," CUNA president William Reid (also a member of the CUNA Mutual board) had told Bergengren in 1942. "It is a sad commentary at national headquarters when things are so haphazardly looked after,

Father J. J. Tompkins, top, was one of Canada's credit union pioneers. CUNA Mutual's Canadian office opened in the kitchen of C. Gordon Smith's home in Hamilton, Ontario in 1944. Smith, bottom, served many years as the society's manager of Canadian operations.

Roy F. Bergengren

Managing Director
CUNA Mutual Insurance Society
1935–1945

Bergengren. While most still held him in esteem, they also agreed he should no longer be managing director. West tried to discuss the executive committee's concerns with Bergengren, but the managing director told West, in so many words, that West was not big enough in the movement to tell him what he should or shouldn't be doing. Bergengren had beaten the CUNA executive committee once, and he could do it again.

In September 1944, Edward Shanney, president of CUNA Mutual, and Karl S. Little, president of CUNA Supply, met with the CUNA executive committee to discuss Bergengren. The consensus was that all three organizations needed new leadership. They tried to think of other solutions but finally agreed the only way was to fire Bergengren.

It was a dangerous decision. The executive committee knew it might split the movement, and some directors cautioned patience. "You can hire business managers, but you can't hire enthusiasm," said Harold Latham of North Carolina. "Bergengren's enthusiasm and interest and inspiration has covered this continent too damned well to dispose of it with a snap of the finger."

It was true. Bergengren was the movement's spiritual force. No one had done more to inspire credit union people. Like a traveling evangelist, he had a gift for speaking and an ability to create memorable phrases about credit unions. None was more famous than his statement that "credit unions prove, in modest measure, the practicality of the brotherhood of man."

Bergengren also saw credit unions as a practical method of Christianity, and he seldom began a speech without a text from the Bible. "It is pretty hard to read the New Testament without concluding that Jesus Christ would, if living and walking about this earth again, find more of his principles being carried out practically in an efficient and properly operated credit union than in most churches."

Like most evangelists, Bergengren knew how to sway people's emotions. Early in World War II, he was at a state league meeting, trying to drive home the point that granting loans to servicemen and their families, though restricted by Regulation W, was patriotic. Suddenly he pulled a piece of paper from his pocket.

but I realize it is difficult to teach old dogs new tricks."

Reid's successor as president of the national association, "Doc" West, a young executive from Decatur, Illinois, talked to many people about

"I have a letter from my son in North Africa," he said as he began reading an emotional account of the war. The letter was full of patriotism, faith, and hope; it urged the folks back home not to forget the boys overseas and to keep making loans. When Bergengren put the letter back in his pocket, there was not a dry eye in the crowd. During the speech, one of his associates on stage got a closer look at the paper the managing director read from. It was blank.

Like the best salespeople, Bergengren was not above bending the truth or acting to get his way. Early in his career, after a shouting match with Filene, Bergengren had seemed close to losing control, shouting and stomping his feet. Later, outside Filene's office, he immediately turned calm, to the amazement of Dora Maxwell, a field organizer who had witnessed the tirade.

Bergengren winked. "How did I do?" he asked.

On another occasion, field worker Charles Eikel was scheduled to attend a meeting with Bergengren when the managing director decided to go to a movie.

"But we'll miss the start of the meeting," Eikel said. "I thought you were the featured speaker."

"That's okay."

The two men sat through the entire movie and were half an hour late for the meeting, where Bergengren had the crowd eating out of his hand. "When you're late to a credit union meeting, the anticipation builds. By the time you walk in, they're so relieved you can convince them of anything," Bergengren said.

Bergengren's persuasive talents were bolstered by his ability to transform common stories into unforgettable parables. He often told the story of a power company lineman who had been electrocuted, leaving two coworkers to cover an unpaid credit union loan because his wife and family could not. "The Lesson of the Lineman" was frequently cited as the reason CUNA Mutual was organized. Countless stories of comparable tragedies had also spurred the development of CUNA Mutual. Some, recalling Bergengren's penchant for fabrication and the lack of evidence for the Lesson of the Lineman, wondered if he made it up. Whatever the case, the story inspired action.

"The purpose of a speech is not to satisfy the speaker with a consciousness of his literary skill," Bergengren said. "The purpose goes much deeper than that; it is to reach the mind and the heart of the listener or reader."

Though much of his life was spent in front of crowds, Bergengren kept his home life private. His family was extremely important to him, and though he loved speaking, he regretted being away from his family so much.

Before he left on day trips, his wife, Gladys, often asked whether Bergengren would be back for lunch. If the answer was yes, she put one cigar in his pocket; if no, he received two. Bergengren's cigars lasted as long as possible, thanks to a penknife he used to hold the stubs.

Bergengren always took the train or had someone else, occasionally his wife, drive him on his trips. Years before, he had backed out of the garage, not realizing his young daughter was playing behind the car. She was killed. Bergengren never drove again, and he told only a few people why.

Before leaving on road trips, he drew cartoons on his children's blackboards, illustrating lessons about being good, obeying their mother, helping each other. In later years, his daughter Dorothy and her family lived next door. Every night he was home, no matter what else was going on, Bergengren read to his grandchildren.

Raised in a straitlaced, conservative Swedish home, Bergengren did not drink and he rarely swore, traits that distinguished him from some other credit union leaders. Gurden "Dutch" Farr, a CUNA Mutual director, was once a supper guest in the Bergengren home. Gladys Bergengren served apple pie for dessert. "That's the best damn apple pie I ever tasted, Mrs. Bergengren," Farr said. Bergengren was shocked and let Farr know it.

Bergengren never felt at home with most credit union leaders, and that accounted for some of his political problems. A Dartmouth graduate, he tended to disparage the opinions of those less educated. He always wanted to be right, and he had difficulty accepting that people he had brought into the movement were telling him what to do.

Neither could he accept working for Tom Doig. In September 1944, after the CUNA exec-

Roy F. Bergengren's face betrayed his emotions after Thomas W. Doig praised Bergengren for his twenty years of credit union service in 1941. Doig was speaking at a dinner of the Florida Credit Union League on May 3 in conjunction with CUNA's seventh annual meeting in Jacksonville.

utive committee decided he must be replaced, Bergengren was offered the position of promotional advisor at five thousand dollars per year. He seemed willing to consider the proposal until the committee said it was backing Tom Doig as his successor.

"I won't work for Tom Doig," he said.

Though Doig and Bergengren had once been close, their relationship had grown distant, as had Bergengren and Filene's. Bergen-

gren had brought Doig into the movement, then watched as Doig, who continued to travel throughout the country, began to garner grassroots recognition. Doig often chafed under Bergengren's command, and he openly criticized his administrative abilities.

Unwilling to work for Doig, Bergengren nevertheless recognized he was in trouble. He asked that he be allowed to stay on as managing director until January. Then he would resign gracefully. The executive committee agreed and postponed action until its next meeting. Still it seemed Bergengren would not let go without a fight. That fall, he took the train from Madison to Decatur, Illinois, and spent a long evening protesting the decision of the executive committee to R.A. West, the CUNA president. Bergengren had no money for supper, so West paid.

The next morning, Bergengren started where he had left off. Again, he had no money, so West paid for breakfast. The managing director continued to protest as he packed, but he could not find any cash then, either. West paid the hotel bill.

At the train station, Bergengren told West he did not have enough money to get out of town. Bergengren was vague, so West handed him a twenty-dollar bill.

"This will get you wherever you're going."

"Actually," Bergengren said, "why don't you just buy me a ticket to Madison? I'll keep the twenty; I'll need it."

When West sent his expenses to Hyland at national headquarters, he included a note chastising Hyland for letting Bergengren travel without enough money.

"What are you talking about?" Hyland wrote back. "Bergengren turned in his expenses already. He probably had a hundred-and-fifty bucks in his pocket when he saw you."

Bergengren continued his psychological punishment of the executive committee in the following months. In December, he formally declared that he would not be a candidate for re-election and asked to be retained as managing director until May 1945. But he had changed his mind by March. Recalling Bergengren's ploy of several years earlier, director John Eidam moved that he be dismissed immediately. Bergengren said he would accept the position of promotional advisor if he could retain his old title until the annual meeting. Eidam withdrew his motion but reintroduced it the next day. Bergengren was fired, and Tom Doig was unanimously elected managing director.

Bergengren continued to fight, but wartime restrictions prohibited the national directors from meeting that year. Though several state leagues protested the decision and a few threatened to withdraw, the decision was not rescind-ed. By the time the national directors reviewed Bergengren's protests, Doig had been managing director more than a year.

Bergengren was bitter. He did not criticize the executive committee publicly, though he told friends he was thinking of writing a book titled, "Now It Can Be Told." He retired with his wife to a farm in Vermont and continued to speak and travel. He wrote several books about his experiences in the credit union movement, spending many hours hunched over the old typewriter he had rescued from Filene's office.

President Harry S Truman, at the podium of the University of
Wisconsin Fieldhouse, helped dedicate Filene House, the new
headquarters of CUNA, CUNA Mutual, and CUNA Supply, on May
14, 1950. The event brought national attention to the credit
union movement.

CHAPTER THREE

An Idea Worth Sharing

The service we render humanity is our only real claim to immortality.

—Thomas W. Doig

By the fall of 1945, World War II was over, and many of CUNA Mutual's employees in the service were coming home. Several letters to Tom Benson had been returned by the government, prompting speculation that he was already on his way back. Ralph Peterson was somewhere in the South Pacific but would soon return. A few employees, like Art Sanborn, had decided to take jobs elsewhere.

Earl Rentfro had retired. He had taken several extended leaves during the war because of heart problems, and his condition was not getting better.

"I will have completed ten years of service in a job that has unlimited possibilities for service, and it is not easy for me to walk out on it," he told the board. "But I do not feel I am physically able to give my work the complete attention it so richly deserves."

Tom Doig was now the managing director of CUNA, CUNA Supply, and CUNA Mutual. Some CUNA board members, noting Doig's strong grass-roots support and high profile in the movement, had feared he might be as independent-minded as Roy Bergengren had been. Several CUNA executive committee members tried to persuade Doc West, president of CUNA, to take the job, but West refused. He believed Doig had earned the chance to be managing director on a trial basis.

The CUNA Mutual board was concerned about Doig, too. Some members believed the insurance job had become too complex for an administrator unable to give full attention to the job. The board approved Doig but not until after its president, Edward Shanney, spoke with him privately. Much was expected of Doig as an administrator, Shanney said. If Doig did not measure up, the board would not likely be as patient with him as it had been with Bergengren.

Doig's appointment reflected the desire of the CUNA and CUNA Mutual boards, which had expended what some believed was unnecessary energy arguing over control of the insurance company, to work more closely together.

Postwar cooperation was essential for response to new opportunities for growth. Government lending restrictions were being lifted. Veterans and civilians were beginning to make home improvements and purchases delayed by the war. As consumption increased sharply, so did the need for low-cost credit union loans.

As loans increased, so did CUNA Mutual coverage. After dropping from $106 million in 1941 to $73 million in 1943, coverage rebounded to $130 million by the end of 1946 and nearly $200 million the next year. In 1948, federal credit unions became eligible for the first time to purchase Life Savings insurance. The move, combined with CUNA Mutual's decision to increase Loan Protection limits to $5,000 and emphasize individual life insurance sales, boosted the society's total coverage to $291 million at the end of the year.

By 1949, CUNA Mutual had become the eighty-second largest life insurance company in North America in coverage, and it was growing faster than any on the continent. Insurance rating agencies gave CUNA Mutual the highest marks possible for security, and the society returned almost ninety cents of every premium dollar to members through claims payments, dividends, or reserves, nearly double the industry average.

Despite these achievements, Doig realized that CUNA Mutual's prospects for growth depended not only on its performance but also on

getting its message to a higher percentage of credit unions. Of 11,000 credit unions in the United States and Canada, only 7,000 were affiliated with CUNA, and of those, 4,600 were covered by CUNA Mutual.

Doig knew that CUNA Mutual could not just depend on increasing participation among existing credit unions. By demonstrating that Loan Protection and Life Savings insurance were viable products, CUNA Mutual had unintentionally encouraged commercial companies to enter the field. Because of this competition, the society would not grow unless more credit unions could be organized.

The task would not be easy. Thousands of dedicated volunteers had worked for years to organize the credit unions already in existence. Despite their effort, most of the public still did not know what a credit union was. Doig decided to place additional emphasis on advertising and promotion.

One early idea for generating publicity came from Charles F. Eikel, Jr., a former CUNA field organizer who in 1946 had been named assistant managing director of CUNA, CUNA Mutual, and CUNA Supply. In 1948, he proposed a national celebration called Credit Union Day.

Eikel did not know that Bergengren had tried to start a credit union day in Massachusetts on January 17, 1927. Slated for the anniversary of the birthday of Benjamin Franklin, the "father of thrift," the event never gained popularity. After a few years, Bergengren's Credit Union Day had been forgotten.

Eikel's plans for Credit Union Day extended far beyond the modest goals of the first event. On this day, credit union workers would take the day off and local chapters would hold dinners across the continent. At the meetings, donations could be collected for future public relations, organization, and publicity campaigns. If the credit union movement became large enough,

Members of the CUNA and CUNA Mutual staffs met in 1947. From left: Vaughn E. Liscum, Ruth E. Ryan, Thomas W. Doig, Charles F. Eikel, Jr., and Charles G. Hyland. On the wall are pictures of credit union pioneers Alphonse Desjardins, Hermann Schulze-Delitzsch, and Roy F. Bergengren.

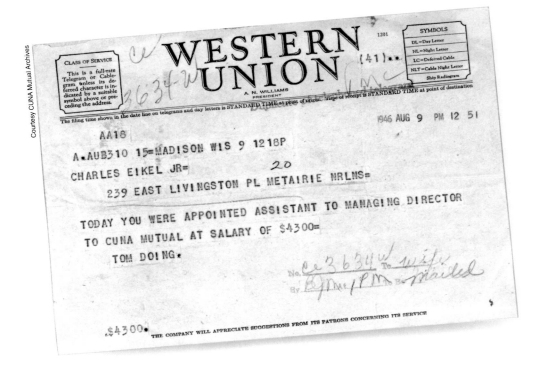

Courtesy CUNA Mutual Archives

Thomas W. Doig (his name is misspelled on the telegram) informed Charles F. Eikel, Jr., a field representative for CUNA, that he had been named an assistant to the managing director in 1946.

Eikel theorized, Congress might eventually make Credit Union Day a national holiday.

Radio seemed the key to Credit Union Day success, but neither CUNA nor CUNA Mutual was ready to approve the funds needed to finance a national broadcast. Then Eikel learned that J. L. Kraft, chairman of the Kraft Foods Company, whose employees had several credit unions, had praised the movement at a recent Georgia league meeting. His company sponsored one of the country's most popular radio programs, "Kraft Music Hall."

It seemed a natural connection: Kraft could sponsor Credit Union Day on its radio program in October 1948. Eikel knew it was a long shot, but he decided to pay the chairman a visit.

Eikel, a New Orleans native who had organized credit unions in the South as a field representative for CUNA, was used to difficult selling jobs. Though many companies and groups were anxious to organize credit unions, anti-union sentiment was high in the South during the late 1930s. Any proposal that included the word union raised an immediate red flag with some employers.

Typical of these incidents of hostility was Eikel's experience at a cracker factory in New Orleans. The owner's son thought a credit

union would be good for employees, but he warned Eikel that his father was set against the idea. The owner was waiting at the door when Eikel arrived.

"Don't you come any farther!" he shouted. "I don't want any damn union in this place! I want you off these premises, and I want you to stay off, and if you ever come back, I'm gonna call the cops!"

"Beg your pardon?" Eikel said innocently.

"Don't beg my damn pardon! Just get the hell out of here! I don't want any damn union around here!"

"I don't understand, sir. What have you got against unions? Aren't you a citizen of the United States, the forty-eight states of the union?"

"That's different!"

"It is? What about the union of marriage? You got anything against that?"

"Of course not!"

"When you die, do you think you'll go to heaven?"

"I hope so."

"Doesn't your religion tell you that you'll be in union with God?"

"That's different!"

"Let me just ask you one more question, sir. Have you ever worn long underwear?"

"It's none of your business, but yes I have. So what?"

"Long underwear is called a union suit."

"That's different and you know it!"

"The credit union is different, too. You don't even know what it's about. Why don't you at least give me the chance to tell you about it?"

The man calmed down enough to let Eikel make his pitch. Eikel did not organize a credit union that day, but the cracker factory employees eventually got a credit union.

Eikel did not always get the chance to use his persuasive talents. Once he was escorted out of a railroad yard in Hattiesburg, Mississippi, by an irate superintendent with a loaded shotgun. When he got back to his hotel, his bags had been packed and the sheriff was waiting with a message for him: Leave town immediately or spend the night in jail.

On his way to organize a credit union for a black Baptist church in Mississippi, Eikel stopped at a gas station to get directions. The white attendant eyed him suspiciously. Though Eikel had lived all his life in the South, his New Orleans accent at times made him sound like he was from Brooklyn, and hostile prospects had accused him of being a carpetbagger. Asking about a black church, in the days when segregation was strictly enforced, only reinforced the attendant's mistrust.

"Why do you want to go to that church?"

"Because I'm going."

"You can't go there!"

"I can go anywhere I please," Eikel said. "Are you going to give me directions or not?"

The attendant reluctantly complied. Eikel found the church, parked across the street, and was opening the trunk to get his credit union literature when two cars pulled up. Two men got out and asked Eikel what he was doing. He told them.

"You ain't gonna organize anything," one of the men said. "I think you better get on back to New Orleans."

Eikel headed for Louisiana. The cars followed for a short distance, then turned around. Eikel did the same but took a different route back to the church. This time three cars, each with four men inside, pulled up.

"Don't even get out of the car," the leader said. "We're gonna personally escort you to the state line." And they did, one car in front of Eikel and two behind him.

After such experiences, Eikel figured convincing Kraft of the value of Credit Union Day would be easy by comparison. He was right. The chairman liked Eikel's proposal, including having the president of the United States and the prime minister of Canada deliver messages during the broadcast; he especially liked the part about the chairman of Kraft serving as master of ceremonies.

Kraft's advertising manager showed less enthusiasm. "I don't know, Mr. Kraft," he said. "The idea has merit, but sponsoring a radio program costs a lot of money. You've got to get some big results for that kind of investment."

"You could make your investment back in no time by the gratefulness of credit union people," Eikel interjected.

"Businesses run on profits, not gratitude. Besides, we've already scheduled Al Jolson for

the October show," the manager said. "What's he going to say when I tell him we've decided to turn his show over to credit union people?"

"You could use Al Jolson like nobody's business!" Eikel said. "He could sing a few numbers. I'll bet he'd even say a few words on behalf of credit unions."

The advertising manager was still not convinced. He told Eikel to do more research and return in one week, ready to show the effect a Credit Union Day broadcast would have on Kraft sales.

A few days later, Eikel (with the help of Mary Jean McGrath, a writer on the CUNA staff) wrote the manager an impassioned letter. The broadcast was likely to pull in more than ten million credit union members and their families, he said. More important, the movement would respond where it counted most—at the grocery store.

"After this program, not one credit union housewife will push her cart through the supermarket past the Velveeta and Miracle Whip without remembering Kraft products and their sponsors as behind the credit union idea," Eikel said. "They will want to buy Kraft products because Kraft backs ideals and policies they agree with."

"CUNA Mutual is founded upon the rock of faith. Individually, we and our credit unions were weak. Together, we cast our bread of protection upon the waters of life, and it has returned to us a hundredfold."

J. L. Kraft still liked the idea, but his advertising manager remained unconvinced and the company's advertising agency was adamantly opposed. Even if the company sponsored the broadcast, the agency advised, Kraft should not host the show because he did not have professional training. Disheartened, Kraft bowed to the wishes of the agency. He would have to give the program a lot more thought, he said.

CUNA already had selected the third Thursday in October, when the Kraft Music Hall was scheduled to air, as the official date of Credit Union Day. That night, thousands of credit union chapters held dinners across the country. Though it never was as successful as Eikel had originally hoped, for the next three decades Credit Union Day was useful at the chapter level for reminding people of the movement's principles and ideals. It would continue to be observed into the 1990s.

The Kraft setback did not dampen Eikel's enthusiasm. The boards of CUNA and CUNA Mutual had recently approved the construction of a new headquarters, and Eikel decided that if he could not get North American leaders together on a credit union broadcast, he would convince them to help lay the building's cornerstone. Friends told Eikel he was crazy.

Some had thought the same of Bergengren's trying to build a new headquarters. Shortly after Filene died, Bergengren convinced the CUNA national directors to designate 1938 as Filene Year and to use the occasion to solicit donations from credit union members around the country for a national headquarters. Although passions still ran high over whether to stay in Madison, the directors finally okayed the city for the permanent headquarters.

To make sure the directors did not change their minds, in 1940 the Madison credit union chapter paid for the land previously optioned by Bergengren and gave it to CUNA on the condition that it build there. The site, known as the

Malt House property, was located near Lake Mendota in east Madison. Once used as a brewery, the Malt House stood over several tunnels used to store beer, one of which had been painted for use as an underground nightclub. The building would be rented as a tavern until the new headquarters was built.

Between 1938 and 1941, credit union members had donated about $150,000 to the headquarters fund, but arguments about how and where to build persisted. Some leaders, including Doig, wanted to move to Chicago. The debate was postponed when the United States entered World War II. To satisfy the opposing factions, a trust agreement was drawn up to safeguard the fund, which grew to $160,000 in the next four years.

By the end of the war, bickering over Madison had subsided. The office on East Washington Street was too crowded, and a new building was necessary to keep up with postwar growth. The problem was that wartime inflation had made it almost impossible to build a headquarters large enough to house CUNA, CUNA Mutual, and CUNA Supply for $160,000. By 1948, the price of such a building was more than $300,000.

This problem was compounded by the trust agreement, which prohibited CUNA from soliciting additional donations or borrowing more funds. The national directors considered dissolving the agreement, but they could not do so without giving back the original $160,000 to the donors.

Lawyers finally determined that the trust agreement allowed CUNA to sell a ninety-nine-year lease on the land and building to CUNA Mutual for $150,000, boosting the trust funds to $310,000. But the Wisconsin insurance commissioner balked at the arrangement. An insurance company could not invest money in a building without receiving title, he said; the deal amounted to a subsidy for CUNA, which the state insurance department had fought for years. CUNA solved the problem in 1949 by giving CUNA Mutual title to half the building for the society's $150,000 contribution.

As construction of the headquarters, known as Filene House, finally began in 1949, Eikel began campaigning to convince President Harry S Truman to attend its dedication. He had

Filene House, the national headquarters of CUNA, CUNA Mutual, and CUNA Supply, was completed in 1950.

Courtesy CUNA Mutual Archives

met Truman the year before, when the president gave a campaign speech in Madison. Eikel had presented him then with an honorary CUNA membership.

The CUNA staff had conceived the idea of making Truman an honorary member only the day before the president arrived. The proclamation calligraphy was done in record time the next morning. But there was no frame for it and no time to get an art studio's help. Truman was scheduled to speak in three hours. Then someone spotted a photograph on Orch Edgerton's desk—in a frame of just the right size. In a few seconds, an Edgerton family portrait was replaced by the proclamation.

With construction underway Eikel urged national Democratic party organizations and legislators to join him in inviting Truman to the May 1950 dedication. With the president still unsure in March, Eikel told his friends he would change his religion, his political affiliation, anything to get Truman to Madison. Credit union leagues and members flooded the White House with telegrams. Doig, noting the movement's increasing work in foreign countries, appealed to Truman's penchant for international cooperation.

"Mr. President, if this were just another commercial building or purely an event of local significance, we would not presume to call upon you," he said. "But Filene House is more than just a memorial to an individual. It is really a 'little United Nations,' where citizens from many countries work together with good will and cooperation for a better way of life. Surely, this is a forerunner of peace among nations."

Doig's mention of the possible disappointment of five million credit union members may also have had an effect. In April, Truman's secretary told Doig the president's train would stop in Madison while returning from political appearances on the West Coast.

Although representatives of Prime Minister Louis St. Laurent had said he would like to attend if Truman did, a Canadian embassy official in Washington advised against the trip. It would not be wise, the official said, for the prime minister to get involved with an American political tour, even though the dedication was not considered a partisan event.

As construction crews worked toward the

Courtesy CUNA Mutual Archives

dedication, the U.S. Secret Service arrived in Madison a week before the event. An agent took CUNA employees John A. Colby and William B. Tenney to inspect the president's tour route and arrange for security. The agent also told a surprised Ford-Mercury dealer that the president needed fourteen limousines ready for Sunday.

Preparations generally went smoothly, although the Secret Service agent had some trouble with a local Democratic party official who insisted the itinerary be changed so he could meet the president aboard his train. When the agent refused, the official showed up at the agent's hotel room to press his cause. When the official refused to leave, the agent jumped out of bed, naked, threatening to physically eject the intruder.

Truman arrived in Madison Sunday morning with his wife, Bess, and daughter, Margaret. He met the next morning with dignitaries including Doig, Eikel, the chairpeople of the three CUNA organizations, and Oscar Rennebohm, governor of Wisconsin. After attending church, the president addressed delegates of the CUNA organizations in town for annual meetings, at the University of Wisconsin Fieldhouse.

Truman lauded the work of credit unions, but his mind also was on cooperation in international affairs. The North Atlantic Treaty Organi-

President Harry S Truman waved to the camera enroute from the University of Wisconsin Fieldhouse to the Filene House dedication. With Truman in the back seat of the limousine were CUNA president John E. Eidam, obscured, and Oscar Rennebohm, governor of Wisconsin.

zation had recently formed to counter Soviet aggression; in a few months, America and several other countries, backed by the United Nations Security Council, would send troops to counter the Communist invasion of South Korea.

"No one nation can bring about peace," the president said. "Together, nations can build a strong defense against aggression and combine the energy of free men everywhere in building a better future for all of us."

Despite rain, a crowd estimated at more than twenty thousand lined the streets from the fieldhouse to Filene House. Most onlookers were content to wave and yell, "Hi, Harry!" But as Truman entered his limousine, an overly enthusiastic supporter ran toward him, probably to shake his hand. Secret Service agents tackled the man a few steps from the curb.

The motorcade, including several Lincoln convertibles lent by dealers in southern Wisconsin and northern Illinois, made its way to Filene House. The roof on Truman's yellow convertible kept going up and down. The president offered his hat to Governor Oscar Rennebohm, a Republican, whose hat blew off along the way. Later he insisted Rennebohm keep it.

At Filene House, the president and his family were escorted to Doig's second-floor office, the only one in the new headquarters yet furnished, as the University of Wisconsin band played the "Missouri Waltz" outside. Truman,

President Harry S Truman enthusiastically participated in the laying of the cornerstone in Filene House. Left to right: Truman showed the trowels he would use, as John E. Coyne, foreman for the Filene House project, and Thomas W. Doig, seated, watch. Then, Truman placed mortar in the cornerstone opening. After lifting the cornerstone into place with Coyne, the president again displayed the ceremonial trowels.

Courtesy CUNA Mutual Archives

Courtesy CUNA Mutual Archives

expected to take a place at Doig's new desk, chose to relax on a plain folding chair.

CUNA had asked Hoffman House, one of the leading restaurants in Madison, to cater the event, complete with silver tea service, fancy hors d'oeuvres, and petit fours. But the restaurant, swamped with customers in town to see the president, mixed up the order and passed it along to a little coffee shop.

The coffee shop dispatched a gray-haired woman wearing a white waitress uniform to Doig's office. Carrying a huge pot of coffee, oatmeal cookies the size of saucers, and plain white

napkins, she nearly dropped the entire load when she saw the president. "This is terrible," she told CUNA public relations employee Mary Jean McGrath; then she left suddenly without explanation.

McGrath did her best to keep the president and the rest of the reception party engaged in conversation. The gray-haired woman returned some time later with napkins decorated with colorful flower stickers hurriedly applied at home.

The Trumans did not appear to miss the fancy appetizers. The president contented himself with a cup of coffee. Margaret asked for a Coke, declining a glass, and sipped from the bottle.

Courtesy CUNA Mutual Archives

CUNA Mutual reached first billion dollars of coverage in force.

Mrs. Truman did not want anything to eat. "I just had lunch," she said, patting her stomach.

After the "luncheon," Roy Bergengren, CUNA's managing director emeritus, gave the dedication address. His oratorical skills had not diminished in the years since he had left Madison. His speech was so stirring that President Truman later wrote him for a copy of it.

"Our founder was no Alexander or Napoleon, marching across the world of their time, triumphantly into oblivion," the former managing director said of Filene.

"He was, rather, a courageous little shopkeeper, impersonating St. George and tackling with limitless courage a dragon with as many monstrous heads as the problems that bedeviled his time.

"Usury was a dragon's head, all sharp fangs, drooling with the lifeblood of innumerable victims. In the credit union this restless, inspired prophet found an idea that synchronized with his practical concepts of democracy. Here was a school that could train vast numbers of people in the democratic control and management of their own money. Here was a way to unite people who differed on every other subject under the sun. Here was the perfect defense against Fascism, the greatest potential bulwark against Communism.

"On us he unloaded the responsibility of proving that the credit union has the strength to endure, the capacity for constant self-improvement. On this spot we honor the past, which honored itself in unselfish, patriotic devotion and made the present possible. Here we pledge our sacred honor that what they created shall have eternal life."

After Bergengren's speech, CUNA secretary Marion F. Gregory of Illinois handed two trowels to the president. Preparing for the laying of the cornerstone, President Truman pushed up his shirt-sleeves, smiled broadly, and said, "Now I've done this a lot, probably more times than you. Let me show you how."

John E. Coyne, a member of the Madison city council and the construction foreman for Filene House, placed mortar on the bricks in the opening provided for the cornerstone. Truman bent down to smooth the mortar. Coyne placed a CUNA time capsule in the wall's open-

ing, and struggled to lift the cornerstone into place.

"Want me to help you?" the president asked.

"Yes," Coyne said.

Truman took hold of one end of the stone and Coyne the other. Together they counted to three, picked the cornerstone up, and set it in the wall of Filene House. The president left for Chicago a few minutes later.

The president's visit and resulting national publicity impressed on Doig the possibilities of increased promotion. In 1952, CUNA started its first official public relations department. CUNA and CUNA Mutual each paid 40 percent of the department's budget; CUNA Supply paid 20 percent. During the next few years, the department played a consulting role in all three organizations, advising management about the public relations value of programs and policy decisions.

The department also offered promotional tools to local credit unions, including sample news releases and radio spots, pamphlets and brochures, and ideas for speeches. Every national credit union meeting became a major production. The 1953 annual meeting in Atlantic City opened with the entrance of a drum and bugle corps. With lights turned off and spotlights turned on American and Canadian flags, "The Prayer of Saint Francis of Assisi" was recited (and still is today), and the audience sang patriotic anthems.

In 1953, the movement produced its first movie, *King's X*. Made by a Hollywood company for a hundred thousand dollars, the film was often shown outdoors in small towns with no theaters, bringing the credit union story to hundreds of thousands of people. At about the same time, CUNA Mutual issued a comic book featuring Mr. CUNA, a character with a mustache and derby hat who explained the society's services.

Sometimes the movement was overambitious. CUNA Mutual director Joe DeRamus once got the idea of having Tom Doig run for president of the United States. The national Republican chairman from Illinois assured DeRamus that credit union members would not necessarily vote for the managing director for political office. Though DeRamus gave up the idea, public relations writer Howard C. Custer was assigned to gather material in hopes of convincing *Time* magazine to do a Doig cover story. The magazine declined.

While CUNA and CUNA Mutual had advertised extensively in credit union publications like *The Bridge*, they had never used much external advertising. The attitude of many credit union leaders toward promotion was epitomized in a Tom Benson memo evaluating a possible advertisement: "Some of the copy does create the impression, though carefully footnoted, that the panacea of all family problems can be solved through this type of plan. I do not believe the credit union movement must now stoop to this type of promotional effort. People organize, operate, and use credit unions because they believe and know what they are doing, not because they are influenced by words, color, and catch-phrases."

Some feared outside advertising might invite more outside criticism. As the movement had grown, so had the number and variety of its opponents. A Chicago insurance broker told a Kiwanis club in Florida that credit unions, along with all mutual insurance companies and cooperatives, were part of an international conspiracy to overthrow the United States. He told Marion Gregory, hired in 1953 as CUNA's director of public relations, that his proof was locked in a vault. He would have presented his findings to Senator Joseph R. McCarthy's subcommittee investigating Communist activities in America, he said, except its members were afraid he wanted to take the investigation too far. The press had not picked up the story "because they were in on it."

More worrisome were the criticisms of banks and small-loan companies. Credit unions had once served a useful purpose, they claimed, but had become obsolete when banks and other financial institutions became willing to supply working people with small loans. Since credit unions no longer were unique, the banks argued, they should not be exempt from taxes; at the least, they should be supervised more closely.

Courtesy CUNA Mutual Archives

CUNA's public relations staff spent much of its time in the early 1950s countering these and other arguments. Banks had started handling small loans only after credit unions showed the way. If credit unions ceased to exist, would the banks still serve the working poor? The average credit union loan was less than three hundred dollars, much too small for a bank to make any profit. Some recalled the newsboy whose bike broke down. He applied for a fifty-cent loan in the morning, fixed his bike, collected from customers, and returned that afternoon to repay his loan. The surprised credit union staff met for several minutes before deciding it should not charge a penny in interest. Would a bank have even bothered with the newsboy?

As for taxes, the CUNA public relations staff argued that credit unions were unique, nonprofit volunteer organizations. No outside capital was involved. Only members could deposit their savings in a credit union, and only members could borrow from its pooled resources. Just as interest was paid on bank savings, dividends were paid on credit union savings; just as banks were not taxed on the interest they paid depositors, credit unions were not taxed on dividends they paid savers. Moreover, the government already taxed credit unions through

The CU-Notes, a choir composed of employees of CUNA, CUNA Mutual, and CUNA Supply, often entertained at credit union events and around the Madison area. Outside Filene House in 1952 with assistant managing director Charles F. Eikel, Jr., are, first row, from left: Kay Moore, Velma Thompson, Charlett Morgan, Betty Welsch, and Jane Thoma. Second row: Leona Hasse, Pat Sparks, Donna Levenick, Nan Gifford, Lydia Vivian, and June Nesberg. Third row: Gladys Hall, Darlene Ott, Beverly Shepard, Clara DiLoreto, Loretta Sullivan, and Madonna Remick. Fourth row: Armella Ring, Elaine Richgels, Lillian Theis, Margaret Manthei, Deloris Walsvick, Jeanne Buechner, and Marcella Sturgis.

Among the vehicles used to promote CUNA Mutual in the 1950s was a comic book, "Protecting Your Family," and a matchbook with a picture of Filene House, below.

personal income taxes on the members who "owned" the credit union.

"In a sense, you might call credit union groups 'do-it-yourself' financial projects," Gregory said. "To tax members on the savings they are able to make through this specialized method of operation would be comparable to taxing the savings an individual makes when he spends time and effort building his own home, rather than paying for outside help."

Despite the efforts of credit unions to maintain a low profile in the early 1950s, Congress had considered several bills to levy taxes on cooperative groups, as well as mandatory deposit insurance on credit union shares. Many credit union leaders decided national advertising would give credit unions a better chance to answer critics and explain their unique features and contributions.

In 1952, using funds set aside in a publicity reserve fund six years earlier, CUNA Mutual began sponsoring a national radio advertising campaign in the United States and Canada. Radio was still the main source of news and entertainment for most people. It was also the most inexpensive way to reach them. For the cost of a phone call, the most popular radio programs reached a hundred homes.

For the next three years, the credit union movement, using CUNA's name and CUNA Mutual's advertising funds, sponsored Gabriel Heatter's Tuesday night news commentary over the Mutual Broadcasting Network. The movement sponsored a similar program in Canada hosted by Lorne Greene, later famous as rancher Ben Cartwright in the television series "Bonanza." Greene had helped start a credit union at the Academy of Canadian Radio Arts in Toronto. CUNA Mutual also sponsored "Twenty Questions."

Heatter and Greene were among the most popular broadcasters of their time, each reaching several million listeners. In a few weeks, CUNA and CUNA Mutual received nearly 27,000 inquiries about credit unions. Despite the enormous interest, not everyone favored the campaign. Its first year cost more than $600,000 and some leagues wanted the funds shifted to other activities. Bergengren, watching from Vermont, told a friend that if he had initiated such a campaign, he would have been "halved, quartered and burned."

Many questioned the campaign's scattergun approach. The managing directors of some state leagues weekly received dozens of invitations to talk about organizing credit unions. Many of the initial postcards came from the sick, unemployed, and elderly, all in need of money and enthralled by the messages of announcers they trusted. Few were in any position to organize a credit union.

The public relations staff had warned that a significant time lag between the sowing and the reaping was likely. Credit union organizers typically required several contacts to get an application signed; the same must be expected of advertising. One message did not usually sell a person; neither did two or four or even ten. People were exposed to thousands of impressions every day. Only through repetition would the credit union message get through.

The number of inquiries was only one indication of the effectiveness of the campaign. Radio advertising was making credit unions more recognizable and dispelling misconceptions about them. CUNA field representatives reported that employers and other groups were becoming more willing to listen to their story. Some league managing directors even asked that CUNA Mutual's insurance coverage not be mentioned further because they could not keep up with the inquiries.

At its 1953 annual meeting, the CUNA Mutual board voted to ask policyholders whether they supported the advertising campaign. Almost five thousand favored continuing the program; fewer than two hundred were opposed. Buoyed by the support, the board stepped up advertising in magazines such as *Business Week*, *Time*, and *Newsweek*. Leading businesspeople like Eddie Rickenbacker, World War I flying ace and president of Eastern Airlines, testified about the benefits of credit unions for employees. J. L. Kraft also gave his endorsement.

The radio and magazine campaigns eventually paid off. From 1952 to 1954, almost six thousand new credit unions were organized, at least one-fourth of them directly attributable to advertising. The percentage of credit unions affiliated with CUNA also increased, to nearly 80 percent.

CUNA Mutual had even more spectacular results. In 1952, just sixteen years after it was founded, coverage totaled a billion dollars, the fastest any insurance company had reached that mark. Three years later, coverage reached two billion dollars, making CUNA Mutual one of the twenty largest life insurance companies in North America in total insurance in force.

The radio campaign came to a close in 1954. Because nearly the entire cost was borne by CUNA Mutual, some CUNA executive committee members feared that the society was taking over duties that belonged to CUNA. CUNA directors voted to shift more of the cost of advertising to the national association. Not long afterward, Doig announced that CUNA Mutual had discovered it could not sponsor radio programs in states where the society was not li-

censed. It maintained its magazine advertising, focusing more on magazines like *Reader's Digest* and *Life*.

CUNA and CUNA Mutual turned increasing attention to television but delayed advertising plans upon discovering that a TV campaign would cost more than a million dollars a year.

A Common Servant

The decade following the end of World War II would one day be known as the Golden Age of Credit Unions. It was a time of unprecedented growth, increased awareness of credit unions, and harmony within the movement.

Most agreed these achievements were a reflection of Doig's time as managing director of CUNA, CUNA Mutual, and CUNA Supply. Despite initial concerns about his leadership, Doig had avoided many of the inevitable political disagreements that made the job so difficult.

Doig succeeded because he respected the democratic wishes of the movement. He fought hard for his ideas, but when other proposals won, he supported them with enthusiasm. He rarely sprang new plans on the boards he served, wisely choosing to discuss his theories first.

During the early 1950s, CUNA Mutual sponsored national radio news broadcasts in the United States and Canada. The society's Canadian spokesman was Lorne Greene, right, later famous as rancher Ben Cartwright in the television series "Bonanza." C. Gordon Smith, manager of CUNA and CUNA Mutual's Canadian operations, is at left.

Courtesy CUNA and Affiliates Archives

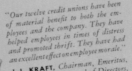

Thomas W. Doig

Managing Director
CUNA Mutual Insurance Society
1945–1955

As an administrator, Doig delegated freely, saving most of his energy for that which he did best—inspiring the movement. Like Bergengren, Doig was a gifted orator, though less polished and loquacious than his predecessor. Slightly nasal, his voice was nonetheless resonant and powerful. While Doig lacked much formal education, he was a voracious reader. He often took as his inspiration the Bible, and his speeches usually sounded like sermons.

"CUNA Mutual is founded upon the rock of faith," Doig wrote in the society's 1946 annual report. "Individually, we and our credit unions were weak. Through union and the exercise of courage we developed strength. Having gained strength, we offered and still offer to others the protection afforded by our strength. We cast our bread of protection upon the waters of life, and it has returned to us a hundredfold."

Doig was a persuasive evangelist, not only because of the power of his prose but also because he lived what he preached. Unlike Filene, who loved humanity but had trouble with individuals, Doig related to others on a personal level. Unlike Bergengren, who sometimes belittled the opinions of his peers, Doig was eager to listen and learn from others.

Doig was an unabashed idealist. He believed the foundation of credit unions to be moral, not economic. Committed to creating a financial institution with a soul, he never forgot to do the same in his own life.

"You can throw money out the window, and it will come back to you," he often said. Doig threw so much money, to friends in need, to strangers, that many thought him naive. Doig did not care. The credit union philosophy—that the vast majority of people are honest—was his philosophy. Far better to be burned occasionally than to refuse to help for fear of disappointment.

Yet Doig was not simply an unworldly doer of good deeds. Allies and opponents knew him as a savvy political operator, a hard bargainer, a skilled builder of coalitions that helped him maintain power. Few politicians worked a roomful of potential supporters as well as he did.

Unlike many politicians, however, Doig applied his wiles less to personal promotion than to the advancement of the movement. A friend said Doig reminded him of the biblical passage in which Christ advised followers to be as wise as serpents and as harmless as doves. During the radio advertising campaign, Doig wanted figures on what other financial institutions charged for loans. Though there were state limits on loan charges, some banks and loan companies found ways to charge more. So Doig put on work clothes, planted dirt under his fingernails, and visited several lending institutions. In a few hours, he had all the evidence he needed for the ad campaign.

The credit union movement during Doig's tenure was social as well as political. Sometimes credit unions were organized and political problems solved in the wee hours, over a few drinks or more. Doig was certainly not the only credit union leader who drank, but his habit occasionally affected his ability to give speeches (some claimed him more eloquent after a few drinks) or led him to make embarrassing remarks.

If such incidents sometimes made Doig's friends unhappy, he did much more to earn their loyalty and trust. Doig was an easy man to forgive because he forgave others; he was an easy man to love because he loved. "We're all human," a friend said of Doig, "and Tom was as human as anybody."

Though he was not a crusader, Doig was an advocate of equal rights. The credit union movement, like most segments of society, was far from free of prejudice. Some leagues refused to accept black credit unions as members. Doig criticized arrangements to keep them at a distance at a national meeting, putting himself in political hot water. His actions did not immediately change things, but they helped pave the way for the future.

Doig also believed in equal opportunities for women. Several women had made significant impact on the credit union movement, among them Evelyn Higgins, the first woman to serve on a credit union board; Agnes C. Gartland, the assistant executive secretary of the Credit Union National Extension Bureau; and Louise McCarren, the young Kroger employee who had surprised Bergengren on the train to Estes Park and later became managing director of the Ohio Credit Union League. Other league pioneers included Harriet Berry of North Carolina, Elizabeth Lynch of Florida, and Caro D. Coombs of New York.

Perhaps the most prominent woman in the credit union movement was Dora Maxwell, one of six children of a Jewish peddler in New York City. Bergengren hired her as a field worker in the eastern states after his first choice, a man, did not work out. Maxwell became one of the top organizers in the movement, once organizing 120 credit unions in five months.

Maxwell was an active supporter of social causes, including the cooperative and pacifist movements. She vehemently opposed the internment of Japanese-Americans during World War II, and she championed civil rights when the movement consisted of only a few brave blacks and eastern liberals.

Maxwell did not wear her beliefs on her sleeves. She often traveled with Doig and Hyland, watching patiently as they spent free time playing pinball. Maxwell never played. Instead, every time they put a coin in the pinball machine, she took a nickel from one pocket and put it in the other.

"What the heck are you doing?" Hyland asked Maxwell.

"None of your business."

"Aw, c'mon. It can't be that big a deal," Doig said.

"If you must know, I'm giving money to charity," Maxwell said. "When you put a nickel in the machine, I put a nickel in my pocket, and it goes to a charity for kids. That's money I'd be spending playing pinball with you. So you might say I'm getting my charity for free."

Doig and Maxwell became close friends. When he was named managing director, he appointed her head of CUNA's organization department; she later headed the education

---

SERVING THE MOVEMENT

By 1949, CUNA Mutual was growing faster than any life insurance company on the continent. Insurance rating agencies gave CUNA Mutual the highest marks for security, and the society returned almost ninety cents of every premium dollar to members, double the industry average.

---

department as well. In 1947, the executive committee, believing Doig was spreading himself too thin, pressured him to pick an assistant managing director. He nominated Maxwell.

The executive committee balked at the choice. Maxwell was an excellent, committed worker, they admitted, but she was not the right person for the position. Her political views, which bordered on socialism, were bothersome. Her feminist beliefs—she was married but still used her maiden name—also made many credit union leaders uncomfortable. But the main strike against Maxwell was that she was a woman.

Maxwell took the pressure off Doig, who

The Filene Memorial trustees, the Filene House Advisory Committee, and the administrative bodies of CUNA posed on the steps of the national headquarters in August 1950 after giving the signed deed to John E. Eidam, CUNA president, and Moses C. Davis, CUNA Mutual president. Front row, from left: Thomas W. Doig, Elmer J. Christoph, Moses C. Davis, Gurden P. Farr, W. Arthur Dunkin, John L. Moore, and C. Frank Pratt. Middle row: attorney John E. Roe, the Rev. J. D. Nelson MacDonald, William Reid, Willard L. King, Joseph Rothschild, John E. Eidam, W. O. Knight, Jr., and Harold C. Moses. Back row: Charles G. Hyland, Marion F. Gregory, Harry C. Lash, H. B. Yates, Paul D. Deaton, William W. Pratt, R. A. West, and Jack W. Burns.

Buttons like this one, identifying the wearer as a credit union member, were sold for about a penny in the late 1940s. Many credit unions distributed the buttons to members on Credit Union Day.

had threatened to resign over the issue, by quitting first.

"Frankly, I am reluctant to resign," she told Doig. "I would prefer to stay and see this thing through. However, I am unwilling to be the cause of any rift between you and the executive committee. You have a great future. The credit union movement has a great future. I am sorry I shall not be a part of it." She returned to field work for CUNA and CUNA Mutual and retired in 1955.

In a subsequent letter to *The Bridge*, Florence Lancaster, president of the St. Martin's Federal Credit Union in New York, criticized the magazine for printing an announcement of Maxwell's resignation without explanation. She noted a recent item about a league that was taking applications for managing director. "The first requirement for this position was that the applicant be male," Lancaster said. "Would this have been printed in *The Bridge* if it had been specified that the person applying must be white or Christian or non-Catholic or some other unfair discrimination? The fascists believe that woman's sphere should be confined to children, home, and the church. We fought a war

over these ideas and licked them. Or did we?"

The magazine responded: "*The Bridge* would not print an advertisement or notice that to obtain a position a person must be white or Christian or non-Catholic. With due respect to feminist thinking and with genuine sympathy for that point of view, *The Bridge* feels that the type of discrimination involved in the letter is not of the insidious nature of the other types mentioned and that employers may with no evil intent decide that a position should be filled by men."

Maxwell's resignation was one of only a few unhappy incidents with employees during Doig's tenure as managing director. Doig was popular with the employees of CUNA, CUNA Mutual, and CUNA Supply. He placed a rose, which he paid for himself, on the desk of each woman employee on her birthday. He started credit union accounts for the new babies of workers and deposited five dollars in each. He occasionally went to watch employee bowling teams and took them out to dinner afterwards. But Doig's concern went beyond gifts and pleasantries. One day, he told the employees he wanted them to join a labor union.

"But we don't need a union," a worker said.

"Our pay is as good as anybody's in town, and we are treated better."

"I hope I am good to work for," Doig said. "But I make mistakes. Maybe I'll give somebody a raise and miss people who deserve it more. Maybe I'll die and somebody else comes in who isn't so great to work for. I think you should join an established union, whichever one you think is best. Then, within a few months, be ready to negotiate a contract."

Doig once negotiated the entire wage settlement for CUNA Supply at the Hoffman House restaurant, the unofficial hangout of his employees. Over drinks, he asked the employees on hand about the pay scales at local print shops, then pledged to go 5 percent higher than the highest rate. The amazed employees, expecting stiffer negotiations, gratefully bought Doig several drinks.

If Doig made Filene House a good place to work, he expected much in return from his employees. CUNA Mutual existed for service, he insisted, and employees were expected to follow the Golden Rule. Doig demanded that claims workers take extra time to fully explain claims problems to members. Doig was also known to overrule his claims department and approve settlements, especially when a credit union made a mistake that invalidated a member's claim. The claim might be technically invalid, but that did not mean CUNA Mutual was not morally responsible.

Under Doig, the society also began to stress the importance of stability and quality. "When you compare CUNA Mutual with the competition," he said, "don't just look at our prices. Check our reserves, security, and ratings." His goal was to make CUNA Mutual as secure as any life insurance organization in the country, and by 1955 the society was well on its way.

As CUNA Mutual and CUNA grew stronger, Doig grew weaker. Friends blamed his lifestyle: too much work, too many late nights. A man only could take so much. As a field organizer and assistant managing director, Doig often was on the road for a month or more, at home for a few days, then back on the road again.

Doig also paid an emotional price for his commitment to the credit union movement. On the road when his first child was born, he told his companions that sometimes he'd like to "chuck this job in the river and go home." Years later, Doig told young employees not to make the same mistake he had.

Doig had a heart attack in 1953. He returned to work several weeks later—the entire staff stood and cheered when he walked into Filene House—but he was never the same again. Two years later, Doig became ill. He delayed seeking treatment, in part because his family was Christian Scientist. But he became weak and gaunt. Some days he put his head down on his desk, coughing so hard he had difficulty sitting up again. Finally, in the fall of 1955, Doig went to the doctor and learned cancer had spread through his body. He was fifty-nine years old and had only a few months to live.

Thomas W. Doig and Dora Maxwell.

Differences of opinion are the essence of democracy, Roy F. Bergengren said. In 1956, the credit union movement found itself engaged in an emotional debate about a consultant's report calling for dramatic changes in CUNA management. Fallout from the debate ultimately led to a split between the leaders of CUNA Mutual and CUNA. One of the most passionate encounters was the CUNA national meeting in Milwaukee in May 1956, where the national board considered the merits of the report.

CHAPTER FOUR

A Report of Conflict

It is a very human thing to cry when something you love is in pain. And our organization, the vehicle we use to turn dreams into realities, was in very deep pain.

—J. Peter Harris

"**D**ifferences of opinion are the very essence of democracy," Roy Bergengren wrote in his book *Crusade*. The credit union movement had not been free of political differences under Tom Doig's leadership, but complaints were muted by the successes of the era. By the fall of 1955, however, as Doig neared death, long-simmering differences began to surface.

Some members of the CUNA executive committee voiced the most significant complaints. Many agreed Doig had been more responsive than Bergengren to the direction of the executive committee (though a few, still angry that Bergengren had been forced out, blamed Doig). Nevertheless, some members claimed they still lacked enough control to guide the movement.

The committee's frustration was aggravated by the depth of its own accountability. In many organizations, delegates selected a board for four years or more, granting it authority to carry out the organization's strategy with a fair amount of autonomy. But CUNA's delegates were the directors. Nearly two hundred national directors, representing fifty-nine American and Canadian leagues, met annually and selected from their number an executive committee. While the CUNA bylaws gave the committee power to conduct business between national meetings, the committee was expected to follow closely the mandates of the national board. Failure to do so would almost certainly prompt a flurry of criticism within the movement. Thus, some executive committee members felt caught between the national directors and management.

At the same time, some CUNA national directors argued that something was deficient at Filene House. The movement had achieved un-precedented growth in recent years, but it also had problems: too many credit unions dormant or liquidating, legislative pressures, a need for better publications and educational programs. Some claimed the CUNA and CUNA Mutual staffs, the majority of which had been hired from within the movement, did not have the specialized business and administrative skills needed to solve these problems.

Questions of board control and staff qualifications collided at the 1954 annual meetings, held at Estes Park, Colorado, to mark CUNA's twentieth birthday. A few directors campaigned for a management consulting firm to study the strengths and weaknesses of CUNA, CUNA Mutual, and CUNA Supply. Others voted them down.

At the next year's meeting, in St. Louis, the national board seemed open to a management study of CUNA. But it balked when Melvin H. Widerman, a store manager and director from Maryland (who would be named CUNA president later that day), moved that the report, when completed, be referred to the executive committee with "power to act" on its findings. "It seems to me you are asking the executive committee to practically check on itself," one director said. The national board approved doing the management study but stipulated that its recommendations be submitted to the national directors for approval, amendment, or rejection.

The study was finished in the fall of 1955, in time for the quarterly meetings of the CUNA executive committee and the boards of CUNA Mutual and CUNA Supply. The three boards also met jointly to review shared problems, coordinate plans, and eliminate potential misunderstandings, a practice Doig had encouraged.

The main topic at the 1955 joint meeting

was Doig's illness. No one expected him to resume his position, and some executive committee members, eager to act on the management report, wanted to select a new managing director for the three organizations as soon as possible. Others, including most CUNA Mutual board members, were strongly against the idea. Widerman finally told the joint boards that action on a new managing director would be deferred until the next joint meeting, in February.

Most expected Doig's successor to be Charles Eikel, the assistant managing director. Eikel had been acting manager for several months in 1954 while Doig recovered from a heart attack, and he had been in charge during the past few months in 1955.

Like most credit union leaders of the time, Eikel was not an administrative expert. But he had taken night courses in business, accounting, and law, and his intelligence and passion for credit unions made him a fast learner. Eikel also had a quality that could not be taught: the ability to inspire loyalty.

But Eikel's relationship with some members of the executive committee had recently deteriorated. In August, Widerman had taken Eikel out for lunch. Widerman had just seen an early version of the management consultant's report, he told Eikel, and the news was not good: Operations at Filene House were "chaotic," and CUNA staff members were not trained to move to positions of greater responsibility. Quickly naming a replacement for Doig to implement the report's recommendations was critical to turning the situation around, Widerman said.

Eikel was honest and temperamental, qualities that made him a superb motivator but a poor diplomat. He reacted angrily to Widerman's assessment.

"You're wrong," Eikel said. "The staff may not be perfect, but it's doing a fine job under difficult conditions. It sounds like you don't think I've got the experience to be managing director, either."

"Well, that's what some of the boys think."

"If the executive committee doesn't want me as managing director, that's their right. You can tell me you don't like the tone of my voice or the way I part my hair. You can even tell me you don't like me. But don't tell me I don't have the

Courtesy CUNA Mutual Archives

Charles F. Eikel, Jr., was assistant managing director of CUNA and CUNA Mutual in 1955.

experience. I'm as ready for the job as anybody you could name."

"If that's true, why don't you ask Tom to resign? It's terrible, but everybody knows he's too sick to come back. Tom and his family will be well taken care of. We need to get this organization moving again."

Eikel, who was extremely loyal to Doig and had been visiting him nearly every night after work, shook his head.

"Mel, if you think I'm going to go to my boss and ask him to resign, you're nuts."

"Will you at least do me a favor? Will you keep me posted on what's going on at the office? You guys in Madison never let us know what's going on there."

Eikel said he'd think about it but changed his mind a few days later. He was not in the habit of writing confidential reports, he told Widerman, and was not about to start now.

On November 11, 1955, the day after the joint meeting, the CUNA Mutual board decided to continue with Eikel as assistant managing director until it considered candidates for a new managing director with the CUNA executive committee and CUNA Supply board at the next joint meeting. (During the session, word arrived that Bergengren had died.)

The next day, the CUNA executive committee voted, "reluctantly, in consideration of the report of his doctor," to retire Doig at full salary and, upon his death, to give his widow an annual annuity of $2,500 for the rest of her life. The committee elected a new managing director, H. B. Yates, a retired high school history teacher from Dallas, who had preceded Widerman as CUNA president.

The committee went into closed session and called in Eikel. Yates had agreed to take the job temporarily, he was told, until matters relating to the management report were resolved. Eikel agreed, but he angered a few directors when he observed that the CUNA Mutual board would not be happy about the decision.

Eikel was right. The CUNA Mutual board called a special meeting in December to talk to Widerman. Upset that the CUNA executive committee had not waited to retire Doig as Wider-

man had promised, the CUNA Mutual board declined to name Yates as its managing director, as Widerman now urged. The board reaffirmed Eikel as the society's assistant managing director.

Yates, thin and subdued, quietly assumed the CUNA managing director's job in Madison on December 12. His reception was polite but not warm. Though the employees worked hard to help him learn his duties, most were unhappy that Eikel did not get the job. A bachelor, Yates spent much of his time in the office alone, a situation some attributed to his penchant for brevity. If a question could be answered yes or no, that was generally all one got from Yates. He had not been a supporter of Doig, but some employees noticed that he seemed genuinely sorry when he learned Doig died on December 19.

During his first week, Yates saw little of Eikel, who was about to leave on an extended vacation. The two had not gotten along for several years. As a CUNA field representative, Eikel did not mind correcting league representatives when he felt it was warranted. His relationship with some leaders in the Texas league, including Yates, had been rocky, and he had been booted out of meetings by local representatives who resented his advice.

When Eikel returned from vacation, Yates gave Eikel a copy of the management report, which had been seen only by the executive committee and a few other political allies.

"You'll probably blow your top when you read it," he said. "But I want your reaction."

Eikel was unhappy with the report, which was critical of the CUNA staff in many areas. According to the consulting firm, the office did not have clear administrative policies and departments operated as distinct entities with "little, if any, regard for the activities or cooperation of other departments." CUNA's labor policies were more liberal than those of any other organization the consultant knew. Personnel controls and reporting records were "lackadaisical."

Though the report lauded employees for their spirit, it said most department heads had no "outstanding ability, education, or experience to merit the salaries they received." Eikel was commended for his promotional talents, but the consultant believed his "ability to coordinate departmental activities is missing."

From left: William B. Tenney, J. Orrin Shipe, and Charles F. Eikel, Jr. enjoyed a meal at Eitel's Old Heidelberg Restaurant in Chicago, about 1950.

Courtesy CUNA Mutual Archives

Yates and Eikel met a few days later to talk about the report. "Knowing you, I'm sure I'm going to get an honest opinion," Yates said.

"You're right about that," Eikel said. "I think this report stinks to high heaven."

When Yates said he supported the report and intended to make organizational changes in CUNA, Eikel decided the rest of the office should be made aware of the report. That weekend, he met with most of the CUNA staff in the home of Marion Gregory, the director of public relations. Eikel had promised he would not show the report to anyone, he said, but he hadn't said anything about reading it out loud.

The group was puzzled by what it heard. The report consisted mostly of vague generalizations, like "underdeveloped functional assignment," "good basic policies," and "lack of general management direction," with almost no specific examples, the employees claimed. One employee said the report could have won a Pulitzer Prize in abstract writing.

Several workers said the consultant had not even talked with them; others claimed he had spoken with them less than five minutes. Several department heads said the consultant had talked to them less than thirty-five minutes and mostly about his hobby, raising horses.

Some employees said the report had serious factual errors. For example, the consultant criticized the office for high expenses, claiming an average $47.30 per day. But he subtracted Saturdays and Sundays from his calculations, forgetting that many of the meetings and trips were on weekends. Adding those days brought the expense rate down almost $12.00 per day.

The employees were most disturbed by what they considered the report's reliance on speculation. The consultant had said of Doig: "The managing director has placed greater emphasis on the development of CUNA Mutual so that between the three organizations there is not the proper balance." That was ludicrous, the staff said. Doig had believed in a strong CUNA Mutual but he had been much more occupied with CUNA business.

The staff also was angered by the report's criticism of Doig giving flowers to the women employees on their birthdays. Doig had paid for the flowers out of his own pocket.

Several employees were especially opposed to the consultant's recommendation that most CUNA departments be placed under a development director. Along with the managing director and executive committee, the development department was to supervise and coordinate the work of the other department heads and "thoroughly teach these men the fundamental policies, principles, aims, desires, problems, and their solutions of the credit union movement."

"There is one man in the Madison office who stands out head and shoulders above all the others, who could with the proper guidance, head up this new development program," the consultant wrote. "He is thoroughly familiar with the credit union movement, is a hard and tireless worker, has a good and broad vision of the entire CUNA organization, and its affiliate activities, knows where he ought to go, and knows what to do when he gets there." The man was J. Orrin Shipe, supervisor of the CUNA advertising and promotion service.

Shipe started his credit union career in Buffalo, New York, at age twenty-two and joined the CUNA staff as a field organizer in 1939. He eventually started the national association's first education department and edited *The Bridge* magazine. After navy duty in World War II, he became a special representative for CUNA Mutual.

Shipe's talents and energy were acknowledged throughout the movement. In 1952, he received an offer to join a commercial insurance company at a much higher salary but turned it down to stay with the movement. Like many coworkers, Shipe was aggressive and forceful and not afraid to back up his opinions with physical force. As a young field organizer, Shipe and a few others had sometimes wrestled each other to the floor spontaneously, in a sort of initiation rite.

Shipe and Eikel had been very close friends. They lived a few blocks from one another, often rode to work together, and socialized regularly. Eikel was godfather to one of Shipe's children; Shipe was a confirmation sponsor of Eikel's son.

Courtesy CUNA and Affiliates Archives

CUNA president Melvin H. Widerman spoke at the national meeting in Milwaukee in May 1956.

Eikel often defended Shipe against critics of Shipe's aggressive style; Eikel had his own critics. But their relationship had cooled as each moved up in the organization. One reason may have been Doig. Eikel was devoted to him. Shipe, a close friend of Bergengren, was not.

Courtesy CUNA Mutual Archives

J. Orrin Shipe, above, was temporarily named development director of CUNA in 1956.

The recommendation of Shipe for development manager was only one of the issues on Eikel's mind when he met again with Yates to talk about the consultant's report. Rumors, especially that Yates was about to begin implementing the report's recommendations, were floating around Filene House.

Yates wanted to know whether Eikel had changed his mind. Eikel said he still believed the report was so slanted as to be useless.

"You're bucking the executive committee, the national directors, and the managing director," Yates told Eikel.

"I am just giving you my opinion. As for the national directors, they were supposed to see this report before you acted on it. Most don't even know what's in it."

"You're playing politics! You're using the staff to campaign for you as managing director!"

"The management report said I had trouble getting the department heads to cooperate. How is it, all of a sudden, that I am able to convince all these people to work for me?"

The next morning, Yates called Eikel into his office again to try to change his mind about the report, but the assistant managing director said he had no intention of supporting the recommendations. Yates suggested that Eikel resign. He refused.

Later that morning, Charles Hyland, the CUNA comptroller, asked Yates whether he intended to implement the recommendations of the management report before the next meeting of the national board. When Yates said he did, Hyland called Melvin Widerman, CUNA president and head of the executive committee, reminding him of the national board's resolution in May 1955.

"As comptroller, it has always been my posi-

tion not to let anything happen that would be a surprise to the national directors," Hyland said. "This should be referred back to them."

"Charlie, I can appreciate your position, but you are going outside the responsibility of your position."

"That sounds a little bit like a threat."

"No, Charlie, this is not a threat, and I don't want you to take it in that light, but we are all very anxious and want to see that everybody is treated right. Decisions have been made that are not going to be to the liking of everybody. We have one thing in mind, and that is to make CUNA a strong organization that we can be proud of. Some people will not like it, and they will think we are stepping on their toes. You have to be broad-minded about things that are being done."

"What are you thinking when you go ahead and ignore the resolution?" Hyland asked.

"It is going to be submitted to the board of directors. It would be senseless to wait until May to do what must be done now. As long as I've been with the national association, we waited until it was too late to do things that have been costly to us."

When Hyland pleaded with Widerman to call the executive committee before taking action, Widerman asked him to write him a letter with the request.

A few hours later, Yates called Eikel, Shipe, and several department heads into his office and announced the formation of the development department.

Marion Gregory, head of the public relations department, said he did not think it fair that decisions had been made on the basis of a report he had not had a chance to read (he had heard it read) and that he thus was in no position to defend himself.

"There is nothing derogatory in the report," Yates said.

El Watkins, the editor of *The Bridge*, protested. Watkins was known for his passionate views and sometimes spoke without considering the consequences. He could not, he said, in good conscience go along with the report's findings because it had not been approved by the national board. He refused to work with Shipe as development director and urged that the report be made public so it could be checked for accuracy.

Yates refused; the executive committee had made its decision, and the consulting firm was insisting that action be taken. Minutes after the meeting ended, news of the new department spread through the office.

Yates became concerned enough about morale that he called a CUNA staff meeting a week later. Some misleading rumors had been spread about the management consultant's report, he said. Most of the staff should not be concerned about the report for it contained no recommendations to change working conditions or salary levels. The report was not being made public because it "reflected unfavorably" on a few supervisors, Yates insisted. Still, the reason for establishing a development department was not that CUNA departments were "poorly operated," he added paradoxically.

News of the consultant's report was made public for the first time in the February 1956 issue of *The Bridge*. Yates praised the leaders who had brought the credit union so far but emphasized that the missionary spirit was, by itself, no longer adequate to solve the movement's problems. He noted that CUNA Supply and CUNA Mutual had recently voted to undergo management surveys.

"The missionary spirit does not usually find administration to its taste," Yates said. "CUNA has grown up without developing coordination. Responsibilities have been assigned to individuals on personal grounds rather than in line with sound organizational structure. Department heads have often been left free to follow their own inclinations rather than given defined objectives."

"If all this sounds alarming, it is reassuring to remember that despite the lack of coordination between departments, CUNA has recorded substantial achievements," he continued. "That this was possible was due entirely to the fact that by and large the personnel are not only thoroughly dedicated to credit union objectives but also have rich experience and articulate philosophy of service."

But dissatisfaction at Filene House continued. Yates required that all expense accounts come to him before going to Hyland, the comptroller. Disgruntled CUNA employees began to

contact national directors on their own time, and Yates began to receive a flurry of letters. Some were supportive. Others were angry that Doig had been retired, in the words of one state league official, "on his deathbed." Many directors believed Yates and the executive committee were moving too fast.

"I am not inclined to feel that this particular management consultant firm, or any other for that matter, can know all the answers to our problems," said W. Arthur Dunkin, a CUNA national director from Missouri and CUNA Mutual board member. "In a voluntary movement such as ours it is very easy to start an internal disagreement that can develop out of all proportions to its importance."

Yates responded tersely that the bylaws gave the executive committee authority to execute the powers of the board of directors between meetings. "I think you will find that any standard text on parliamentary procedure makes the same statement," he said, adding that the national board "will still have the final say" in May.

Tension was high when the CUNA executive committee and CUNA Mutual and CUNA Supply boards attended the joint meeting in Chicago in February 1956. Despite earlier concern about choosing a common managing director,

Outgoing CUNA president Marion Gregory (right) posed with H. B. Yates, the new president, in July 1953. Gregory later headed CUNA's public relations department and worked for Yates, the managing director in 1956, before resigning in protest.

the item did not appear on the February agenda. William H. Burke, a CUNA Supply director, objected to the CUNA executive committee's selection of a new managing director in November and asked for a unified decision. But his speech was not placed in the minutes.

Two days later, CUNA employees delivered a statement, signed by about twenty staff members, to the executive committee. The statement said the employees would not continue to work for CUNA if Shipe were appointed development director.

That same day, at the CUNA Mutual board meeting, several directors proposed that the board elevate Eikel to managing director. William Reid of New York objected, not because he did not think Eikel deserved the job but because he believed the CUNA executive committee and CUNA Mutual board still had a chance to select a common managing director. William Pratt of Pennsylvania and Art Dunkin agreed.

But the rest of the board was anxious to fill the position. Besides, Harold C. Moses, a director from Louisiana, pointed out that no matter the title, the matter of a common managing director would be settled in May at the annual meetings. The CUNA Mutual board elected Eikel managing director.

Eikel said he appreciated the vote but believed no person was important enough to split the credit union movement. He asked the directors to reconsider and name him acting director until May. The directors congratulated him for his gesture, though a CUNA executive committee member later told Eikel he thought his gesture insincere. When Widerman met Eikel on the elevator later, however, he said Eikel had done a "wonderful thing."

At a special joint meeting that night, Widerman told the CUNA Mutual board that CUNA was struggling with its budget. He asked the society to pay half of Yates's salary. He also hoped, since Yates was managing director of CUNA, that the CUNA Mutual board would elect Yates managing director as well.

Gurden Farr, president of CUNA Mutual, said the society did "not see fit" to accept Yates and thus did not provide for his salary in its budget. CUNA Mutual director Joe DeRamus then criticized Widerman for "conflicting state-ments." The CUNA president insisted that the changes proposed in the management recommendations required immediate action, yet he had known about the findings well before the November meetings. If the changes were so important, DeRamus asked, why hadn't the joint committee discussed them at that meeting? He also said several executive committee members had told him they were not implementing the report, yet Yates had signed a *Bridge* article saying he had already started making those changes.

Reid asked Widerman to see the management report. How could they hold a reasonable discussion without knowing what was in the report? Widerman had allowed one CUNA Mutual director, William Pratt, to see it. Why not the entire board?

The joint committee went into executive session to discuss the report, finally reaching a compromise: Though Eikel was still working as assistant managing director for CUNA, CUNA Mutual would pay his entire salary. In exchange, the CUNA executive committee would delay implementation of the management report until after the national meeting in May.

A few days later, a notice, suspending the appointment of the development director, appeared on the office bulletin board at Filene House; Yates said Shipe suggested the move. Over the next few weeks, copies of the management report were sent to the national directors.

The argument over Yates's salary, among other matters, brought to the surface long-standing disagreements between the two organizations. Some believed CUNA Mutual should contribute more to CUNA activities, allowing the national association to lower league dues. CUNA Mutual countered that the Wisconsin insurance department still monitored closely the relationship between CUNA and the society.

Despite the insurance department's criticism, the organizations had found many ways to work together. Not only had they a common managing director, but they shared the payment of his salary. CUNA Mutual and CUNA also shared many other salaries, from receptionists to secretaries to switchboard operators. Field representatives on CUNA's payroll continued to boost CUNA Mutual contracts, and CUNA Mutual sometimes paid expenses for employees on

| Gurden P. Farr, President Detroit, Michigan | Harold C. Moses, Vice President New Orleans, Louisiana | J.D.N. MacDonald, Secretary Dartmouth, Nova Scotia | John L. Moore, Treasurer Oakland, California | Joseph S. DeRamus, Director Chicago, Illinois |

| Moses C. Davis, Director Atlanta, Georgia | William W. Pratt, Director Harrisburg, Pennsylvania | William Reid, Director Brooklyn, New York | W. A. Dunkin, Director St. Louis, Missouri | A. P. Quinton, Director Hamilton, Ontario |

CUNA business.

But not everyone was happy with this arrangement. Critics, pointing to CUNA Mutual funding of the radio advertising campaign and other services, believed the insurance society was taking control of activities more properly controlled by CUNA. As president of the national association, Yates had noted these risks in 1954.

"The credit union movement is entirely too important to serve as a kite tail for any life insurance company," he said. "If CUNA Mutual continues to shoulder the expenses, there is danger of the national board degenerating into a debating society with no power." Soon thereafter, CUNA dues from state leagues were increased.

Even the most strident critics had accepted that it was too late to convert CUNA Mutual into a stock company controlled by the national association, and in 1945 the two organizations had signed a statement asserting that neither group was "empowered in any way to control or dominate or direct the affairs and activities of the other." Yet many of the arguments over control, which had dominated discussions a decade earlier, still existed in 1955.

"All of you are aware, I believe, of the great abuses created by a few people in large insurance companies and corporations where they entrench themselves in office and reap huge profits, salary bonuses, and power," Albert W. Marble, managing director of the Michigan Credit Union League, had told the executive committee in 1953. "I can see a barrier here that we could build behind billions of dollars of our people's money, built by a few people anxious to entrench themselves in office to perpetuate themselves and where they will sit in judgment upon the executive committee of the Credit Union National Association, the national board, and credit union people."

Marble, a passionate and visionary organizer who had built the Michigan league into one of the largest and most powerful in the country, was a strong advocate of cooperatives. As Bergengren had quietly preached a decade before, Marble believed credit unions should work closely with the cooperative movement. He was critical of what he saw as a growing campaign to establish a distance, respectful though it might be, between the two groups.

Some saw distance as necessary to credit union growth. They worried that a closer affiliation with the cooperative movement, whose leaders often criticized big business, might

Most of the 1956 CUNA Mutual directors had fifteen years of experience or more on the board.

erode support in industries where many credit unions were being organized. Because remnants of McCarthyism still existed, some credit union leaders were concerned about being linked with an organization a few characterized as socialistic, for the charge was occasionally leveled at credit unions as well.

In the early 1950s, some cooperative leaders, discussing tax matters with the government, intimated that the cooperative agenda was supported by the credit union movement. The CUNA national directors then passed a resolution emphasizing that credit unions and cooperatives were distinct and separate entities.

CUNA Mutual's directors maintained an even greater distance from the cooperative movement. Cooperative supporters criticized the society for not investing more of its surplus in cooperative ventures. The president of a Canadian cooperative union proposed that CUNA Mutual turn over its Canadian reserves to a Canadian cooperative insurance company.

If the CUNA Mutual board was sensitive to the criticism of cooperative supporters, it did not take kindly to the notion that it was trying to take over the credit union movement. All the directors were longtime credit union people, and most had served terms with the CUNA executive committee. The CUNA Mutual board respected CUNA's position as head of the movement, they said, and had supported the national association, recognizing that the fortunes of the two organizations were inextricably linked.

Two of the most fervent defenders of CUNA Mutual during this period had been among its most vocal critics several years before. Joe DeRamus, a director since 1937, and William Reid, a director since 1939, had not originally liked the society's mutual structure. When it became clear CUNA Mutual could not be reorganized into a stock company without complex legal and logistical problems, they accepted the society's design and ultimately became committed to it.

DeRamus was born in Alabama, where, he later told doubtful friends, he had clubbed snakes over the head when they came through holes in the floor of his family's modest house. His father died when he was a boy, and the family moved to Peoria, Illinois. Young DeRamus was a gifted musician and he trained to be a concert violinist. But he fell in love with his accompanist and gave up the instrument in a fit of rage after their romance soured. Tall and gangling, DeRamus was also a talented golfer who shot in the seventies despite holding the club cross-handed.

After serving in the U.S. Army Aviation Corps in World War I, DeRamus became editor of the Rock Island Railroad's monthly magazine. For several years, he rode the line from one end to the other, writing about the "little guys" who made the railroad run smoothly. DeRamus found a new outlet for his concern for working people when he met Bergengren in 1925. When the depression of the 1930s forced the railroad to halt publication of the magazine, DeRamus refused a position in another department and went to work, at a hundred dollars per month, for the Illinois Credit Union League.

While his wife and two daughters stayed home in Pullman, Michigan, DeRamus moved into the tiny league office near Chicago's loop. His expense account was fifty cents per day, and he slept on a cot on weeknights. During the day, he traveled the Chicago area, spreading the credit union gospel to a population then in the midst of the Great Depression. His message often fell on deaf ears, but he organized enough new credit unions to merit a raise and move his family to Chicago.

DeRamus had two sides, one soft and gentle, the other tempestuous. He loved to write poetry, published a collection of poems, and was dubbed by Bergengren "the poet laureate of the credit union movement." Although most of his compositions dealt with credit unions ("The service we render our fellow man is truly the best investment plan."), DeRamus also wrote about CUNA Mutual's employees, including an ode to the "laughing eyes" of Elaine Richgels, who recorded the minutes of the society's meetings .

DeRamus's temper was even more legendary than his verse. He argued with foes and allies alike and was often hardest on his closest

Joseph S. DeRamus, above, served on CUNA Mutual's board for more than two decades.

friends, especially Doig. An associate once described De-Ramus as a good listener and a hard talker, willing to hear all sides of the argument but likely to erupt if he disagreed. Although his temper earned him detractors, DeRamus was respected for his dedication, knowledge, and vision. He did not miss a CUNA Mutual board meeting in nearly two decades, and he had pushed hard for the radio advertising campaign over the initial objections of other directors.

William Reid was less turbulent than DeRamus but no less committed. Born in Pennsylvania, he left school at fourteen, deciding he could work and educate himself at the same time. Every morning, he walked two miles to a coal mine, where he put in a full day as an office boy before walking home. After supper, he walked back to the mine office to take high school equivalency courses.

Reid came to New York City in 1912, passed his civil service exam, and became a bookkeeper for the city. He rose to chief accountant in the comptroller's office, then to auditor of disbursements, and he became one of the leading fiscal advisors to Mayor Fiorello La Guardia. He was appointed deputy mayor of New York City and chairman of the city's housing authority, earning the unofficial title of "the world's biggest landlord."

Reid also played a leading role in the development of one of the country's first group medical plans, the Health Insurance Plan of New York. He became active in the city's municipal credit union in 1921 and was one of the few people to serve as president of both CUNA and CUNA Mutual.

A slightly built man with sandy hair and a thin mustache, Reid was perhaps the most in-

Courtesy CUNA Mutual Archives

timidating presence on the CUNA Mutual board. Thoroughly prepared, he expected the same of all who sat with him. He sometimes disagreed vehemently with those whose positions he actually supported as a way of measuring their commitment and illuminating the validity of objections. Although this technique helped him make better decisions, it often infuriated fellow directors and CUNA Mutual staff.

Once, after Reid unleashed a barrage of objections and criticism, Hyland and Bergengren threatened to resign together. Reid calmed them down and said, "It's obvious to me that we've been putting too much stress on Mr. Hyland and Mr. Bergengren. They're irritable. They're not amenable to reason. I move that we insist that each man take a two-week vacation with full pay, so they can come back in a proper frame of mind."

Reid, DeRamus, and the other CUNA Mutual

Dedicated and volatile, Joseph S. DeRamus started his credit union career as an employee of the Rock Island Railroad. He became one of the most influential forces in the credit union movement.

directors, even the diplomatic Harold Moses, were less conciliatory with their political detractors. Upset by accusations that the society was trying to take over the credit union movement and with five directors up for reelection at the upcoming annual meeting, the board issued a series of defensive letters in the spring of 1956. "An effort is being made," one said, "by the broadcast of casual statements, to discredit the motives and objectives of the board."

The letters defended the society's accomplishments, pointed to its "mutually beneficial" relationship with CUNA, and urged policyowners to support the board's nominees. "Experience with and understanding of the problems of the society and demonstrated ability to help solve those problems are highly desirable qualifications of board members," the board said. "Being a director of a business like CUNA Mutual, or of any cooperative business, is not primarily an honor to be passed around but a very real and important responsibility for which we should always strive to find and retain the best and most experienced leadership available."

"We don't say we should blindly elect incumbents," it continued. "We do say we should commend rather than condemn those directors willing to continue their service with accumulated experience, and that we should give their candidacy our grateful and even preferential consideration, with due regard of course for the records and qualifications of other candidates."

A few weeks later, on April 23, nine CUNA Mutual policyowners filed suit against the society in U.S. District Court, alleging that the board had "authorized and participated in the negligent, lavish, and unlawful use of corporate funds for noncorporate purposes, i.e., to influence the election of the individual director candidates" at the annual meeting on May 11, 1956.

The policyowners requested a preliminary injunction to stop CUNA Mutual from engaging in campaign activity until the suit was considered. The judge, Patrick T. Stone, granted the injunction and set a court date of May 4.

William Reid, deputy mayor of New York City, was president of CUNA and CUNA Mutual during his credit union career.

Seven of the nine policyowners were national directors. Two of the plaintiffs, Leonard R. Nixon of Connecticut and Alonzo J. Snell of Minnesota, were members of the CUNA Supply board, and a third, Henry Claywell of Florida, was on the CUNA executive committee.

Nixon, a legendary figure in the Connecticut league who had organized more than three hundred credit unions and been a national director for twenty years, had been one of the leading voices for change at Filene House. A close friend of Bergengren, Nixon had emphasized at the February joint meetings that Doig had been treated far better than Bergengren. "When Mr. Bergengren was fired, it set the movement back many years," he said.

CUNA Mutual was represented by the Madison law firm of Roberts, Roe, Boardman, Suhr and Bjork, which had worked for CUNA and CUNA Mutual. Much of the preliminary work on the case was done by Glenn Roberts, one of the senior partners, and Robert Curry, a young attorney just a few years out of law school. Curry's role increased when another senior partner, who usually handled CUNA Mutual business, suffered a nervous breakdown.

The suit had two main charges, that CUNA Mutual had used society funds illegally by sending out brochures on behalf of the incumbent candidates and that it had paid its field representatives to interfere in CUNA and CUNA Supply elections.

The defense argued that CUNA Mutual was legally bound to nominate and support its candidates for election. The board had contacted the insurance commissioner before sending the offending letters. The commissioner said they were legal. CUNA Mutual had even sent a letter to policyowners explaining how independent candidates could be nominated (the bylaws required a hundred policyowner signatures). Such activity by a mutual company on behalf of independent nominees was actually against the letter of the law, the defense said, but CUNA Mutual had done it to guarantee democracy.

The defense did not deny that some field organizers, employed jointly by CUNA and CUNA Mutual, were upset by changes in the organization. The plaintiffs alleged several instances in which field representatives criticized the CUNA

IT'S PART OF OUR AMERICAN TRADITION
TO WORK THINGS OUT TOGETHER

ADVERTISED IN
LIFE

Bringing in the Catch

Pooling their boats and nets, early New England fishermen put to sea in groups. The catch they shared far outweighed what they could haul in singly.

How today 10 million of us
help keep dollars from getting away

FROM some hands, dollars escape like fish in the sea. Yet these individuals may well not be at fault. For money troubles can come even to the most foresighted people. Before they realize it, they are lost in a fog of debt and doubt.

But today, in America, certain groups of people have been able to secure a remarkable degree of protection against money troubles. These groups are called *credit unions*.

A credit union is simply a group of people with a common bond, such as employment in the same company, who operate their own borrowing and saving system under supervision of state or federal agencies. The plan was first used over

100 years ago. Now, some 20,000 credit unions serve nearly 10 million Americans.

Saving together, members build a fund from which loans are made to help those of their group who need money for worthwhile purposes. As a credit union exists solely for the benefit of its members, loan cost is low and a good return is earned on savings.

Thus, the credit union serves a two-fold purpose, encouraging thrift and providing a convenient source of credit. Those who belong to credit unions are economically more secure. They can improve their living standard without getting into financial difficulties. And by being better

able to meet their financial obligations they are better citizens.

The entire credit union idea is democracy in action—people working things out together with dignity of spirit. Management, labor, church and government all heartily endorse credit unions.

Any group of 50 or more people can usually operate a Credit Union (in some areas groups of 100 or more are required).

SEND FOR FREE BOOKLET. A credit union can help you and your friends where you work or live. Write today for free booklet that tells you how. Send your name and address to **Credit Union, Dept. 102, Box 57, Madison 1, Wisconsin.**

This Ad appears in Life -- July 11, 1955

    PRINTED IN U.S.A.   11

Following the successful radio campaign of the early 1950s, CUNA and CUNA Mutual continued advertising in national magazines during the mid-1950s. This ad appeared in *Life* magazine on July 11, 1955.

executive committee and the managing director, Yates, during travels around the country.

But what was politics and what was not? The most cited case involved Jack Burns, assistant manager of the Canadian offices of CUNA and CUNA Mutual and a former member of the CUNA executive committee and CUNA Mutual board. National staff members were often asked by league personnel to help fill time-consuming volunteer jobs by recommending qualified people and convincing them to accept. During one meeting, a league official requested that Burns ask a potential candidate whether he was interested in running for the CUNA Supply board. The candidate apparently had his eye on another job and gave Burns no answer. The next day the candidate told a member of the CUNA executive committee that Burns had been "playing politics." He later withdrew his complaint, but at the November 1955 executive committee meeting Yates brought a resolution instructing management to "issue a cease and desist order to stop these practices." Eikel later maintained he was never told what the practices were.

If some field representatives had opposed any candidate, the defense asserted, they had done so "on their own time and on their own responsibility." None of the CUNA Mutual directors had assigned political chores or even heard of any such incidents.

Though the society's lawyers were confident of their defense, they took nothing for granted. Seven of the ten CUNA Mutual directors, along with employees Charles Eikel, Elaine Richgels, Tom Benson, and O. H. Edgerton, made the three-hundred-mile bus trip on May 4, 1956, to Superior, Wisconsin, where district court was in session.

Roberts and Curry hoped the accomplishments of directors like Reid and DeRamus would dazzle Judge Stone and bolster their legal arguments. After opening arguments, in which he effusively praised the board's record and dedication, Roberts asked the directors to stand, listing each term of service, which in the majority of cases was fifteen years or more.

The judge was visibly impressed, a reaction that led Carroll Metzner, lawyer for the plaintiffs, to protest what he called maneuverings to "overwhelm and overpower us."

"Your Honor, we have just as many people as they have brought in today," Metzner said.

"What is that?" asked Judge Stone, who wore a hearing aid (and occasionally turned it off when he tired of a lawyer's argument).

"I said we have just as many outstanding people who will support this action."

"I don't care about that. They are making accusations here against an honorable group of men who have done a magnificent job with this insurance company—and men who are doing it without pay. You should not be permitted to unseat those men by a lot of would-be politicians who apparently would like to grasp this company from the present management. I don't approve of it."

"We are not here to grasp anything from anybody, Your Honor," Metzner said. "We have no representative seeking election to the board. We just want this other matter [politics] discontinued, and I think that is the gist and the purpose of our complaints."

Metzner had sought a preliminary injunction to postpone the CUNA Mutual election until after the case was concluded, but Stone denied the request. Sensing an opening, Curry asked Stone to dismiss the complaint. Stone complied, until Metzner reminded the judge of a rule that gave him ten days to respond to defense arguments.

Roberts made a final attempt to convince Stone to dismiss the suit, emphasizing that it was "still a cloud upon us."

"Well, what I have said here today about this board of directors, I think, ought to dissipate the accusations," Stone said. "These men have erected a monument here that speaks more eloquently than anything that can be said about the fine work they have been doing. And I don't like to see them smeared or stigmatized or removed from office. We all recognize that their accomplishments have been magnificent. They should be applauded for it and not criticized."

The CUNA Mutual directors left the courtroom elated. They got back on the bus and celebrated all the way back to Madison.

The national directors gathered in Milwaukee a week later for the annual meetings of CUNA, CUNA Mutual, and CUNA Supply. The directors represented many factions with widely

disparate views and agendas. Some held the middle ground, believing that while the executive committee's motivations had been good, the attempts of some members to push recommendations of the consultant's report had resembled, in the words of one national director, "a herd of pachyderms attempting to dance the minuet."

Gradually, however, the delegates found themselves being drawn into what was being called the "national camp" or the "Mutual camp." Delegates leaning toward the national camp believed the executive committee was just trying to improve CUNA. The consultant's report said employees had extremely liberal benefits and few administrative controls. It was no surprise that employees should fight hard to preserve these conditions, they said.

Some Mutual supporters believed the management report was politically motivated and could have been written without consultants. They pointed to a confidential consultant report to Widerman with personal observations about Eikel and others, seemingly unrelated to job performance.

"In conversation, Eikel indicated that it was customary to elevate the assistant managing director to the position of managing director," the consultant reported. "If and when he was elected to this position, he was not going to have the executive committee or board of directors tell him how to operate CUNA. He was going to run it his way or else."

Mutual supporters also discovered that the consultants had done work for a Florida credit union for which Claywell served as treasurer. Claywell was one of the group that had sued CUNA Mutual.

The national meetings resembled political conventions even in the calmest years, and both the CUNA Mutual and CUNA boards found themselves locked in vigorous arguments with delegates. At one point, CUNA Mutual president Gurden Farr, reporting to policyowners on the suit, let his emotions get the better of him.

"The sooner people of the type that brought this action are eliminated from the credit union movement," he said, "the sooner we will be in a position to go forward."

Several policyowners called for Farr's re-

marks to be stricken from the record.

"We do not live in Russia," one said. "We live in America. We live in the greatest democracy in the world."

Delegates began to applaud.

"We have every right to criticize the board of directors of CUNA Mutual if we are policyowners or representatives," the director continued. "I think the president should be censured for stating that they should be eliminated because to us that is terrible language."

"Is there any further discussion?" Farr asked.

The policyowners considered two resolutions against the "unjustified use" of premium money to campaign and one supporting the campaign literature. Al Marble, managing director of the Michigan league, said that even if the court ruled it permissible to send out campaign literature, "I still maintain from a moral standpoint that it is not a good practice."

The ensuing discussion turned into a lengthy argument over the merits of the suit. Finally, as the argument threatened to get out of hand, Al Bauman, a director from Missouri, moved that future campaign information consist only of biographical sketches of the candidates.

He pleaded for a halt to "this long and

H. A. Busse, manager of the service and supplies department at Filene House, updated a policyowner address on the addressograph machine in 1956.

Courtesy CUNA Mutual Archives

drawn out argument that—please, God!—may someday end as to whether CUNA Mutual is trying to control the national association or whether certain people in the national association are trying to control us. I think we have sense enough to know without any propaganda from either side by letter—and I have a stack of them this high at home—or any argument in the hallways or private rooms as to how we are going to vote and select a man for this board."

Bauman's appeal quieted the crowd, and his motion passed. The policyowners quickly passed a motion commending the board for its efforts, and the meeting adjourned.

The next day, at the CUNA national board meeting, Widerman started where Bauman had left off. The movement had a responsibility to move forward, he said. "It is especially tremendous since, at the present time we disagree how to do it. Some of us have grown bitter in the struggle. There have been heated statements made during the last few months. There will undoubtedly be some more during the sessions today and tomorrow."

"Yet I think there are a great many things in which we all agree," he continued. "Our differences are not differences of principle, or principles of objective, but mainly the kinds of differences that spring up out of personal frictions and personal loyalties. On matters of principles we are all deeply united."

Hyland, whom the management report had characterized as a dedicated "watchdog" whose lack of accounting education nevertheless limited his effectiveness, did not agree. After giving his comptroller's report, he criticized the executive committee for moving too quickly with the management report and noted several factual errors. He passionately defended Doig. And he said he was resigning.

Hyland's announcement shocked the crowd for he was one of the last remaining credit union leaders with intimate ties to the movement's founders. Karl Little, a director from Utah, pleaded with Hyland not to quit. The mood was explosive. William Reid waited to rebut the management consultant's report, soon on the agenda.

But the meeting bogged down in a discussion of building negotiations between CUNA and CUNA Mutual. The insurance society had been thinking of building a new headquarters behind Filene House and selling its share of Filene House to CUNA. But the national association rejected CUNA Mutual's asking price. Art Dunkin, who had been defeated in his bid for reelection to the CUNA Mutual board the day before, defended the society, finally leaving the room to find his building committee files.

By the time Dunkin finished a chronology of the negotiations, almost an hour had passed. The crowd had lost much of its emotional edge. Reid had a plane to catch, and he left before delivering his speech.

Discussion of the CUNA management consultant's report was businesslike. The directors passed a motion concurring with the report but then approved only a few of the recommended bylaw changes, among them the creation of the development department. They tabled or rejected several proposals they believed would bypass their authority, including having the comptroller report directly to the executive committee.

The board also tabled a bylaw amendment giving the executive committee the right, after a full hearing, to remove any employee who "influenced or attempted to influence the election of any candidate" of the three CUNA organizations. Several directors said the proposal held "dynamite" and would be equivalent to an espionage network. "You would not dare go home and tell your wife that the president made a mistake," one said.

Despite subdued discussion of the management report, tensions rose as the directors prepared to elect the CUNA executive committee. Widerman was nominated again for president, as was John L. Moore, a Californian who had been a signer of the CUNA constitution at Estes Park and a member of the CUNA Mutual board since 1935.

It was a clear ideological battle, Moore representing the Mutual camp and Widerman the national camp. The two had run against each other for the same CUNA office the year before. At that time, the director who nominated Widerman had said that if the national directors were happy with the way Yates had run things, they should vote for Widerman.

After the vote was taken, the tellers reported that one director had returned a ballot with two names, one with an X next to it. A tense discussion followed: Should the ballot be thrown out? The directors voted to accept it, then learned Moore and Widerman had each received ninety-three votes. As the two sides lobbied furiously for votes, Little moved that Hyland be elected comptroller unanimously. Reluctant, Hyland nevertheless agreed to stay on "to do everything in my power to bring this movement back together." The second ballot for president came in amid rumors that several directors had changed their votes, but there was still a tie. Lobbying continued. It was nearly 7:00 P.M. On the third ballot, a few more directors changed their minds, and Moore lost by four votes.

Eikel's supporters on the CUNA staff believed they had lost as well. Patricia Cornell, a secretary, left the meeting in tears. J. Pete Harris, a national director from Georgia, saw Cornell leave. Concerned, he asked her identity and was told mistakenly that she was secretary Martha Ann Dolohanty. A few days later, Dolohanty got a letter from Harris.

"Most of us held our tears until we reached our rooms," Harris wrote. "I do not believe there was an individual yesterday, in that room, that did not weep. It is a very human thing to cry when something you love is in pain.

And our organization, the vehicle we use to turn dreams into realities, was in very deep pain."

Still, Harris said, "I cannot believe that any of us would shut off the growth of the credit union movement to avoid growing pains. It takes the clash of ideals to strike the rust of complacency from our ideals. I do hope these thoughts will help you to understand, and that you realize that we will soon have a far stronger and more capable organization than we have ever hoped for before."

The national board reconvened the morning after Widerman's election. A few directors tried to pursue complaints about the management consultant's report, including one accusation that it was "anti-union," but the board quickly moved on to the next order of business.

Personnel and executive secretaries in 1956 included, from left, Patricia Cornell, Charlett Chezik, Kay Moore, Elaine Richgels, Nan Lee, and Martha Ann Dolohanty.

Courtesy CUNA Mutual Archives

After the meeting, the new executive committee gathered in a corner of the room to elect officers. Yates was named managing director. He thanked the committee for its confidence, then announced his choice for assistant managing director. Eikel had just walked over and was sitting down as Yates spoke.

"I can't hear very well down here," a committee member said.

"They just appointed Orrin Shipe as assistant managing director," said another.

Eikel had just lost his job. The meeting adjourned a few seconds later.

Immediately after the meeting, Widerman walked into the joint committee meeting and

"Our differences are not differences of principle, but mainly the kinds of differences that spring up out of personal frictions and personal loyalties."

said Yates had been reelected managing director of CUNA. Leonard Nixon added that the CUNA Supply directors had chosen Yates its managing director. The implication was clear, but the CUNA Mutual directors refused to name Yates.

H. E. McArthur, a member of the CUNA Supply board from Illinois, wanted to know what the charges were against Eikel. "Nothing has been brought up, but the man is fired? Are you going to fire the rest of the people?"

"Definitely, Mr. Shipe is to replace Mr. Eikel," Yates said enigmatically. "I want to get the record straight on that. I don't think we have to have a trial when a man is replaced."

While the three boards could not agree on a common managing director, the executive committee proposed a plan to accomplish that goal: a committee made up of two members each from the CUNA executive committee and CUNA Mutual board and one from the CUNA Supply board to recommend a candidate. The CUNA Mutual board showed little interest in the proposal when it met in New York on June 16. The majority of the CUNA Supply board was politically aligned with the executive committee, several directors argued, and CUNA Mutual would be outvoted three to two on any common candidate. The directors rejected the plan and named

Eikel managing director of CUNA Mutual.

Morale at Filene House continued to deteriorate. When Yates arrived back at the office after the annual meeting, his secretary, Martha Ann Dolohanty, and stenographer, Patricia Cornell, said they could no longer work for him. Yates could not fire Dolohanty for, while she worked for the managing director, she was on CUNA Mutual's payroll. Upset by the upheaval in the movement, Dolohanty had decided after the convention to seek a credit union job in Arizona, but Eikel later convinced her to stay with CUNA Mutual.

The surprised Yates told Cornell, who was on CUNA's payroll, that she could be fired if she did not take Dolohanty's place as executive secretary. Cornell resigned anyway, as did several others. The executive secretary's job, which paid more than any other secretarial position, was posted on the bulletin board, but none of the secretaries in Filene House applied. The position was filled by an outside applicant.

Yates became increasingly isolated. A generally congenial though taciturn man, he was perplexed by the staff's loyalty to Eikel. A department head told him the reaction was not based on loyalty but on the conviction that Eikel was most qualified to be managing director of CUNA. But Yates had his own loyalties to consider. The executive committee, the democratically elected leadership, had given him a difficult assignment, and he was determined to complete it.

"I must be doing a good job," Yates told one visiting national director. "Nobody talks to me except the janitor."

Relations were better among CUNA employees. Although some had decided to fight and others believed the dispute was none of their business, they rarely questioned each other's choices. Relations also remained congenial, if more reserved, between the CUNA and CUNA Mutual staffs, for most viewed the matter as a dispute between the elected leadership.

Still, Yates was concerned enough about what he called "false rumors" to call the CUNA and CUNA Supply employees into the cafeteria on May 22, where the management consultants were waiting. Using a chart, Yates attempted to show how CUNA and CUNA Supply elections were democratic but CUNA Mutual's was not.

Bill Tenney asked a question. "You've shown us how the credit unions elect the national directors to represent them, and CUNA Supply works the same way. And yet these same national directors are the ones who carry the ballots of the policyowners, who are members of the credit union movement, and who elect the CUNA Mutual board. What makes this democratic on one side and not on the other?"

The meeting ended quickly.

A week later, Yates fired Jack Burns, the Canadian assistant manager who had been accused of politicking, and Jim Yates, a CUNA field representative (who was no relation). No reason was given for the Yates firing, though the managing director offered to give him a recommendation, saying he had always thought highly of him.

Yates also removed El Watkins as editor of *The Bridge*, saying that many national directors felt the magazine needed dramatic improvement. Though the magazine's circulation increased from 22,000 to 38,000 under Watkins, Yates said it had not kept pace with credit union growth. Yates offered Watkins a job as a *Bridge* staff writer, but Watkins refused. The incident set off a labor dispute, with the office workers' union arguing that the firing violated the union contract. Union and management could not resolve the dispute, and it eventually went to arbitration, the first in CUNA history. Watkins eventually won reinstatement as editor, but refused to accept the terms of the settlement. He also received retroactive pay. Characteristically, Watkins refused to cash the check as a matter of principle, but eventually he relented.

Several top managers had hoped the turmoil at Filene House would lead to reevaluation of the changes, but the CUNA executive committee indicated at its August meeting that it was generally pleased with management direction. A few days later, five leading CUNA managers resigned.

Among the five was Marion Gregory, the energetic, ambitious, and often controversial director of public relations and former CUNA president. Gregory had a fair amount of nerve; a few months later, he submitted his name to the CUNA executive committee as a candidate for the managing director's job. Others who resigned were William B. Tenney, a tough ex-

Marine and detail man who managed the education department; Clifford O. Skorstad, director of organization, the widely venerated field organizer whose credit union career went back almost as far as Doig's; Vaughn E. Liscum, the assistant comptroller who often sang the national anthem at annual meetings; and C. Gail Keeton, who headed the legislative department.

The mass resignation stunned the movement. In one day, the CUNA staff had lost most of its experienced managers. Combined with several other resignations, the staff was seriously depleted. The five resigning managers told the national directors they had resigned with reluctance and regret.

Several CUNA managers resigned or were fired during the political upheaval of 1956. Among them were, clockwise from top left, Clifford O. Skorstad, Elbert "El" Watkins, Vaughn E. Liscum, and C. Gail Keeton.

"You should know that the people who left CUNA did not do so to satisfy their personal desires; they left because they were thoroughly disappointed and concerned about the sad state of affairs in the Credit Union National Association," they said.

But others perceived a different motive, especially when Eikel hired all five of them. Eikel had been free with his criticism of Yates and the leaders of the executive committee, and he had canceled the insurance licenses of three of the men who had sued the society—Leonard Nixon, Harold Iversen, and Alonzo Snell.

Several national directors from New York sent an angry letter to the CUNA Mutual board in late August, saying the hiring was "in bad taste" and "not conducive to bridging the breach which exists between the society and CUNA." The directors were upset with Yates, too, and asked him not to accept the resignations until the movement's leaders could consider the matter.

Eikel flew to New York to meet with the directors. The hiring of the five was poorly timed, they argued, and only gave credence to accusations that CUNA Mutual was trying to take over the movement. Eikel said he had nothing to do with the resignations: The problem was that management had alienated the resigning managers. If the five men were so valuable, he said,

why had Yates not seen it? Why had some of them been prohibited from traveling?

"It is my job to find the best people for CUNA Mutual," Eikel finally said, "and if these men are available, I'd be a fool not to hire them."

Eikel said he had talked other CUNA employees out of quitting. One of them was C. Gordon Smith, who oversaw CUNA and CUNA Mutual operations in Canada. The political fight was hotter in Canada than in the United States, pitting the mainly agricultural, pro-cooperative leagues in the western provinces, which supported CUNA, against the primarily industrial leagues in middle and eastern Canada, which favored CUNA Mutual.

Smith, an Ontario resident, was an unyielding, almost bellicose supporter of CUNA Mutual. Indicative of his uncompromising stance and the polarization of the time was that his supporters described him as always smiling while critics later said he wore a perpetual frown. Smith's backing of Eikel and CUNA Mutual would play a part in the decision of the Canadian national directors to divide the management of CUNA Mutual and CUNA in Canada. Smith was offered the job as CUNA's Canadian manager, but he turned it down, keeping his CUNA Mutual position.

If Eikel urged employees to stay with CUNA, he did not do the same with Yates. Several days before the resignations, a deputy sheriff had delivered an eviction notice to the CUNA managing director, giving him thirty days to vacate his office, which was owned by CUNA Mutual. The eviction notice was signed by Eikel.

CUNA and CUNA Mutual had been discussing the property for some time. In 1954, Tom Benson had suggested that the society, whose number of employees had doubled since Filene House opened, would soon run out of space. CUNA Mutual eventually decided to build on the lot behind Filene House, provided it could sell its portion of the building to the national association, which was seeking more room for CUNA Supply.

The CUNA Mutual board considered selling its half of Filene House for the price listed on its books, $159,000, but its lawyers said the insurance commissioner might veto the deal as another CUNA subsidy unless the society could

Several CUNA and CUNA Mutual employees watched in 1949 as O. H. Edgerton countersigned a CUNA Mutual check for $150,000, the society's portion of the costs for Filene House. Behind Edgerton, from left, are Thomas W. Doig, Charles G. Hyland, Bert F. Beales, Thomas B. Benson, R. Eugene Cotterman, Charles F. Eikel, Jr., and C. Gordon Smith.

Courtesy CUNA Mutual Archives

prove the property was not worth more. One appraisal showed that portion of the building as being worth $202,192. The CUNA executive committee balked at that price and ordered its own appraisal; it totaled $208,250.

The CUNA building committee recommended accepting CUNA Mutual's asking price, but the executive committee wanted to negotiate further. The CUNA Mutual board offered a thirty-five year mortgage on the property at 4 percent interest, later lowering it to 3 percent.

But by May 1956, the building committee had decided it would not buy the building for more than $159,000. At the national meeting, Yates unveiled a plan to build a new CUNA Supply building for $250,000. He made no mention of CUNA buying any property from CUNA Mutual.

In the meantime, CUNA Mutual still had a space problem. The board had hired a consulting firm, which recommended that the society make use of all its space, including the office used by CUNA's managing director. Edgerton and Benson met with Yates on June 26 to discuss the problem. Yates and Shipe said it would take a little time to rearrange space on the CUNA side of the building to make the office available.

A week later, Yates told Edgerton and Benson that he had called Widerman and Nixon, who advised him to "sit tight." Yates then handed the men a memo. He had determined that CUNA had the right, as long as Filene House should stand, to have its managing director occupy the executive office.

"I have found that the foregoing rights were not granted to or reserved for CUNA in the deeds from the trustees," he said. "I am satisfied that they were left out of such deeds by reason of mutual mistake or oversight and that CUNA's interests were inadvertently slighted."

Eikel shook his head when he got the memo. He said Doig had often talked of moving out of the office—too cool in the winter, too hot in the summer, and too noisy all year—and creating a new office in the adjacent conference room on the CUNA side. Counsel advised Eikel that the only way to get Yates to move was a court order, and Eikel signed the eviction notice.

The CUNA Mutual board eventually decided that the negative publicity about the incident

Courtesy CUNA Mutual Archives

was too great. At the August 15 quarterly meeting, the CUNA Mutual board voted to let Yates stay in the office in exchange for seventy-five dollars a month in rent.

Another ray of hope for healing the movement emerged at the August joint meeting when director Al Bauman, who had played peacemaker at the national meeting in May, presented a new plan to choose a common managing director. The CUNA executive committee and CUNA Mutual would each appoint two members to the committee, which would then choose two more committee members; the group of six would select and recommend a candidate.

But any hope of unity ended shortly after the first meeting. The committee, composed of CUNA executive committee members William O. Knight of South Dakota and Lawrence Kilburn of Connecticut and Joe DeRamus and Harold Moses of CUNA Mutual, could not even agree on the final two committee members. Typical was their discussion of one of CUNA Mutual's committee candidates, Frank Graner, dean of the school for credit union personnel at

In 1959, William O. Knight, Jr., presented Harold C. Moses, right, with a citation honoring him as the only CUNA national director to serve twenty-five consecutive years. The two men served on a committee that failed to find a common managing director for CUNA and CUNA Mutual in 1956. As presidents of CUNA Mutual and CUNA, respectively, Moses and Knight later agreed that separate managing directors were necessary.

the University of Wisconsin.

"Graner has a mortgage with CUNA Mutual," Knight said.

"Oh my God, what else!" said Moses. "I don't know who has and who hasn't . . . "

"For his house."

"You'd think we'd foreclose if he didn't pick somebody . . . "

"No, but I'm talking about the possibility of having a preconceived notion," Knight said. "Anyone who lives in Madison is bound to have some pressure, either personal or professional, that is going to influence them."

Moses tossed out another name.

"What objection could you have to Oscar Rennebohm, former governor of Wisconsin? I don't know of any connection he has with the movement."

"Well, he was the guest at CUNA parties at Filene House, and he was very much in the foreground when we opened Filene House."

"So was the president of the United States. Would that disqualify him?"

"Pardon?"

"So was the president. Would that disqualify him?"

"Well, it might. I think you can understand that to be a little different."

The meeting went downhill from there. DeRamus and Moses rejected all the CUNA committee candidates because they were connected with the cooperative movement. Knight and Kilburn rejected all of CUNA Mutual's candidates, most of them on the staff of the University of Wisconsin, because they felt Madison residents could not be objective in choosing a managing director.

Frustrated at the standoff, league officials took matters into their own hands. On November 7, 1956, the eve of the quarterly joint meetings at the Sheraton-Blackstone Hotel in Chicago, thirty-seven state league representatives met there to find a solution. If CUNA and CUNA

J. Deane Gannon, top, rejected an offer in November 1956 to become managing director of CUNA, CUNA Mutual, and CUNA Supply. By the time Gannon reconsidered, CUNA had hired H. Vance Austin, bottom.

Mutual did not settle their differences, the officials warned, "CUNA will fall apart" and a new national association might emerge. Some leagues were talking about withholding dues until the dispute was resolved; if that happened, widespread cancellations of CUNA Mutual insurance would occur. The first step to solving the problem was a common managing director.

After learning of the meeting, Eikel called the CUNA Mutual directors together that night.

"In the past year, we have been living in an atmosphere not conducive to happiness and good health," he said. "Our uneasiness and unhappiness has penetrated our family lives. It is beginning to have its effect on the children. Recognizing my responsibility to the people who work under my direction, I do not believe I can stand as an obstacle in the path of their happiness and the happiness of their families."

If it would help them find a managing director acceptable to all three organizations, Eikel said, he would "gladly and willingly" step down as CUNA Mutual's managing director. It was the second time he had made the offer.

If Eikel could make such an offer, the directors decided, they were willing to find a common managing director. At the joint meeting the next day, the three boards found a name that everyone approved: J. Deane Gannon, longtime director of the Bureau of Federal Credit Unions. Gannon was flown in, and he arrived at the hotel about 10:30 P.M. Some executive committee members were at the opera; when they returned to the hotel around midnight, a joint meeting was convened and Gannon was offered the job.

Gannon, a Madison native and former supervisor of credit unions for the Wisconsin Banking Department, was highly regarded by nearly everyone in the credit union movement. He had much experience with credit unions and had scrupulously avoided involvement in the current controversy. He was interested in the job, and CUNA Mutual prepared a press release announcing his appointment.

But Gannon apparently had been watching the dispute more closely than anyone knew. Mindful of the political pressures inherent in the job, he asked for a longer contract than the boards were willing to give. In late November,

Gannon told Widerman he could not accept the offer.

Gannon changed his mind three months later, but by then CUNA had hired as its managing director H. Vance Austin, manager of the Colorado Rural Electric Association. Austin, a longtime credit union volunteer with close ties to the cooperative movement, had avoided public involvement in the split. Despite Austin's apparently neutral stance, CUNA Mutual remained committed to Eikel. A few months later, the chairmen of CUNA and CUNA Mutual, Knight and Moses, agreed that separate managing directors were necessary. They issued a statement expressing the hope that Eikel and Austin would work together for the good of the movement.

The policyowner suit against CUNA Mutual was settled in December 1956. A hearing had been held in June, at which Judge Stone denied the society's motion to dismiss the case. The trial opened on December 10. Three plaintiffs—Nixon, Snell, and Iversen—and five other witnesses testified about alleged political activity by CUNA and CUNA Mutual field representatives. Before CUNA Mutual could present its side of the case, Judge Stone called both sides into his chambers, recommending that the case be dismissed in the best interest of the credit union movement.

In court, the judge, who had defended the CUNA Mutual board so vociferously a few months earlier, evened the score.

"While there was justification for the institution of this action," he said. "and there has been proof of some improper activities on the part of some of the employees of the society, such as entering the politics of the other organizations, nevertheless there is an absence of evidence on the part of the officers and the defendants in this case. However, they are chargeable with the acts of their employees which they have knowledge of. I have been assured by defendants that these improper activities have been abandoned, and will not be resumed in the future.

"I feel you have all learned something from this investigation and it would be a good thing if all your difficulties and troubles that have arisen out of this lawsuit should be buried here as of this moment. I hope that the men in this organi-

zation who have been friends for so many years may iron out their difficulties and renew their friendship and former close cooperation for the benefit and welfare of your organizations."

Stone dismissed the case on its merits, without costs to either party.

For several years after CUNA Mutual built a new headquarters
on the western edge of Madison in 1960, most of its neighbors
were cows and the tallest structures were cornfields.

CHAPTER FIVE

An Expanding Mission

Human service really is the only reason for the existence of our credit unions.

—Charles F. Eikel, Jr.

As the credit union movement struggled with political factionalism following the CUNA management consultant's report, CUNA Mutual turned its attention to its own consultant's study. CUNA Mutual board president Gurden Farr had written to a well-known consulting firm, O'Toole Associates, on December 13, 1955, the day after H. B. Yates assumed his duties as CUNA managing director. O'Toole was hired to begin a study in early 1956.

O'Toole's preliminary report was favorable: Management, policies, and procedures were solid. The society had grown rapidly, reaching $2.4 billion of insurance in force by the end of 1955.

But the consultants also warned that CUNA Mutual faced increasing competition in nearly every field of insurance. More than forty companies actively competed against the society already, and the list was growing daily. Given the volatile political situation, the preservation of old business, not just its expansion, was a priority.

Managing director Charles Eikel emphasized to the CUNA Mutual board in July 1956 the need to "instill in the minds of our members that a CUNA Mutual contract is the best contract for the safety and protection of the credit union and families of credit union members." He recommended intensifying the campaign to sell individual life contracts and becoming qualified to sell in every state. He also proposed two new departments: Policyowner Relations and Field Operations.

The society had first employed its own field representatives in 1947. Before that, CUNA field organizers represented CUNA Mutual, and policies were sold by state league and credit union personnel who served as licensed agents. In areas where CUNA Mutual was not licensed, the society continued to sell by mail.

But William Reid had insisted that CUNA Mutual actively seek more business. "We have over 10,000 credit unions in this country, and we have policies with just 4,300," he said in 1947. "The time has come when you have got to do something about it, not just sit back and let it roll in." He recommended hiring two field workers.

With the insurance society already seen as getting out of the control of the national association, however, CUNA Mutual representatives might be perceived as competing with the CUNA field staff. A CUNA executive committee member warned that the move would create "two distinct organizations," leading to antagonism and "a rift" in the movement.

Sensitive to such criticism, the CUNA Mutual board brought the matter to the CUNA executive committee and CUNA Supply board in 1947. But most executive committee members favored the plan, including Leonard Nixon, a licensed CUNA Mutual agent in Connecticut. "Is it going to be possible for the CUNA Mutual people to organize a credit union once in a while to repay for the insurance we sold for them?" he asked.

When told the CUNA Mutual field workers would be under Tom Doig's direction, Nixon moved that the joint committee approve the plan. The motion passed. CUNA Mutual added several field representatives to its payroll in the late 1940s and early 1950s, among them Henry L. Timme, Hasell R. Hood, Charles C. Compton, Ted Davis, and Willard R. Johnson. All of them split their work between CUNA and CUNA Mutual, and some years the CUNA Mutual representatives organized more credit unions than they sold Loan Protection contracts.

Combining these duties was viewed favorably in periods of harmony. But in the scramble for power following Doig's death in 1955, allegations of political misdeeds by the CUNA Mutual field staff were raised in the suit against the society by several policyowners, including Nixon.

By July 1956, Eikel saw a clear course. CUNA Mutual must expand its field staff to fight growing competition but move away from organizing credit unions. He informed Tom Benson that the field department must not be referred to as a "field force" in any financial statements or documents lest it create the impression the department was actively competing with CUNA.

Eikel addressed these issues at a training course for the new field department in October 1956. Twenty-two representatives, several of whom had recently resigned from CUNA, attended. Among the instructors was Richard M. Heins, a business professor who had just driven 2,300 miles from California to join the faculty of the University of Wisconsin. Asked to teach the course, Heins begged off, saying he was too tired and hadn't even gotten settled in Madison. But the society, which had many contacts at the university, convinced one of Heins's fellow professors to pressure him until he accepted.

At the course, Eikel delivered a long, emotional speech defining CUNA Mutual's new direction. "You will be watched very closely," he said, reminding his audience of a similar admonition from H. B. Yates, the CUNA managing director, earlier that morning. "But we desire to be closely watched because more credit union people will learn of the effectiveness of our work on behalf of the credit union movement."

Though he would tolerate no political activity from the field representatives, Eikel emphasized that they would do more than sell insurance. The only way to stop the false assumption that CUNA Mutual was trying to take over the credit union movement was "personal contact with people." When confronted with hostile league personnel wanting CUNA Mutual to stay out of their state, he said, "We're going in!"

Eikel admonished the CUNA Mutual representatives to remember they worked for the credit union movement first. "We believe in this movement of ours," he said. "Otherwise we wouldn't be here. The national association is

good, and they've been good to CUNA Mutual. We know the importance of the national association; therefore we don't want to wreck it. We want to build it with everything we've got."

CUNA Mutual insurance could not be sold without first selling the credit union movement, Eikel said. He did not have to convince his representatives, for they had been hired primarily for their dedication to the credit union movement. Most were longtime credit union volunteers. Some, like Cliff Skorstad, the assistant director of the new department, had been organizing credit unions for more than two decades. Few had much insurance knowledge, and they did not view themselves as insurance agents.

John Colby, a huge, gentle bear of a man, was the department's first director. As a CUNA field representative, he had earned a reputation for putting to maximum use his stop-overs between trains. He once killed a few hours in Ontario organizing a credit union with only nineteen members, one short of the legal requirement. Just a few minutes before the next train left, Colby signed himself as the twentieth incorporator. He remained a member of the credit union well into his retirement.

Colby and his assistants, James R. "Speed" Cooper and Skorstad, had little time for formal training sessions with their representatives, who were scattered around the country. Usually the representatives developed their own selling materials and learned from each other through impromptu critiques. Training was secondary to enthusiasm, for they weren't selling a product so much as a religion. A typical practitioner of the style was Hasell Hood, who served several southern states. Once asked by his wife to see a Presbyterian minister about joining his church, Hood reluctantly agreed. When the two men emerged from the pastor's office, Hood was not a member of the church, but the preacher's hands were filled with credit union materials.

Like most representatives, Hood found that his work took him far from his family for weeks. Hood covered twelve states from the Carolinas to Texas. Once while on the East Coast, he received a call instructing him to travel to El Paso. "Why don't you ask your Chicago representative to go?" Hood asked. "He's closer than I am."

Besides selling insurance, a CUNA Mutual

MILESTONES

1956 Field Operations and Policyowners' Representatives departments established.

1960 New home office building dedicated May 12 at 5910 Mineral Point Road in Madison.

CUMIS Insurance Society incorporated May 23 to provide property and casualty insurance.

1962 CUNA Mutual ranked seventeenth among North American insurance companies in coverage in force.

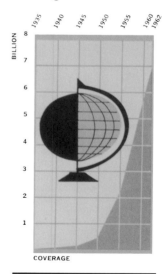

COVERAGE

Hasell R. Hood

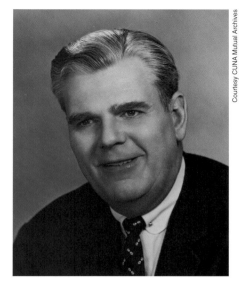

John A. Colby

James R. "Speed" Cooper

representative's job was to be available for anything the credit union wanted. Representatives met regularly with local officials and treasurers to inform them of new services and deliver promotional kits designed to help credit unions grow. They tried to convince prodigal credit unions to reaffiliate with their leagues. They taught treasurers to be more aware of potential risk exposure and showed them how to file claims, something few insurance companies did. They talked up CUNA Mutual insurance, but they also talked up the movement.

Sometimes they sold without talking at all. Arthur C. Webb, a CUNA Mutual representative in southern Illinois, called on one credit union husband and wife who were deaf. Determined to sell them the society's family security plan, Webb communicated with them on more than a hundred sheets of legal paper over four visits. The couple bought the plan after comparing it with others. By then, Webb and the couple had begun to understand each other's hand signs well enough to communicate without paper.

As Webb and other representatives began taking CUNA Mutual to its policyowners, the society also brought its policyowners to Madison. In 1957, CUNA Mutual's Policyowner Relations Department, headed by Marion Gregory, started a league and chapter policyowner representative program (POR). The POR program was designed to inform policyowners about the

services available through CUNA Mutual and to get their opinions so the society could serve them better.

The CUNA Mutual board, fearing political fallout, initially voted the POR program down. The CUNA national directors, tired of fighting over which organization did what, had recently approved a vague code outlining the proper functions and authority of CUNA and CUNA Mutual. It said, essentially, that the two organizations should stick to their own business and try to cooperate. Because education was one of CUNA's traditional jobs, the CUNA Mutual directors feared the POR program would be perceived as an infringement on CUNA territory.

But Gregory cornered Joe DeRamus after the vote and convinced him of the merits of the POR program. CUNA Mutual could serve the credit union movement only by conserving business; since the society sold only to affiliated credit unions, it could grow by expanding its business among present policyowners. The advantages of better two-way communication with policyowners outweighed the liabilities of potential political criticism. DeRamus went back to the board and got the program passed.

In December 1957, fifty credit union league representatives and observers from the United States, Canada, and several other countries attended the first POR program in Madison at CUNA Mutual's expense. During the three-day conference, they learned the history of the society, its operations, claims, and underwriting procedures. Seminars on family finances and more efficient credit union operations were held.

Armed with filmstrips and other materials from the Madison conference, the policyowners' representatives gave reports to meetings of chapter representatives, who passed the information to local credit union officials. This process ensured wide communication, Gregory said, and increased the policyowners' feeling of ownership of the society. CUNA Mutual also sponsored a policyowners' advisory committee to study the society and make suggestions for improving service.

Though the POR program and field operations department were well received by policyowners, others viewed them as political vehicles designed to help CUNA Mutual steer an independent course. Eikel did his best to keep Vance Austin, the new CUNA managing director, apprised of the new programs. Austin spoke at the

first POR dinner, and the managing directors maintained a civil, if not cozy, relationship for several months. They tried to cooperate in little ways, as when Austin graciously refused Eikel's offer to pay for the copies of *The Bridge* that CUNA Mutual had always received for free.

"Certainly it will not be possible for us to be in complete agreement with the other's beliefs, methods, and procedures," Eikel wrote Austin. "Nevertheless we should try. I for one would like very much to bring about a spirit of unity and cooperation among our three national bodies."

But the times conspired against unity. In August 1957, William Knight, CUNA president, wrote to Harold Moses, his counterpart at CUNA Mutual, upset that the society had implied CUNA was a sponsor of the POR program. CUNA had never been consulted about the program, he said, nor had it ever expressed approval or disapproval. Knight and Moses exchanged caustic correspondence until Moses announced CUNA had not approved the POR program. Satisfied it

Courtesy CUNA Mutual Archives

CUNA Mutual representative Arthur C. Webb communicated by pen when he sold a Family Security insurance policy to Mr. and Mrs. Bert Oliver, a deaf couple who were members of the Hunter Employees Credit Union in East St. Louis, Illinois. From left: Mrs. Oliver, Webb, Mr. Oliver, and the Oliver children, Garry and Larry (both of whom had normal hearing).

In the late 1950s and 1960s, CUNA Mutual used a variety of tools, including brochures and movies, to promote the credit union movement. In 1960, the society introduced a cartoon character, Oswald Dogood, in *The Scrapbook,* a twelve-minute film. Oswald helped viewers learn about credit unions, family finances, and CUNA Mutual's services.

would no longer be bypassed, the CUNA executive committee eventually voted to support the program—but only after CUNA Mutual made a modification allowing the leagues, not the insurance society, to choose which policyowner representatives from their states attended the POR conference. The move was intended to make sure CUNA Mutual did not only select policyowners who were politically sympathetic to the society.

Controversy over the CUNA Mutual field department was not solved as easily or quickly.

Courtesy CUNA Mutual Archives

Eikel had said at the first training conference that representatives were not to get involved in elections but were to diligently defend the society from its critics. Given the sharp political split, drawing a line between politics and business was difficult. Everyone had an opinion; every conversation was potentially tinged with political pronouncements; every CUNA and CUNA Mutual election was fought on ideological grounds. Some league managing directors did not want CUNA Mutual representatives to meet with their boards, much less talk with any credit unions in their states.

If Eikel said he did not believe in politics, he did believe in survival. Five members of the CUNA Mutual board were up for election in 1958. Of the remaining five, two were sympathetic to current CUNA executive committee leadership. To the passionate Eikel, the implication was clear.

"We have got to go out and sell CUNA Mutual to such an extent that, regardless of who is elected in 1958, the policyowners of this company appreciate the valuable services rendered to them by this staff so much that the board of directors dare not tamper with this program," he told the representatives. "Oh, they may throw management out, but the program itself must go forward and that's the important thing."

Thus, in some eyes the CUNA Mutual representatives, known as Eikel's Army, avoided politics by promoting and defending the society, while in other eyes these activities constituted little more than politics. Among the duties of the representatives was running area policyowner elections for the CUNA Mutual board. Policyowners opposed to CUNA Mutual leadership often tried to land their own candidates on the board but rarely succeeded. They charged that Eikel's Army checked ballots in the hotel rooms and, if results were not to their liking, substituted forged ballots.

But tactics like those alleged were hardly necessary. CUNA Mutual policyowners could vote instructed ballots, telling the national directors, who represented them at the annual meeting, whom to vote for. Policyowners also could vote uninstructed, leaving the decision to

the director. One key to gaining support for CUNA Mutual-backed candidates was making sure uninstructed votes were represented by supportive directors.

But political practices were only part of the reason for criticism. CUNA Mutual had started its field and POR departments to conserve business, but in doing so it had opened itself to claims that money spent on these departments would cause premiums to rise and dividends to fall. Some leagues, believing inexpensive CUNA Mutual insurance was a prime incentive for league membership, feared outside competitors might underbid CUNA Mutual, selling to credit unions, which might then drop out of their leagues. A study showed that 60 percent of the credit unions who dropped CUNA Mutual also dropped league membership the same year.

Many large credit unions also wanted experience-rated contracts. CUNA Mutual gave all credit unions, no matter their claims experience, the same premium and dividend rate. The larger credit unions argued that if their claims rates were lower, they deserved lower premium rates, a common industry practice. If CUNA Mutual would not give them better rates, outside companies would be more than willing.

CUNA Mutual argued that experience rating was anathema to the credit union philosophy of sharing risks. It might even affect a credit union's ability to serve its members. Would a credit union treasurer grant a loan for a serious operation knowing that if the member died the credit union's rates would go up? By offering the same premium and dividend rates, CUNA Mutual assumed that risk instead. Still, others said the society's talk about "loyalty and harmony" was simply a way to avoid competition, the natural consequence of independence.

Unhappiness with CUNA Mutual policies came to a head in 1958, when two credit union leagues decided to look elsewhere for insurance. In September, the Oregon league signed with Occidental Insurance Company as an alternative carrier. In December the Michigan league bought a controlling interest in the First National Life Insurance company. The company, intended to provide insurance services similar to CUNA Mutual's Loan Protection and Life Savings to Michigan credit unions, was renamed

League Life Insurance Company.

Both leagues had complained about excessive costs generated by the POR and field departments, duplication of CUNA services, and lack of cooperation with league leadership. Outside companies, offering more benefits and lower costs, had approached them first, the leagues said. Moreover, the decision to offer new coverages did not prevent credit unions in their state from purchasing CUNA Mutual insurance.

CUNA Mutual charged that the leagues failed to give an accurate picture of its operations, which showed that actual costs were exceedingly low compared with other companies. Some saw a deeper motivation for the move away from CUNA Mutual, pointing to the close relationship between Al Marble, managing director of the Michigan league, and Murray Lincoln, president of the Cooperative League. Eikel claimed in a newspaper interview that the cooperative movement, with close ties to the CUNA executive committee, was trying to replace and "farm out" CUNA Mutual business to cooperative carriers.

Cooperative leaders dismissed such claims, saying recent developments within CUNA simply represented a legitimate contest between one group wanting a closer relationship with the

Top: Participants at CUNA Mutual's first Policyowners' Representatives Program conference in 1957 listened to managing director Charles F. Eikel speak. Bottom: Mildred S. Boyd of California was one of the first chairs of the Policyowners' Advisory Committee that studied the society annually and made suggestions for improving its services.

cooperative movement and another desiring greater distance between the traditional allies.

After the moves toward new carriers in Oregon and Michigan, the CUNA Mutual board demanded that CUNA censure the leagues. But the executive committee, after studying the situation, refused. CUNA Mutual had been unresponsive to the leagues, Knight said: "The action on the part of these leagues was careful, long negotiated, protracted, deliberate, and was done for reasons they felt were for the best interests of their credit unions."

But some credit unions did not agree. CUNA Mutual received numerous inquiries from credit unions in Oregon and Michigan, asking whether they could still get CUNA Mutual insurance if they declined to pay league dues. Fearing the loss of business in leagues with hostile leadership, CUNA Mutual decided to waive, in Oregon and Michigan, its underwriting rule restricting sales to league-affiliated credit unions. "We sincerely hope you will retain membership in your league," Eikel told Oregon credit unions, "but we will not cancel your CUNA Mutual contract if you withdraw." Eikel emphasized that the new policy applied only in states where leagues sponsored another insurance carrier.

Criticized for selectively waiving the underwriting rule, CUNA Mutual soon found itself defending the original policy. An attorney from the antitrust division of the U.S. Department of Justice appeared at Eikel's office in December 1959. He said the department had received a complaint about the underwriting rule from a credit union unhappy about having to join its league to get CUNA Mutual insurance. The rule probably violated the Sherman Antitrust Act, the attorney said. Richard Uphoff, an investigator for the Federal Bureau of Investigation, was sent to sift through CUNA Mutual's files and correspondence. Impressed with his thoroughness, the society later hired Uphoff as its chief claims examiner.

The government said CUNA Mutual could avoid an investigation by dropping the entire un-

When the government challenged CUNA Mutual's policy of selling only to credit unions affiliated with CUNA, the FBI's Richard J. Uphoff, above, was assigned to the case. Impressed with his thoroughness, the society later hired Uphoff as its chief claims examiner.

Courtesy CUNA Mutual Archives

derwriting rule, but the board refused, turning the defense over to its legal counsel, Robert L. Curry. Curry found that the underwriting rule was adopted by the original CUNA Mutual board in 1935. Included in the first Loan Protection and Life Savings contracts, the rule had been removed in 1942 at the insistence of the Michigan state insurance department but continued as a voluntary policy.

Curry argued that the underwriting rule was intended solely to maintain a strong, united movement and was necessary for the society to continue selling policies on a group basis without experience rating. No legislation and no CUNA Mutual policy required a credit union to retain its contract with the society. Credit unions were free to get insurance from other companies.

In January 1961, after Curry presented his arguments to federal officials at the antitrust division in Washington, D.C., the government decided not to prosecute. Curry successfully defended CUNA Mutual from similar charges in other states before the matter was forgotten.

The decision of the Michigan and Oregon leagues to sponsor other insurance companies and CUNA Mutual's subsequent waiver of the

SERVING THE MOVEMENT

The Policyowners' Representatives program helped inform policyowners about the services available through CUNA Mutual and ensured better two-way communication so the society could serve policyowners better.

underwriting rule in those states raised the specter of a movement torn apart. Fears increased when CUNA and CUNA Mutual became physically separated for the first time.

Lacking room to grow in Filene House, the CUNA Mutual board had planned to build a new headquarters adjacent to Filene House but decided the land was too marshy and the site too small. The society instead bought eighteen acres on the west edge of Madison, where the tallest structures were cornfields and cow paths were more plentiful than roads. Some critics called the move "crazy," but Tom Benson, who scouted the area, believed city development would soon move west to meet the site.

In 1959 construction began on a building that included a main wing of four floors and a two-story executive wing, with 55,000 square feet of space and a parking lot for 300 cars. The land and building cost $1.6 million. Included in the purchase was land that CUNA Mutual hoped would one day be occupied by CUNA and CUNA Supply.

More than a thousand credit union leaders and 160 CUNA Mutual employees attended the dedication on May 12, 1960. Ivy Baker Priest, United States treasurer, and Ellen L. Fairclough, Canada's minister of citizenship and immigration, gave the principal speeches. The building was dedicated to Roy Bergengren.

A Question of Risk

In November 1959, a few months after construction began on the new headquarters, Eikel recommended that CUNA Mutual organize a property and casualty company as a "running mate" of the society. "This is not a conclusion hastily reached," he told the board, "but comes as the result of long and exhaustive research."

The main reason for the new company was competition, Eikel said. Many insurance companies were combining casualty and life operations, often through mergers, and many insurance departments welcomed the trend because it encouraged consumer savings. Because of efficiencies created by merging several, formerly distinct coverages under one management structure, companies with multiple lines could offer comprehensive insurance plans at reduced cost.

Since CUNA Mutual sold only life products, many credit unions bought general coverage from outside companies. If these companies now offered life insurance as well, the competition might get its foot in the door and replace CUNA Mutual's Loan Protection and Life Savings coverage. CUNA Mutual would lose its effectiveness if it sat and did nothing, Eikel said, and "anything that damages, injures, or impairs

the effectiveness of CUNA Mutual also damages, injures, or impairs the credit union movement."

The movement needed a property and casualty company for other reasons. Richard Heins, the professor who taught at CUNA Mutual's first training course for field representatives, had recently completed a study showing that up to 90 percent of all credit unions had little or no liability insurance.

According to Heins, personal property risks faced by credit unions often represented a substantial portion of their assets. A fire or boiler explosion, for instance, could bankrupt the

Top: Ivy Baker Priest, United States treasurer, and Ellen L. Fairclough, Canada's minister of citizenship and immigration, helped lay the cornerstone of CUNA Mutual's new home office on May 12, 1960. From left: Priest, CUNA Mutual chairperson Rev. J. D. Nelson MacDonald, Fairclough, and Charles F. Eikel, Jr. Bottom: The home office at night appeared on the cover of the society's 1960 annual report.

CUNA Mutual director Paul D. Deaton, at the head of the table (left), led a meeting of policy-owner representatives in 1959.

credit union. Even worse, many credit unions were located in buildings owned by others. If a fire started in one of these credit unions and destroyed the building, the credit union would be liable.

Credit unions were legally obligated to cover employees injured on the job. They were liable for accidents at the credit union, liable for injuries caused by cars driven during credit union business, and liable for actions resulting from the decisions of the board. Many small credit unions operating out of homes thought they were covered by personal or residential liability policies, but they were not.

Heins found that half of all credit unions carried no insurance on their personal property, including records. Many mistakenly thought they were covered by CUNA's 576 Bond, sold to credit unions by Employers Mutual of Wausau from the early 1950s. But the 576 Bond covered loss or damage due to theft or embezzlement. It did not cover fire, explosions, or acts of God.

CUNA Mutual's new property and casualty company would cover all these potential risks through a comprehensive package that could be paid in one monthly payment. Eikel said the company would be capitalized with two million dollars and formed as a Wisconsin stock company,

with all the stock initially owned by the society.

The CUNA Mutual board favored the plan, but CUNA president Julius Stone of Massachusetts, sitting in on the meeting, did not. He reminded the directors that CUNA was already thinking of starting its own bonding and casualty company. Though Eikel said CUNA Mutual's new company would not write policies already covered by the 576 Bond, Stone wondered whether the company represented a further attempt to take over the work of the national association.

Stone urged the CUNA Mutual board to delay any decision about the new company until after the CUNA national directors met in May. "CUNA Mutual came into existence because the movement felt there was a need for it," he said. "The movement should also have its say about the property and casualty company. No one should speak for the credit union movement except CUNA and its duly elected officers."

"I thought the CUNA Mutual policyowners were part of the credit union movement," DeRamus said. "They should decide whether they want this company. A few representatives who head the national association should not decide for them."

CUNA Mutual director William Pratt suggested the board delay the start of the company for three months to advise leadership of the movement. The board agreed to wait.

Stone quickly called a special meeting of the CUNA executive committee in Chicago in December 1959. A prominent Boston attorney, he had recently dedicated a memorial in Boston Commons to another committed credit union leader, Edward Filene. Like Filene, Stone was fierce in his convictions. But he was conservative to the bone, a traditionalist who believed unequivocally in the democratic processes of the credit union movement and the authority of its elected leaders.

For Stone, the issue was not whether a property and casualty company was a good idea; it was whether an affiliate should have the right to make a decision without submitting it to the democratic processes of the organized movement. Stone took the committee through a long review of the struggle over who should control CUNA Mutual, renewing an old argument.

"If our insurance company had been, from the start, a stock company, owned by CUNA, then much grief that we have had over the years

CUNA president Julius Stone, above, asked CUNA Mutual to delay plans to start a property and casualty insurance company.

He praised CUNA Mutual for its progress but charged that many recent decisions, from the POR program to the waiver of the underwriting rule, revealed a new operating philosophy: "Whatever is good for CUNA Mutual is good for the movement." Although the society had an obligation to its policyowners, Stone said, "If it is true that this duty to the policyowners will overrule the needs of the credit union movement, then CUNA Mutual can no longer be considered to be a part of the credit union movement."

Irett Ferris, a CUNA insurance committee member from Michigan, raised questions about CUNA Mutual's ability to run a casualty company. "The handling of life claims is relatively easy," he said. "The insured is either dead or he is not. He either had coverage or he did not." Running a casualty company, Ferris said, should not be left to "amateurs or men trained in the life field. Would not CUNA Mutual's position be improved if they devoted their efforts to meeting the competition, rather than embarking into an area where they lack experience, in the hope that it will solve their problems?"

Though tense, the meeting was not without moments of levity. Eikel, attending with several CUNA Mutual leaders, was called to the front of the room to report on the new company. "I have been a bad boy again," Eikel said as he passed R. C. Morgan, an executive committee member from Texas.

But Eikel could not change the mind of the executive committee, which voted nine votes to four to request the CUNA Mutual board to withhold action on the new casualty company until the CUNA directors met in May 1960.

The meeting was the first salvo in a battle of words and special releases over the next few months. CUNA Mutual directors, emphasizing that they had cooperated by delaying action on the new company, called Stone's emergency meeting "a sad and useless chapter" in the history of the movement. They pointed out that a stock company owned by CUNA would not solve the

---

SERVING THE MOVEMENT

The job of CUNA Mutual representatives was to be available for anything the credit union wanted. They met regularly with local officials to explain new services, tried to convince prodigal credit unions to reaffiliate with their leagues, and taught treasurers to be more aware of risk exposure. They talked up CUNA Mutual, but they also talked up the movement.

---

would have been avoided," Stone said. "Decisions on insurance matters would have been made by the leagues and by the CUNA national directors, and they would have been carried out without any resistance or animosity."

The charter for CUMIS, a property and casualty insurance company owned by CUNA Mutual, was signed May 17, 1960. At the signing were, front row, from left: Charles G. Hyland, Charles F. Eikel, Jr., and Robert L. Curry. Back row: Richard M. Heins, Marion F. Gregory, and Thomas B. Benson.

Courtesy CUNA Mutual Archives

MILESTONES

1963 Agency system inaugurated to promote individual insurance services. First agency in United States at Granite City, Illinois; first Canadian agency at Toronto.

Members Group Life Plan introduced, covering entire credit union family under one contract. Premiums paid through the credit union by the member.

1964 New wing of CUNA Mutual home office was completed in October.

Canadian coverage passed billion-dollar mark.

problem of control that Stone was so worried about. Running an insurance company was not "a committee assignment." A separate board, responsible for following laws and the mandates of insurance departments, would be required. Misunderstandings between such a board and the executive committee would be inevitable.

The fracas continued at the quarterly meetings in February. The CUNA Mutual directors again delayed organizing a property and casualty company, in effect meeting the executive committee's request to postpone action until May, when the next meeting would be held. But the CUNA Mutual board also refused to acknowledge the executive committee's request, a breach of etiquette Stone called "a long, long step in the direction of severing CUNA Mutual's relationship with the credit union movement." He told the insurance committee to have a proposal for a CUNA-owned casualty company ready by the national meeting. CUNA also

should consider starting its own life insurance company, Stone said, "should the movement find itself without the services of a facility for providing credit life insurance."

Most believed the suggestion was less a threat than a bluff. Though the CUNA insurance committee studied the impact of competing with CUNA Mutual, Stone made it clear that the national association had no plans to form its own life company. "It is not a question of one group controlling another group," he said, softening his rhetoric. "It is a question of free discussion, free debate, established voting rights, parliamentary procedure clearly spelled out, fair play, and majority rule."

Both sides came well armed to the national meeting in Madison in May 1960. CUNA Mutual had conducted a survey of policyowners about its proposed property and casualty company. Eighty percent of member credit unions approved.

The CUNA executive committee had resolutions from sixteen leagues against the move. It also had a recent report from the Alfred M. Best Company, the insurance rating firm. CUNA claimed that Best, which had given CUNA Mutual high marks in recent years, believed CUNA Mutual's surplus was low and slipping. With such a low surplus, Best's said, the society would be "unwise" to start a company in a new field. CUNA Mutual said the report was misleading. The surplus was "low" only because it returned such high dividends to its policyowners. By every other indicator, CUNA Mutual's financial health was robust. Convinced, policyowners voted by a five-to-one margin at the national meeting to start the casualty company.

The CUNA national meeting convened the next day, May 13, amid tension and uncertainty. Leagues from Ohio and New York, upset that CUNA might start its own casualty company, said they were withholding annual dues pending the outcome of the meeting. New York objected to Stone's "rule or ruin" handling of the situation, and Ohio criticized both CUNA and CUNA Mutual for a power struggle it believed could lead to the "ultimate disintegration and collapse of our credit union movement."

No precedent existed for the actions, and it was moved that the two leagues not be seated. Director John Camp of South Carolina asked about CUNA's dues policy. Comptroller John Brady responded that while the deadline for payment of annual dues was May 1, it was enforced only when a league elected a new director.

"In other words, it has been the policy that if the leagues pay their dues by May 1, well and good, and if they did not, there were no questions asked?" Camp asked.

"That is your inference," Stone said.

Camp pressed on. "Has either league withdrawn its membership?"

"Well, I suppose this is a conclusion the chair cannot answer."

Contending the leagues had not withdrawn and observing that eleven other leagues had not yet paid their dues, Camp said New York and Ohio should be seated. A furious parliamentary battle ensued. New York and Ohio were eventually seated, but only after passage of a motion that they pay their annual dues.

A few hours into the meeting, when the CUNA directors finally reached the most important business of the day—the recommendations of the CUNA insurance committee—they moved quickly, narrowly approving a recommendation that CUNA not organize a casualty company "at this time." The recommendation had initially included the same ban on CUNA Mutual, but the directors removed the restriction, freeing the society to move ahead.

Karl Little, Utah director, also moved that CUNA "not start, buy, or enter" into a contract to provide credit life insurance and that CUNA "reaffirm its endorsement" of CUNA Mutual as the movement's credit life company. Little's motion passed; it was an important affirmation of the society by the movement.

The CUNA Mutual board convened immediately after the meeting and voted to start a property and casualty company. Reid was named president. The first choice for a name had been CUNA Mutual's General Insurance Company, but Stone had told the society it could not legally use the CUNA name or trademark without CUNA approval. Hoping to avoid more controversy, the board went with its second choice, CUMIS, derived from the first letters of CUNA Mutual Insurance Society.

John T. Hitt was named the first general manager of CUMIS. The company issued its first policy in the fall of 1960 after James Burke, William Fitze, Jack Lary, and Tom Mitchell qualified to sell CUMIS products. In its first year, CUMIS did business only in Wisconsin, selling 476 policies and earning $78,000 in premiums. CUMIS was registered in eight more states in 1962, when premiums in force increased to $178,000.

The company chose a careful and deliberate course, developing new policies and rating plans unique in the insurance industry. Among its leading developments were the CUMIS Comprehensive Security Policy, providing protection for all a credit union's basic risks, and a homeowner policy for credit union members.

Courtesy CUNA Mutual Archives

John T. Hitt, first general manager of CUMIS.

MILESTONES

1965 Securities and Exchange Commission approved CUMIS common stock issue to credit union members and organizations.

League Assistance Program started to provide financial assistance to Leagues for the organization of new credit unions.

First computer installed in CUNA Mutual home office.

Vietnam emergency claims policy adopted by board to assist credit unions with members in military combat duty.

The company also began marketing the CUMIS Financial Records Policy, which protected against the loss of credit union ledgers and records not covered by CUNA's 576 Bond.

CUMIS premiums rose to $360,000 in 1963. At the same time, CUNA Mutual's insurance in force totaled $7.6 billion. More important, despite the rise of political factionalism in recent years, 93 percent of CUNA-affiliated credit unions carried CUNA Mutual insurance, a tribute to the society's many contributions to the movement.

Desiring to spread the ownership of the company throughout the credit union movement, the directors formed CUMIS as a stock company. They had decided to delay a stock issue until it was clear that the company would succeed. In 1965, after CUMIS began serving its 1,500th credit union, 226,400 CUMIS shares worth $25 per share were offered to credit union organizations and members. CUNA Mutual retained the majority of CUMIS shares.

The early years of CUMIS were not without controversy. Though the actions of the national directors in May 1960 had cooled the political rhetoric, the arguments over CUMIS flared again in 1962 when CUNA Mutual learned from the Wisconsin state insurance department that CUNA was expanding its bond coverage. The society protested, saying CUMIS had avoided overlap with CUNA's bond and auto coverage but the expanded CUNA bond would offer many of the same liability coverages offered by CUMIS. As a matter of self-preservation, Reid said, CUMIS would have to add complete bond coverage.

The executive committee invited CUMIS to submit its own bond proposal but voted seven to six to pursue the CUNA plan; the minority argued that the action violated the intent of the earlier ban on CUNA forming a casualty company. One month later, the CUMIS directors voted to add bonding to its package of property and casualty coverage.

Political arguments were one thing, but direct competition was another. Mindful of poten-

Courtesy CUNA Mutual Archives

Harry E. Manzer, above, was hired in 1963 to build CUNA Mutual's individual life program.

tial consequences, CUNA and CUNA Mutual agreed to stop all action on their respective bonding plans and form a committee to determine who should market property and casualty coverage to the credit union movement.

The CUNA/CUNA Mutual/CUMIS Insurance Study Committee met in a hotel near Chicago's O'Hare Airport on July 13, 1963. Attempting to prevent the flow of more acrimonious correspondence, the two sides agreed not to release any information from the meeting. One verbatim record would be taken and only two reports prepared, for CUMIS president Bill Reid and CUNA president R. C. Morgan. All the participants, especially Eikel and J. Orrin Shipe, were forbidden to speak publicly about the meetings. Shipe had been named CUNA mana-

SERVING THE MOVEMENT

In 1960, up to 90 percent of all credit unions had little or no liability insurance, and half had no insurance on their personal property, including records. CUNA Mutual's new property and casualty company, CUMIS, covered these risks in a comprehensive package.

ging director a few months earlier, after Vance Austin's forced resignation by the executive committee.

The study committee planned to review competing plans developed by Eikel and Shipe. Shipe proposed a brokerage facility, CUNA United Services, Inc., to market CUNA, CUNA Mutual, and CUMIS coverages. The corporation would be controlled one-third by the leagues, one-third by CUNA, and one-third by CUNA Mutual.

"We have had too many family arguments over who determines the insurance needs of the movement," Shipe said. "We need to put insurance back into proper perspective." The brokerage facility would answer critics who said credit unions often were operated just to sell insurance, he said, and again establish insurance as "the servant, rather than the master" of the credit union movement.

CUNA Mutual saw merit in Shipe's plan but feared its political implications. Eikel's proposal was simpler: CUNA Mutual would continue to sell its own coverages, as well as the Employers Mutual bond, through a reinsuring arrangement.

The committee spent little time discussing the merits of the two plans. Instead, early discussion centered on the organizational and financial health of CUMIS, of concern because Best had in its 1962 report failed to give its parent company, CUNA Mutual, a recommended rating.

The CUNA consultant had studied 221 companies, compiling loss and expense ratios for each company during its first two years in business. His figures showed the combined loss and expense ratio to be several times the industry average. "I think the figures speak for themselves," the consultant said. "This was a very costly operation."

Richard Heins, consultant for CUNA Mutual and CUMIS, called the report selective and misleading. The Wisconsin state insurance department, worried about a recent rash of insolvencies, had been urging new companies to carry higher loss reserves. CUMIS operational costs appeared high because the company was being cautious and could not be used as an accurate illustration of long-term expenses. Moreover, CUMIS loss ratios were below the industry average. Depending on how one used the numbers, Heins said, one could make the case that CUMIS was several times weaker than other companies or several times stronger. His numbers showed it was stronger.

Heins's analysis ended argument about the financial health of CUNA Mutual and CUMIS. The CUNA consultant backed off his earlier assertions. "I hope I never gave the impression that I was criti-

cizing the financial position," he said.

The discussion quickly moved from the financial to the political when the CUNA consultant began reading another report. Recent events showed the CUNA insurance services department was doing well, he said, while CUNA Mutual was "engaged in much difficulty and conflict. Why the difference?"

Reid erupted. "I can't sit here any longer and listen to this tripe," he said. He tried to rip the consultant's report in half. Failing, he threw it on the desk. CUNA's Morgan, who had cautioned the CUNA consultant to focus more on solutions, calmed Reid down. But the arguments began anew when the consultant, discussing the potential advantages of stock companies over mutuals, said mutuals were "communistic in nature."

"Where did you get this 'communistic in nature?'" asked Paul Deaton, a member of the CUNA Mutual board.

"It is a common ownership," the consultant replied. "You as a policyholder of CUNA Mutual,

Courtesy CUNA Mutual Archives

After CUMIS began selling common stock in the company to credit union members in 1965, retired comptroller Charles G. Hyland purchased a share for each of his four grandchildren. With Hyland are his two youngest grandchildren, Steven, left, and Daniel Hyland, right.

along with all other policyowners, own it, but you as an individual policyholder cannot say, 'I want my portion of the pie, my portion of the company.'"

Deaton asked that "communistic" be struck from the records. Sensing that the meeting was degenerating into another political argument, Morgan tried to move to other business, but little was accomplished.

The insurance study committee met for the last time on February 13, 1964. Employers Mutual had offered to expand its bond coverage at no cost to CUNA. The expansion would overlap with CUMIS coverage, creating the same situation that had caused the committee to be formed. The executive committee was scheduled to vote on the matter the next day.

Both sides had become resigned to reaching no agreement. Morgan said he hoped the expansion would not be passed. If it were, he said, "I would hope it wouldn't blow up into a big fight, which would be good for no one, because we would be offering duplicate coverages, and you talk about confusion in the minds of credit union people—we would have it."

The CUNA executive committee approved the expanded bond coverage. Soon thereafter, the CUNA Mutual board voted to market a package of policies including all bonding coverages offered by CUNA.

Passion and Faith

Differences between the leadership of CUNA and CUNA Mutual became subdued in the latter half of the 1960s, though they continued to affect nearly every policy decision within the movement. The political machinery of each side became increasingly impenetrable, and the recognized supporters of one organization rarely sought elected office in the other as they had in the past.

Charles Eikel, CUNA Mutual's managing director, was a symbol of the separation, unyielding in his support of the society and unrelenting in his criticism of opponents he believed were trying to destroy it. But many people did not know that Eikel never really wanted the CUNA Mutual job; he wanted to be the managing director of CUNA. "I may not have lasted very long," he said, "but it was an ambition of mine."

But fate and politics had intervened. Given the sharp disagreements in recent years, Eikel probably never would get his wish. So Eikel made a decision: If he could not serve the organization he loved most, he would at least make sure CUNA Mutual did its best to serve the movement.

Critics frequently charged that CUNA Mutual was steering a course away from the credit union movement, but those who knew Eikel were confident that would not happen under his charge. Eikel's driving purpose was promoting and extending the benefits of credit union services to all people. Everything he did and said was measured against that ideal. If a new program met his test, he cared little that it met criticism. If it did not, no matter how financially sound or popular, the plan had no chance.

In a passionate movement, Eikel was one of the most passionate. Properly motivated, he could be a volcano. Anyone who took a position he believed to be against the best interests of the credit union movement had best prepare for a fight to the finish, for Eikel would accept nothing less than total victory.

"I haven't very much talent, but there isn't a man anywhere who can deny my feelings for the credit union movement, and I challenge any man to stop me from doing what I believe," Eikel told a group of policyowner representatives in 1958. "I am going to fight with every damn thing I have inside me and with every possible friend I can get to support me. I am going to fight until I haven't got any legs left or any voice left to fight with, but I can assure you of one thing: those who try to stop me are going to find they are in a helluva scrap."

Depending on their political beliefs, many credit union people completely loved or completely hated Eikel, and sometimes they changed their opinions from day to day. Some were afraid of Eikel, for he never hid his opinions or intentions; his assistants, worried about public relations, were kept busy trying to rein him in.

But volatility was only one part of the man. More important were his sincerity, high principles, vision, commitment, and compassion. Like his mentor Tom Doig, Eikel had an extraordinary ability to inspire loyalty. Credit union people followed him not because he sought

MILESTONES

1966 New Canadian home office dedicated in Hamilton, Ontario.

CUNA Mutual's Western Office in Pomona, California dedicated.

CUMIS Package of Protection introduced.

1967 CUMIS 578 Full Discovery Bond introduced.

First Youth Round Table conference sponsored by CUNA Mutual.

followers but because his spirit and zeal were so infectious.

While Doig had been known as Tom to most of his staff, few of Eikel's employees were comfortable calling him anything but Mr. Eikel. He demonstrated his concern for employees through deeds, not words. He insisted that the lowest-paid employee get the same Christmas bonus as the highest-paid. He respected employees' rights and worked hard for good union relations. In 1968, his appreciative staff made him the first honorary member of the Office and Professional Employees' International Union.

While his credit union family was important, Eikel was even more committed to his own family. Often, after a long day of dealing with the problems of the credit union movement, Eikel retreated with his son to the basement to play with an electric train (he hated riding on real trains). He helped with the dishes, puttered in the garden, and read. His favorite subject was Harry Truman.

Though Eikel tried not to bring work home, his children often heard him talk about the battle between loan sharks and credit unions. When asked what her father did for a living, daughter Lucia, remembering the subject of countless conversations at home, replied, "Dad

is a loan shark."

Nobody controlled Charles Eikel, but his wife, Eunice, exerted the most influence. Two young league managing directors, Jim Jukes of Kansas and Bill Broxterman of South Carolina, once approached Eikel at a CUNA meeting. Their conversations sometimes turned into arguments, and this one did too. Jukes and Broxterman proposed that CUNA Mutual market some of its products through the leagues in exchange for a percentage of the profits. Eikel refused to consider the plan.

Finally Eunice Eikel, patient, gracious, and polite, interrupted her husband, something few people did successfully, and said: "Charley, please be quiet for a minute and listen to these young guys. They're trying to tell you something."

Eikel was uncharacteristically dumbfounded. "Gee," he said, "do you think so?"

He listened. The conversation was the first step in negotiations that ultimately led to CUNA Mutual's successful marketing agreements with

Above: CUNA Mutual president Charles F. Eikel, Jr., was general chairman for the 1966 Madison metropolitan area United Givers Fund. Eikel shared smiles with representatives of several agencies supported by the fund, including the Girl Scouts, Red Cross, USO, and American Heart Association. Above left: Charles F. Eikel, Jr. as a young man.

Charles F. Eikel, Jr.

Managing Director and Executive Vice President
CUNA Mutual Insurance Society
1956–1964

President
CUNA Mutual Insurance Society
1964–1973

the leagues in the 1970s.

Eikel's opinions were deeply held. His staff learned quickly that the discussion was over when the boss said, "Not for five damn minutes are we gonna do that!" and those who pushed too hard were occasionally fired, though only for a few seconds. But a convincing argument could change his mind. An important change occurred in the late 1950s, when Heins came to pick up his check for teaching CUNA Mutual's first training course for sales representatives.

Eikel wanted to see Heins.

"Well, you're so damn smart," Eikel said, introducing a remark he addressed the professor with for years. "What do you think about this organization?"

"Seems like a great company from what I've seen."

"But is there anything we're not doing right?"

Heins hesitated. "Well, uh, there are a few things you're not doing right."

Eikel's face turned red. "First you say we're a good company, and now you say we're not doing things right."

Eikel paused. "Well, what are we doing wrong?"

"First of all, you're charging everybody the same premium. The only way that will keep working is if you have a monopoly of the market or if all your members have the same experience. But if they are different, the ones with better experience will look elsewhere because they can get lower rates. You'll be left with the poorest risks. I'll bet if you look at your books you'll find that the credit unions that are canceling are the better risks."

"I think you ought to know that experience rating is opposed to every credit union concept I believe in," Eikel said. "All credit unions should be treated alike."

"There are two ways of looking at that. By charging everybody the same premium, you're actually treating different credit unions the same way. Some people call that discrimination."

"Do you mean to tell me that we have been preaching the wrong thing for all these years?" he said. "Experience rating is evil!"

Heins considered leaving but pressed further. "Do you know what's really going on in this company? Do you know what the cancellations look like?" The professor told Eikel he reminded him of a famous cartoon of Abraham Lincoln guiding a "ship of state" just before the Civil War. Lincoln was blindfolded.

"You're running this company blindfolded if you refuse to look at these things," Heins said. "You've got to have answers to these questions, or you're going to make the wrong decisions."

Eikel exploded and Heins left hurriedly. "Well," Heins thought as he drove home, "I guess I'll never hear from him again."

But at the urging of his wife, Ruth, Heins called Eikel and said he was sorry he had offended him.

"Yeah, well, I'm still pretty upset," Eikel said. "But I want to see you in the office tomorrow morning to talk about these things." It was the beginning of a long and close working relationship, and Eikel delighted in telling the story of his first meeting with Heins, especially the part about Lincoln's blindfold.

In 1959, the CUNA Mutual board began exploring paying dividends based on claims experience, but policyowners voted down the plan, 4,017 to 2,741. But in 1961, after another policyowner vote narrowly supported experience rating, the society adopted a new method of distributing surplus, basing its dividends on claims, volume of premium and length of contract. Unpopular with some traditionalists, the move nevertheless helped CUNA Mutual remain competitive and retain the business of larger credit unions. The society eventually adopted experience-rated premiums as well.

Eikel's leadership was critical during the next decade. The world was changing. Electronic technology was burgeoning, and some predicted that the credit union movement would fall behind unless it was quick to adopt automated services like credit cards. Because inflation was growing, many argued it was time to remove long-standing limitations on loan rates and dividends. Some suggested credit unions expand their investments to earn higher returns on surplus funds.

Eikel understood the necessity for change but insisted that new directions not compromise the philosophy that had built the movement. He once heard about a machine that judged the merit of a loan application in thirty seconds. "There is a definite danger to our credit union movement placing too much emphasis on techniques and devices," he said. "An organization that numbers its membership in the millions and its assets in the billions obviously acquires responsibilities. The treasurer of a large credit union today cannot operate its affairs out of a hip pocket as was true in the past. Credit union philosophy never was and never can be a cover-up for inefficient operation."

"But our credit unions can never be judged completely by the accepted standards of other businesses," he continued. "Efficiency alone will never be an adequate yardstick for measuring the caliber of a credit union's performance. Human service really is the only reason for the existence of credit unions. We can't simply do it with new buildings, new tools, and new programs. It's got to be done by people—credit union people—who understand credit union philosophy and are burning with the desire to extend its benefits to their friends and neighbors throughout the world."

Under Eikel, CUNA Mutual extended an ever-expanding range of services to credit unions and credit union members. New insurance policies—from mortgage protection plans to group life insurance contracts—were introduced. Its education protection plans helped members send their children to college; to keep costs as low as possible, the member drew only the money needed for semester or annual expenses. Personal insurance counseling services were offered. The benefit limits of Loan Protection and Life Savings were expanded.

As the political situation stabilized and competition increased, CUNA Mutual field representatives spent more time selling insurance, a shift requiring additional training. Some representatives balked at the change, viewing "selling"

"We believe in this movement of ours. The national association is good, and they've been good to CUNA Mutual. We know the importance of the national association; therefore we don't want to wreck it. We want to build it with everything we've got."

as tantamount to prostitution. A few even believed it was wrong to sell individual insurance.

Aware of such attitudes, Eikel sent a memo to each of the representatives: "We have often got the impression that some of you feel there is something repugnant about being classified as a salesperson. This is wrong. The kind of selling you gentlemen have the opportunity to practice is that of the highest and most professional standing, as well as a method by which you can, in truth and action, fulfill the dictates of the creed and philosophy we all work by." Speed Cooper, named director of field operations in 1965, helped to encourage that attitude among new representatives, and Harry E. Manzer, the director of agencies, taught them how to sell.

CUNA Mutual products became increasingly popular with credit unions, as some learned the hard way that competitors did not always deliver what they promised. Credit unions going with outside carriers often found their premiums raised within a year or two, as the companies discovered they could not earn a profit. But CUNA Mutual continued to return almost 90 percent of all premium dollars to its Loan Protection and Life Savings policyowners in claims and dividends, the leading record in the industry.

In 1965, as U.S participation in the Vietnam conflict escalated, CUNA Mutual decided not to charge the deaths of credit union members "serving in any declared or undeclared war" to their credit union's loss experience, continuing a policy the society started in World War II.

A year later, CUNA Mutual opened a regional office in Pomona, California, to better serve policyowners in thirteen western states. The office was headed by Vaughn Liscum. The society also dedicated a new Canadian office in Hamilton, Ontario, under C. Gordon Smith.

In cooperation with CUNA and the leagues, CUNA Mutual started a pilot program to organize more credit unions. By the end of 1966, 31 leagues were participating in the program and 345 credit unions were organized.

CUNA Mutual also turned its attention to getting new credit union members. Statistics showed that by 1970, half of the American population would be under age 25. The average age of credit union members was 41 and rising.

Credit unions had always paid special attention to children. Many credit unions had special savings programs for kids, and a few had junior credit unions run by children with adult supervision. Salvatore Strigari, a junior high teacher in a rough Philadelphia neighborhood, taught his underprivileged students about credit unions to help them learn how to better handle their money.

But more was needed. Some credit union people were hostile to the idea of an infusion of youth into the credit union movement. At one national meeting, a director talked proudly of how he engineered the defeat of a twenty-eight-year-old because he wasn't going to have any "young whippersnapper" on his board. The director apparently did not know that Tom Doig, and many other leaders, had joined the boards of credit unions while in their twenties.

CUNA Mutual believed it critical to reach the breadwinners of tomorrow with the credit union message. It started a

Harry E. Manzer, vice president of agencies, left, shook hands with J. L. Herve Lanctot, CUNA Mutual's Canadian office administrative assistant, as Canadian agents and supervisors, holding their country's flag, arrived by train for the Home Office Agents Conference in Madison in June 1965.

Courtesy CUNA Mutual Archives

Courtesy CUNA Mutual Archives

Several youth leaders from the United States and Canada gathered at CUNA Mutual's Youth Round Table conference April 3-5, 1968 in Madison. From left: Barbara Czechanski, Sheboygan, Wisconsin; Ken Behnke, Verona, Wisconsin; Peter Arroyo, Bridgeport, Connecticut; Danny King, Rice University; Kathleen Curran, Madison; and John McGee, UCLA.

new program offering three times the normal insurance coverage to young credit union members. The society also sponsored Youth Round Table conferences to teach young people about money management, make them more aware of credit unions, and get their ideas for making inroads with the younger generation.

CUMIS sales began to take off during the 1960s, reaching $3.3 million in premiums by the end of the decade. The 578 Full Discovery Bond, developed in 1966, became extremely popular with credit unions. Unlike most bonds, which did not cover liabilities discovered after the bond was canceled, the 578 Full Discovery Bond covered all losses discovered while it was in force. John Hitt played an important role in its development.

In 1967, CUMIS went a step farther and introduced its Package of Protection, covering all a credit union's potential risks in a comprehensive plan. Many called it the most important development in credit union insurance since the introduction of Loan Protection. Credit unions paid for the package with one payment, making bookkeeping easier and decreasing the risk of policy expirations. By 1970, ten thousand credit unions were covered by CUMIS.

Many people contributed to the technical development of these advancements, but Charles Eikel provided the charismatic and principled leadership that made them possible. Eikel knew that if the credit union movement succeeded, CUNA Mutual succeeded. He was a credit union man, not an insurance man, and that made all the difference.

CUNA and CUNA Mutual representatives pledged their unity at the society's board meeting in Madison August 16-17, 1971. From left: CUNA Mutual president Charles F. Eikel, Jr., CUNA Mutual chairman Robert A. Kratt, CUNA managing director Herbert G. Wegner, CUNA president Wilfred MacKinnon, and CUNA Mutual board member P. G. Gooch.

CHAPTER SIX

Healing and Growth

I do not think we have time to do other than work toward common goals.

—Robert L. Curry

After twenty-eight years as a CUNA Mutual director, William Reid retired from the board in 1967. His departure not only signaled the loss of one of the most respected figures in the credit union movement but also symbolized a significant trend. Though the political fallout of 1956 still colored relations between CUNA and CUNA Mutual, the influence of leaders who had participated in the initial skirmishes was decreasing. CUNA Mutual directors Gurden Farr and Harold Moses had died, as had CUNA leader Leonard Nixon. Several other leaders on both sides, including Joe DeRamus and Al Marble, had retired.

As a result, the CUNA Mutual board underwent an extensive turnover. Two new CUNA Mutual directors were elected in 1966 and four more in 1968.

A few months after the 1968 elections, the society revised its board structure. CUNA Mutual business had been governed by a ten-member board. The CUNA Mutual directors also sat on the CUMIS board, along with three others who governed CUMIS exclusively. The three were to include a member of the CUNA executive committee, a CUNA national director not on the executive committee and a state league managing director.

CUNA Mutual and CUMIS board meetings were held together. Because the vast majority of discussion centered on CUNA Mutual business, the three exclusive CUMIS directors often waited for hours before the entire board dealt with CUMIS business. Believing the structure wasteful, the two boards consolidated into one. Two positions were added to the CUNA Mutual and CUMIS directorships already in place, creating a new fifteen-member body.

Thus, in just a few years, the CUNA Mutual board underwent almost total transformation. The average age of the directors decreased dramatically, as did their memory of the events that had sparked the split in 1956.

To the new directors, the enduring "cold war" between some leaders in CUNA and CUNA Mutual was a bit of a mystery. Yes, old friends like CUNA comptroller John Brady and Charles Eikel shared a drink occasionally at national meetings. Yet an invisible Berlin Wall still existed. A little socializing with the other side was fine; too much and one's coworkers might view one as a traitor.

As with most long feuds, few young people understood how this one had started or what it was all about. New employees in both organizations learned, without being told, not to trust the other side. They often adopted feelings of mistrust not on the basis of personal experience but because friends or coworkers felt that way.

Robert A. Kratt, chief executive officer of the International Harvester Credit Union in Rock Island, Illinois, had been elected to the CUNA Mutual board in 1966. He had seen up close the barrier between CUNA and CUNA Mutual. During Kratt's first trip to the annual meeting in Madison, his wife, Betty, took a tour of the city.

"So where were you?" a CUNA Mutual director's wife asked when she returned,

"I went on a CUNA tour," she said.

The director's wife was shocked. "We don't do those things," she said abruptly.

Bob Kratt was determined to find out why. He knew people on both sides of the conflict. All of them seemed dedicated to the same goals. What had happened? Kratt tried to find the answer by reading thirty-one years' worth of CUNA Mutual minutes. But minutes told only so much.

He asked a veteran director whether he could see the director's personal files and correspondence relating to the split. The director declined.

"Those things are a lot of old history," he said. "Bad history."

If Kratt did not completely understand the reasons for the split, he and other new directors like P. G. Gooch of Texas, who joined the board in 1966, did understand the need for an end to the feuding. The financial world in which credit unions operated was changing rapidly. Commercial banks and retail stores were competing more actively for a share of the consumer credit market. Life insurance companies were launching new mutual funds and annuity plans. Banks and savings and loan institutions were offering a variety of savings instruments, like certificates of deposit and savings accounts paying variable rates of interest.

To compete, the credit union movement had to be united, and it could only be united if CUNA and CUNA Mutual leaders were talking to one another, Kratt decided. The time was right for change, for the two organizations were in the midst of a major disagreement over a new CUNA policy statement. The statement said that when a foreign credit union wanted help starting its own insurance services, CUNA would provide such help through its insurance services committee rather than through CUNA Mutual.

The only way to break the impasse, Kratt decided, was to start at the top. During the 1967 national meeting, he walked into the CUNA hospitality suite, introduced himself, and asked to talk to CUNA president A. R. "Rod" Glen. Several CUNA executive committee members were standing nearby; some had never seen a CUNA Mutual director in a CUNA suite. Perhaps antici-

The CUNA Mutual and CUMIS boards met in Asheville, North Carolina, August 4-9, 1969. Seated, from left: Fred L. Crump, P. G. Gooch, Clyde P. Dwyer, the Rev. J. D. Nelson MacDonald, Charles W. Jones, Jr., Sydney B. Wexler, Ray D. Hagen, and Robert A. Kratt. Standing: Lee A. Sell, A. Leonard Tune, Wendell F. Walker, Al J. Day, Paul D. Deaton, Charles F. Eikel, Jr., George A. Swales, Gerald J. Ring, and chairman William H. Scogin.

Several CUNA and CUNA Mutual directors formed a committee in the late 1960s to resolve the differences between the organizations. Among the committee members were, clockwise from bottom left: Robert A. Kratt, P. G. Gooch, Paul D. Deaton, and R. C. Robertson, then a member of the CUNA executive committee and later the CUNA Mutual board.

CUNA Mutual included Kratt, Gooch, Paul D. Deaton of Ohio, and William H. Scogin of Alabama; CUNA members included R. C. Robertson of Arizona, Robert H. Stevenson of North Carolina, Harold Carpenter of Alabama, and Charles F. Bernard of Tennessee.

For the next two years, often at night after other meetings, the committee discussed and debated the history of the credit union movement, the long argument over who should control CUNA Mutual, and the people, issues, and philosophies that had led to the split.

For young directors with little emotional attachment to the split, like Kratt and Gooch and Robertson, the talks were informative. For some veteran directors, they were a catharsis. Emotions and, sometimes, invective flowed freely. At the first meeting, Scogin sat across the table from Carpenter, his longtime adversary and fellow Alabaman.

"Look, you and I both know we don't get along," Scogin told Carpenter. "But we need to make this thing work, and we need to sit down and talk it out. That's the only way to go forward."

As longtime opponents shared their feelings, they began to understand how the feelings had developed. While they still disagreed about many things, they discovered general agreement about the direction the credit union movement should take: CUNA was the central leader of the movement, CUNA Mutual the movement's insurance arm. The organizations had different functions and could operate more effectively by cooperating and avoiding overlap.

After two years of informal talks, the committee resolved many of the differences between CUNA and CUNA Mutual. Yet it was clear that attempts at reconciliation would not succeed unless they extended to management in Madison. It was a tall order. Eikel and J. Orrin Shipe, managing director of CUNA, spoke to one another only when necessary. Kratt and Gooch had been careful about how they proceeded in meeting with the CUNA directors, for Eikel would become upset if he thought they were "betraying" CUNA Mutual. Still, friends knew Eikel wanted the acrimony to end.

Eventually the committee brought Eikel and Shipe together. "This is the way it's going to be," they explained. "We don't care how you feel

pating a nasty argument, the executive committee members quickly left the room.

Kratt and Glen, a director from British Columbia, Canada, and a vigorous supporter of CUNA during the split, talked openly and earnestly that night about the past and future of the credit union movement. But many questions remained unanswered: many strong personalities and wills were still involved. The dispute would not be solved that night; a solution would take much effort and time.

Out of this conversation, CUNA and CUNA Mutual formed a committee comprised of four directors from each organization to discuss their differences. Committee members from about the other guy. We're going to come together for the betterment of the movement." Eikel and Shipe agreed.

The organizations reconciled publicly at a golf outing at the Windsor Country Club outside Madison in the summer of 1969. Shipe and Eikel were to play together and ride in the same golf cart, accompanied by Kratt. They got a fourth when Kratt spotted CUMIS training manager William Phillips, who had stumbled onto the outing while running errands.

Eikel and Shipe were still tense in each other's company, and though they tried to put on the best possible face, they circled each other uneasily. Kratt prayed nothing would go wrong; it almost did on the first hole. As Shipe prepared to chip onto the green, Phillips noticed Shipe had mistaken Eikel's ball for his own.

"Bob," Phillips whispered nervously to Kratt, "Orrin is going to hit Charley's ball."

Kratt's eyes widened. "Well, good grief, let him. We don't want to blow this on the first hole."

Luckily, Eikel did not notice the mistake and hit Shipe's ball. After they putted out, Phillips retrieved the balls and returned them to their rightful owners.

The longer they played, the more Eikel and Shipe loosened up. They understood they must get along for just one afternoon, but neither could let the moment pass without jokingly asserting his independence. After teeing off, the first to reach the cart automatically drove to his ball first, no matter where it fell. Eikel and Shipe were terrible golfers, spraying shots left and right, and they zigzagged the course for eighteen holes.

The managing directors also kidded each other. "I've got a bad back, Charley," Shipe would say mischievously. "Would you pick up my ball?"

"That'll be the day when I pick up one of your golf balls," Eikel would respond with a smile.

The round went well. Afterwards, the directors of CUNA and CUNA Mutual shared drinks, dinner, toasts, and laughs. The ceremony did not end every dispute or settle every disagreement, but it did signal a new era of cooperation.

Each side quickly took steps to prove its commitment to unity. CUNA had already passed a modified resolution calling for joint committees from both organizations to develop insurance programs for foreign credit unions. In November 1970, the CUNA executive committee phased out the CUNA insurance services department. Many of the department's employees were eventually integrated into CUNA Mutual.

While CUNA continued to offer its bond coverage with Employers Mutual of Wausau, the latter soon announced it was terminating its agreement with CUNA. The move drew strong protests and threats of withdrawal from some leagues, but this was not unexpected. Sales of the CUMIS 578 Full Discovery Bond had progressed rapidly, replacing Employers' bonds at the rate of five hundred per month. CUMIS now controlled more than half the market. Because of the high risks of bonding, carriers generally found profitability difficult without control of the bulk of the market. Seeing the rise of the CUMIS bond and its own corresponding loss of market share, Employers Mutual decided to simply turn over its bond business to CUMIS. CUNA then endorsed and recommended the CUMIS bond.

To compete with the increasingly complete packages of services offered to credit unions by other financial institutions, CUNA and CUNA Mutual began working jointly on new marketing plans and risk management programs. During the 1970s, CUNA Mutual increased contributions to the leagues and contributed hundreds of thousands of dollars to CUNA's national advertising program.

Supporting CUNA with "lip service to unity" was not enough, CUNA Mutual chairman Pete Gooch said. He emphasized that financial support was justified for business reasons, since credit union growth led to the growth of CUNA Mutual.

As an offshoot of the original peacemaking committee sessions, the CUNA Mutual executive committee and the table officers of the CUNA executive committee began meeting quarterly. Their primary job was to create closer working and planning relationships between the organizations.

In 1971, CUNA Mutual appointed R. C. Robertson, a recent CUNA president and president of the World Council of Credit Unions, to its board to fill the vacancy created by the death of Ray Hagen of Utah. Robertson's appointment stirred memories of credit union leaders actively participating in the affairs of both CUNA and CUNA Mutual, a trend that resumed in the 1970s. Robertson would eventually head the CUNA Mutual board.

New Directions

Charles Eikel viewed the early 1970s with mixed emotions. After years of political acrimony, he enjoyed the renewed unity with CUNA, and he supported cooperation with the same commitment with which he had once fought political opponents.

Eikel got along well with Herbert G. Wegner, CUNA's new managing director, as did the rest of the CUNA Mutual board. Wegner, a visionary who often eschewed a business suit for a leather jacket and who flew his own airplane, encouraged a "think-tank" atmosphere at CUNA. Under his lead, CUNA developed services, like share drafts and data processing, which would prove essential to credit unions in the 1970s.

Wegner was hired after Shipe, facing an employee labor dispute and resisting the executive committee's desire to modernize the CUNA management structure, was asked to resign by the committee. Shipe later became managing director of the Arizona Credit Union League.

Eikel, who turned sixty-five in September 1972, also knew it was time to think about moving on. He had served the credit union movement for thirty-six years, seventeen as president—a position earlier known as managing director—of CUNA Mutual. He had helped the society grow into a worldwide insurance organization, but the insurance industry was changing. Executives could no longer keep their fingers on every issue and decision as Eikel had done. To keep up with the rapid change, managers had to depend increasingly on specialists, delegate more responsibility, and seek more managerial consensus.

Though he was thinking about retiring, Eikel had not made his plans public, for he did not want to be a lame duck president. The board knew Eikel would be retiring soon, but it did not

push him. Instead it granted the president an exemption from the mandatory retirement age of sixty-five.

In August 1972, after dinner with the board at the Edgewater Hotel in Madison, Eikel asked the directors to join him for a "prayer meeting." Prayer meetings, called only when the most essential issues needed discussing, were rare. The sessions were informal, held late at night and usually into the early morning. Only directors participated, though not all chose to attend. The meetings had become popular during Eikel's tenure as an effective way to hash out problems and air differences without minutes or visitors. They were often emotional, and this one was no different.

"It's time," Eikel told the board. "I'm retiring."

For the next few hours, Eikel poured out his heart. It was time to leave behind something he loved almost as much as his family, he said. Though most of the directors believed it was time for a new leader, they were saddened by Eikel's announcement, for it signaled the end of a colorful and productive era.

Several directors wiped their eyes as Eikel spoke, only partly because of the tear gas drifting through the windows. A few blocks away on Madison's State Street, students were protesting the Vietnam conflict and police had used tear gas to disperse the crowd.

Eikel's announcement answered one important question but created another: Who would take his place? Eikel had several capable lieutenants but no obvious successor. The board kept the news of Eikel's impending retirement confidential and appointed a committee to select his replacement. The selection committee considered several candidates from CUNA Mutual, the credit union movement, and, just to be thorough, from outside organizations. Eikel submitted the names of all his vice presidents, a list numbering almost twenty.

The committee had met for several months, narrowed the field to four candidates, and interviewed them extensively when Gooch, the committee chair, proposed shortening the process. "I don't want to influence anyone, and I'm not recommending anyone," he said. "But we have talked to several people, and it seems like we agree who should get the job. Why don't we all

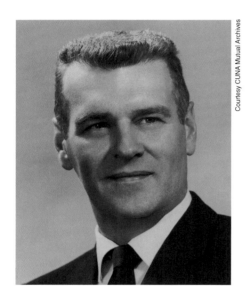

Henry L. "Hank" Timme, above, executive vice president of CUNA Mutual, retired July 1, 1973, because of ill health. Timme joined CUNA Supply in 1939. After duty as a troop carrier pilot and flight instructor in World War II, he became a CUNA field representative in 1947. Timme joined CUNA Mutual as a field representative in 1948 and was later named assistant managing director. He was appointed executive vice president in 1964.

take out a piece of paper and write down our choices?"

The vote was unanimous. The committee made its recommendation to the CUNA Mutual board at the national meeting in St. Louis in May 1973, and the board concurred. The new president of CUNA Mutual was Robert L. Curry, the society's legal counsel.

Eikel retired on June 1, 1973, after thirty-five years of service to CUNA and CUNA Mutual. At the time, CUNA Mutual and subsidiaries had 1,112 employees, 563 at the home office, and its insurance coverage in force totaled twenty billion dollars.

Curry, fifty, was a Wisconsin native. His father was a farmer who developed a skin sensitivity to sunlight. He moved the family briefly to Baltimore, Maryland, then returned to manage a grocery store in Horicon, Wisconsin. The town bordered a vast wetland area where Curry and his two brothers canoed and explored. Life was idyllic, though during the depression of the 1930s the family supplemented its meals with produce that could not be sold at the store.

Shortly after Curry started college at Lawrence University in Appleton, Wisconsin, the Japanese bombed Pearl Harbor. Like his friends, Curry rushed to the recruiting office, only to be told he had a heart murmur. He returned to his studies. In 1942, three friends planning to visit the U.S. Army Air Corps recruiter asked Curry along for the ride. His friends didn't get into the air corps, but Curry did.

Despite volunteering for a new night-fighter outfit, Curry spent the duration of the war as a flight instrument instructor. He often patrolled the California coast at night. One night on the trip home to Sacramento, one of the plane's engines caught fire. The crew turned off the engine and put out the fire but could not hold altitude. For the rest of the trip, the plane climbed and descended, with the crew turning on the engine to regain altitude, then putting out the fire when it started again. By the time the crew made an emergency landing at the airbase, the fire was out of control.

Curry resumed his studies at Lawrence in 1945. Veterans dominated the campus, and Curry was among the busiest, earning three letters as a pulling lineman in football and four as a ballhawking guard who captained the basketball squad. He majored in economics and minored in history but had no idea what he wanted to do after graduation, so he spent a year with the college's admissions department working for Nathan Pusey, who later became president of Harvard.

Curry decided to practice law. He was admitted to Harvard Law School but did not like what he perceived as an uncooperative, dog-eat-dog atmosphere. Neither did Curry, a veteran, appreciate being treated like an undergraduate by acerbic professors. He transferred to the University of Wisconsin Law School. Supported financially by his wife, Muriel, he graduated first in his class in 1953, shortly before his thirtieth birthday.

Curry joined the law firm of Roberts, Roe, Boardman, Suhr and Bjork, which had its origins in a practice started by Wisconsin's Senator Robert LaFollette, a frequent presidential candidate of the Progressive party. Curry developed an active labor practice with the firm but was asked to help senior partner Glenn Roberts prepare the defense for CUNA Mutual after the society was sued by several policyowners.

Curry knew little about the credit union movement, but he was immediately attracted to its purpose and ideals. He was also fascinated by the intense emotions of the time. One of the first credit union meetings he attended was the highly charged CUNA national meeting in 1956. Trained for objectivity, Curry nonetheless told himself that any movement that inspired such passion and fire must be special.

As CUNA Mutual's outside counsel, Curry's law firm did a large amount of work for the society in the next several years, and Curry was assigned to much of it. Eventually he was spending more time at the society than at the law firm, and he became a full-time member of the CUNA Mutual staff in 1967.

Eikel and Curry had a close and occasionally argumentative relationship. "If I'm going to be helpful to you, Charley, I can't agree with you all the time," the young lawyer said. "If I'm wrong, I'm wrong. But I have to be able to challenge you and even play devil's advocate. You need someone in this job who isn't afraid of you."

Eikel grew to appreciate Curry's frankness.

CUNA Mutual president Robert L. Curry was a flight instructor, above, during World War II. After the war, he returned to Lawrence University in Appleton, Wisconsin, where he captained the basketball team, right.

He also valued Curry's friendship. Before tense meetings, Curry and Richard Heins, CUNA Mutual's main consultants, helped Eikel relax by taking him golfing and kidding him unmercifully over dinner.

Curry spent much of his time at CUNA Mutual in the 1960s working on licensing problems and putting out legal fires. One of the most threatening occurred when the Internal Revenue Service (IRS) threatened to retroactively tax a CUNA Mutual reserve fund that had existed for more than thirty years. The fund had been required by the Wisconsin insurance department as a contingency against potential losses from Loan Protection and Life Savings contracts. Curry also learned the reserve had been required as a condition for licensing in some states. Despite the evidence, he was unsure he could keep CUNA Mutual from a large assessment.

Negotiation seemed the most effective route. "Look," Curry told the IRS representative. "We cannot pay a retroactive tax in a lump sum. We do not have the surplus. It will break the company, and a lot of good will be undone." Curry proposed a better way: CUNA Mutual would phase out the reserve over the next ten years, paying back taxes as the fund was shifted into surplus. The IRS would get its money, and CUNA Mutual would stay in business. Both parties would win. The alternative, Curry said, was a messy and lengthy court battle, a battle the society must fight simply to maintain existence. The IRS agreed to the proposal.

Curry's ability to find mutually agreeable solutions to seemingly intractable problems earned him a reputation for fairness and diplomacy among credit union leaders. Because he could talk comfortably with anyone, he was liked and respected by people on both sides of the CUNA-CUNA Mutual dispute. When Curry was introduced to J. Orrin Shipe's wife, she turned to her husband.

"Oh, is this the good guy from CUNA Mutual?" she asked.

"Yeah, well, maybe," Shipe said, smiling thinly. From him, it was a ringing endorsement.

Despite Curry's diplomatic and legal skills, some questioned the wisdom of making him president of CUNA Mutual. Upon his election,

An Evolving Identity

A corporate trademark does more than identify an organization. Used consistently and recurrently, it also illustrates its purpose and philosophy. For more than two decades, CUNA Mutual used the Little Man Under the Umbrella as its identifying mark, with the consent of CUNA, which owned the mark. CUNA Mutual began developing its own mark in 1959, adopting as its logo an M topped by an umbrella-like C.

In 1975, CUNA Mutual adopted an identifying mark that reflected its renewed unity with CUNA. The CM logo was set inside a blue globe as part of CUNA's hands and globe symbol. This design was used until 1990, when CUNA, CUNA Mutual, and the CUNA Service Group adopted a common logo, the hands holding a solid red globe.

CUNA MUTUAL INSURANCE SOCIETY

CUNA MUTUAL INSURANCE SOCIETY

CUNA MUTUAL INSURANCE GROUP

CUNA MUTUAL INSURANCE GROUP

he said: "I believe in the credit union movement and I am deeply committed to its philosophy. I believe in it as a practical working institution which is beneficial for people. I believe that it is essential to work together, for I do not think we have time to do other than work toward common goals."

But traditionalists noted that although he had been a director and president of the CUNA Credit Union in Madison, Curry had not come up through the ranks like other leaders. Yes, he knew the facts, but did he have the vision? Did he have the ability to inspire? Did he have the credit union spirit? A coworker told Curry years later that, at the time, he had judged Curry's selection "a really dumb move." Curry was eager to tackle the job, but even he wondered whether he had the right qualifications.

Curry's managerial ability was tested almost immediately. The field representatives were unhappy about their compensation and talking about forming a union. When Curry met with representatives in British Columbia at the President's Council, an annual meeting honoring the society's top producers, he was taken aback by the level of their anger and dissatisfaction.

Curry suggested that the field staff elect representatives from each of CUNA Mutual's sales districts to discuss their concerns regularly with

him. The group, called the President's Forum, became an important conduit between the field and home office. Curry listened carefully and acted responsively. Suggestions he considered reasonable were not relegated to committees for study. Instead, Curry often made important commitments on the spot.

"Let's see if we can't work something out," he would say. Most of the changes were successful, and the few that failed did so not because Curry was unwilling to try. He quickly earned a reputation as a leader who made promises and kept them.

Curry held the reins of leadership more loosely than did the occasionally autocratic Eikel. As president, Curry freely delegated responsibility. He motivated with praise, not fear, and though he had high expectations, he resisted the temptation to second-guess methods that differed from his own. His door was always open. As a result, Curry made CUNA Mutual's employees feel good about themselves and their work.

Curry's ability to lead and listen were vital during the first two years of his presidency, for he was confronted with several major crises. The most threatening was the society's floundering temporary credit disability coverage.

CUNA Mutual had offered permanent and total disability coverage since 1937. But credit union members suffered more frequently from temporary injuries and illnesses. In 1959, CUNA Mutual added a temporary disability rider to its group Loan Protection contract. For just a few cents more per thousand dollars of insurance, credit unions could supplement their Loan Protection coverage with both permanent and temporary disability.

The coverage was popular but underpriced. Credit disability became a financial disaster, eating half of the society's $3.2 million surplus. Eikel wanted to cancel all existing credit disability coverage, a move that Curry advised was not legal. CUNA Mutual honored existing disability claims but quickly cancelled all new coverage.

Robert L. Curry's willingness to listen as president of CUNA Mutual helped to rebuild once-strained relationships in the credit union movement. Curry, left, listened to CUNA managing director Herbert G. Wegner at a meeting at the Edgewater Hotel in Madison in August 1974.

Courtesy CUNA Mutual Archives

Eliminating the losses did not eliminate the need for credit disability, however, and when credit unions interested in the coverage began looking to companies outside the movement, CUNA Mutual decided to get back into the business. Its credit disability product was dramatically retooled, but the market remained volatile. In 1974, Curry learned the society's credit disability coverage would lose ten million dollars by the end of the year. The only solution was a huge rate hike and restricting coverage to credit unions with excessive claims experience. The leagues were up in arms, and Curry called a series of Dialogue meetings.

Curry pointed out that even with a rate increase, CUNA Mutual still charged much less than commercial companies for credit disability coverage. But his explanations failed to placate the leagues. "Okay, you tell us what to do," he said. "Let's add your ideas to ours, give them a try for several months, then meet again to see what happened and where we should go." By the end of 1975, credit disability was starting to break even.

The Dialogue meetings worked so well they became an annual event. CUNA Mutual also developed new league marketing agreements, shifting from the informal arrangements that provided leagues with financial assistance for their endorsement and sales help to contracts that paid leagues specific percentages for promoting and selling CUNA Mutual products through their field staffs. The Dialogue meetings told the leagues that CUNA Mutual valued their opinions; the marketing agreements told them that the society valued their hard work. The relationship was greatly strengthened in the next few years.

Those who had feared Curry would turn CUNA Mutual into a cold, legalistic organization were pleasantly surprised at his commitment to rebuild relationships and his willingness to listen to all sides, even harsh critics. Like credit union leaders of the past, Curry was an idealist, but his idealism was not narrow or parochial. He sought solutions by building consensus, and after years of partisan divisions, simply achieving consensus was often the solution.

Curry and the CUNA Mutual directors were also willing to take risks on behalf of the credit union movement. In 1974, the society was asked to bail out CUNADATA, a national data processing provider for credit unions started by several leagues in connection with CUNA.

With the rise of automated financial services like electronic funds transfer, direct deposit of payroll, credit cards, and share drafts, credit unions needed data processing systems to compete and survive. But few credit unions could afford their own systems. CUNADATA offered small credit unions the advantage of timeshare data processing through a simple telephone hookup.

When the initial system turned out to be flawed, CUNADATA's sponsors approached CUNA Mutual for help. The decision was difficult. On one hand, the society's directors believed data processing was critical not only to credit unions but to CUNA Mutual, which could automatically process premiums and coverage reports on the system. On the other hand, a study estimated that revamping the system would cost at least eight million dollars over several years. At the time, CUNA Mutual had only thirty million dollars in surplus.

After careful study, Curry and the board decided to support the project because the credit union movement needed it. Electronic Data Systems (EDS), a data processing corporation owned by Ross Perot, took over operation of CUNADATA, refining it to meet special credit union needs.

CUNA Mutual and CUNA eventually sold their CUNADATA stock to EDS. Though the system was operating successfully, it needed steady capital infusions to remain technologically current. The better option, the CUNA and CUNA Mutual directors felt, was to sell the system to EDS, which was interested in continuing to serve the credit union movement. The sale of CUNADATA to EDS was completed in 1981.

Expanding Services

As inflation rates rose at the turn of the 1970s, so did financial competition. Profits were down, expenses were up, and margins were slimmer. Major insurance companies continued to expand their services and marketing activities within the credit union movement. Most offered comprehensive packages. Unless CUNA Mutual

Courtesy CUNA Mutual Archives

Robert L. Curry

*President and Chief Executive Officer
CUNA Mutual Insurance Society
1973–1988*

could supply all a credit union's needs, it risked losing its core business to ambitious competitors who had been content to provide one coverage but now sought to replace contracts traditionally provided by CUNA Mutual. To provide these additional services, CUNA Mutual organized several subsidiaries in the 1970s.

In 1972, the society formed CMC Corporation, a holding company to broker insurance coverages and financial services that could not be provided through CUNA Mutual or CUMIS. After the board discovered that the name CMC was being used by a Wisconsin corporation, it changed the name to CMCI Corporation.

One of the first CMCI programs was the leasing of cars to leagues and affiliates. The corporation's subsidiary, CMCI Underwriters, offered insurance coverage on recreational vehicles, substandard automobile risks, and business ventures.

To help credit unions cope with a rapidly changing financial environment, CMCI contracted with an outside firm to distribute the Financial Planning System to credit unions. A computerized planning model, the system

---

SERVING THE MOVEMENT

The annual Dialogue meetings, which began in 1975, told the leagues that CUNA Mutual valued their opinions. Marketing agreements, which paid leagues for promoting and selling CUNA Mutual products through their field staffs, told them that the society valued their hard work. As a result, the relationship was greatly strengthened in the 1970s.

---

helped credit unions plan for the future by analyzing historical trends and relationships, by changing member needs and economic dynamics, and through new legislation and competition. By allowing credit unions to test "what if" situations and make monthly or long-range forecasts, the Financial Planning System became a popular and valuable service.

CUDIS Insurance Society was formed in 1976 to specialize in credit disability insurance. Though CUNA Mutual had turned around its disability losses, the market was still volatile. An organization focusing solely on credit disability could control these fluctuations, it was felt, and it would legally insulate CUNA Mutual's core business from devastating disability losses.

In the next decade, thanks in large part to

Dick Uphoff, credit disability, a business many had in 1974 wanted to jettison, went from being CUNA Mutual's biggest loser to its biggest winner. The company eventually became the leading seller of credit disability insurance in the world.

In 1980, CUDIS introduced LOANLINER®, a system of consumer lending documents intended to ease credit unions' difficulty in administering loans. LOANLINER was also designed to help credit unions comply with truth-in-lending regulations, which require uniform disclosure of loan costs and other information so borrowers can evaluate lenders' loan terms. A significant innovation, LOANLINER was another example of CUNA Mutual's emphasis on services designed not only to sell insurance but to help credit unions operate more effectively.

The formation of CUDIS and CMCI led CUNA Mutual to organize a new corporate structure. CUMIS, CUDIS, and CMCI became subsidiaries of a holding company called CUNA Mutual Investment Corporation, which in turn was wholly owned by CUNA Mutual Insurance Society. Together the organizations were called the CUNA Mutual Insurance Group.

CUNA Mutual's growth influenced the board to take over management of its investments. For years, at least in part because of the influence of New Yorker William Reid, Chase Manhattan Bank had handled the society's investments. Despite Chase Manhattan's acknowledged record and reputation, some directors did not feel it completely understood the unique mission and needs of CUNA Mutual and the credit union movement. The investments were first brought back to a Wisconsin bank, then to CUNA Mutual's first investment department, headed by Richard Heins, who reduced his teaching duties to join the society full time.

Bolstered by new services, CUNA Mutual experienced steady growth. In 1976, a record year, the disability losses of the previous year were reversed. Total revenue grew to $270 million, and claims increased to $182 million. The next two years were even better. In 1978, total insurance in force jumped to $38.7 billion and CUDIS doubled its assets. CUMIS continued to expand. Among its major additions was CUNET, an employee benefits package tailored to the needs of individual credit unions.

CUMIS also took over the Risk Management Program developed by CUNA to help credit unions better protect their members' assets. Risk management was of concern to all financial institutions, credit unions included. While credit unions had fewer problems than most financial groups, it was a fact of life that a few credit union workers succumbed to temptation.

Some historic embezzlement cases involved people with good hearts but poor accounting methods. As a credit union organizer for the Wisconsin Banking Department in the 1930s, Charles Hyland had called on a Milwaukee credit union whose treasurer was a truck driver. Hyland noticed the financial records were not in good shape, called in an examiner, and told the treasurer to bring his books in. He didn't show up. A few days later, authorities found a bottle on the shore of Lake Michigan with a note say-ing the treasurer had committed suicide. His body could not be found.

Weeks later, a relative of the treasurer called the banking department: If he paid what was missing, could the treasurer come home without charges being pressed? The department agreed. Hyland discovered the man had not stolen any money, but had kept all deposits in a five-gallon jar at home. He had not kept any records, and he panicked when the examiner came. Wisely, the treasurer found another job.

Not all embezzlement and fraud cases turned out as well. Because the average credit union was becoming larger, the average bond claim was rising rapidly. Increasing use of computers and expanded services added to the problem; the more services offered, the greater the risk of fraud.

The CUMIS Risk Management Program became a significant credit union service, working

MILESTONES

1983 League Life and League General Insurance Companies acquired from Michigan Credit Union League effective January 1.

New Western Office dedicated in Pomona, California on March 26.

CUNA Mutual Financial Services Corporation started to make insurance and financial planning services available to credit union members.

Member Direct Marketing program started as joint venture with National Liberty Group.

1984 CUNA Brokerage Services purchased as joint venture with CUNA Service Group.

CMCI introduced Professional Liability insurance.

Courtesy CUNA and Affiliates Archives

CUNA Mutual introduced several new services during the 1970s to help credit unions provide more efficient service.

The NARCUP board in November 1980. From left: Al Jordan, Howard Custer, John McCullough, Frank Kellogg, John Colby, Eleanor Jacobs, Howard Buenzli, Fred Iversen, and Robert Kloss.

MILESTONES

1985 Total assets reached $1 billion.

PLAN AMERICA franchise program introduced.

1986 Business Development Consulting Service launched as pilot project in fall.

1987 CUMIS and CMCI Corp. began providing Travel Accident insurance to credit unions through CUNA Service Group.

with credit unions to reduce embezzlement risk by analyzing their cash-handling procedures and conducting fraud audits, which often uncovered embezzlements normally undetected by standard supervisory audits. CUMIS specialists also helped secure the credit unions' physical security systems.

Charles Eikel watched the expansion of CUNA Mutual services with pride, but by his own choice he viewed them from afar. Upon retiring several years earlier, he had decided he would not subject his successor to the second-guessing that was common among recently retired CEOs. Offered an office at the CUNA Mutual headquarters, he refused.

"If you want to know something or ask me about something, you call me," he told Curry (who did call often). "I'm not coming into the office. The job is yours now. You run it the way you think it should be run."

Eikel remained on the board for a few years and frequently attended meetings as an honorary director after that. Friends marveled at his discipline. Though they sometimes noticed the

hair standing up on the back of his neck when he heard things he did not like, he resisted the urge to dictate. Only once, when the board was considering changing the name of its policy-owners representative program, did Eikel enter the fray, speaking convincingly about the unique character and value of the policyowner name— and then only after he was asked to speak.

Such restraint was difficult. Though happy with retirement, Eikel wanted to contribute. He got his chance in 1977, conceiving the idea for the National Association for Retired Credit Union People (NARCUP). The seeds of the idea were sown in Florida as Eikel sat outside a beauty shop, waiting for his wife and soaking up some sun. While talking to a man sitting nearby, he learned the man was a retired credit union member.

"Now that I left my credit union, I can't get a loan," the man said. "I can't get back in, and it's too far away anyway."

Eikel thought: "Whatever happened to the 'once-a-member-always-a-member' philosophy?"

He took his concerns to the CUNA Mutual

board. In 1977, five retired CUNA Mutual executives—Eikel, Hank Timme, John Colby, Howard Custer, and Frank Kellogg—began studying whether retired credit union members needed their own organization. The group found that many retired members felt they were not fully served by their credit unions. Many fewer retirees than non-retired members had their main savings accounts in credit unions.

These findings led to the development of NARCUP in 1978. The organization helped extend more credit union services, like group insurance, retirement planning, and discounts on travel expenses, to retired members. Eikel was NARCUP's first president. By the late 1980s, it was serving a hundred thousand members across the country.

Vital relationships

As it strengthened its range of services in the late 1970s, CUNA Mutual also paid greater attention to strengthening important relationships, particularly with the Canadian credit union movement. Canadians had played a vital role in the evolution of the society and several, including the Rev. J. D. Nelson MacDonald of Nova Scotia, George A. Swales of Alberta, and A. Leonard Tune of Ontario, had served on its board. C. Gordon Smith had started CUNA Mutual's Canadian operations from his kitchen in Hamilton, Ontario, and charismatically directed its growth into one of the country's largest life insurance organizations.

When Smith retired in 1968, he was succeeded by J. L. Herve Lanctot, a colorful and energetic French-Canadian who had been assistant general manager of CUNA Mutual's Canadian operations. Forthright and fiery, Lanctot was not afraid to speak out about the need for national respect. Earlier in his credit union career, as a CUNA director from Quebec, he rose at a meeting to protest the lack of materials written in French.

Lanctot had spoken in French for five minutes—few at the meeting understood him—then abruptly switched to English: "How in the hell would you like it if you had to take that all the time?" Tom Doig quickly ordered CUNA and CUNA Mutual to produce more French-language credit union materials.

Like many Canadian credit union leaders, Lanctot had high hopes that CUNA Mutual's Canadian operations would one day stand on its own, owned by Canadians. Canadian leagues, once part of CUNA, had organized their own national association. Canadian CUNA Mutual policyowners, tired of criticism that they were part of a foreign company, also felt it was time to take charge of their own insurance operations.

In 1977, the CUMIS Life Insurance Company was incorporated as a Canadian subsidiary of CUNA Mutual. The company was directed by a board of Canadian credit union leaders elected by CUNA Mutual, with Lanctot as president. In 1989, Canadian policyowners acquired majority control of the company, with CUNA Mutual retaining a minority position.

While CUNA Mutual enhanced its relationship with Canada by letting go, it strengthened other bonds by doing the opposite, merging in 1983 with the League Life and League General Insurance companies, both owned by the Michigan Credit Union League. During the controversy over new CUNA Mutual programs in 1958, the Michigan league had acquired a life insurance company to provide members an alternative to CUNA Mutual. The company was renamed League Life. Eight years later, the league acquired a dormant property insurance operation, naming it League General.

Both companies were successful. They were particularly strong in the mass merchandising of insurance. Despite CUNA Mutual's efforts to hold its share of the Michigan market—including the waiving of its underwriting rule for non-affiliated credit unions—the society could maintain just one-quarter of the state's credit union business; League Life and League General had more than half.

But the Michigan league encountered fi-

The Rev. J. D. Nelson MacDonald, top, was the first Canadian to serve as chairman of CUNA Mutual (1959-1961). J. L. Herve Lanctot, bottom, was the first president of CUMIS Life Insurance Company, a CUNA Mutual subsidiary controlled by a Canadian board of directors.

nancial problems after investing in a cooperative housing project in Detroit. Because of recession and massive layoffs in the auto industry, housing demands dropped sharply and losses on the project soared. By 1982, the league needed a quick infusion of cash.

Then Curry entered the picture. Robert E. Vanderbeek, president of League Life and League General, had become friends with the CUNA Mutual chief executive. When the men bumped into one another at a meeting in Singapore, they discussed the possibility of CUNA Mutual acquiring the Michigan companies, working out a possible merger plan on a paper napkin. Curry was later invited to discuss the plan at a special meeting of the Michigan league board and credit union managers.

Many of the participants, remembering the league's difficult relationship with CUNA Mutual after the split, were tense. Nearly all the old guard were upset about selling an organization they had helped create and foster to a large company like CUNA Mutual. But Curry assuaged their fears, emphasizing that the society was not interested in dominating any arrangement.

"This has to be a 'putting together' of our organizations," Curry said. "It has to develop into a partnership. If it is going to work, there has to be enthusiasm from both sides."

Curry's words and his reputation for fairness impressed the group. It voted unanimously to sell League Life and League General to CUNA Mutual. Although it took some time for the sales representatives of both groups, vigorous rivals for years, to fully accept the merger, they eventually started carrying CUNA Mutual policies in one pocket and League contracts in the other. Few League Life and League General employees were displaced. In just a few years, the companies were integrated into CUNA Mutual while maintaining their own identities.

The movement also benefited from ever-improving relations between CUNA Mutual and CUNA. Curry's diplomatic efforts repaired

Courtesy CUNA Mutual Audio-Visual Services

Robert E. Vanderbeek, above, president of the League Life and League General Insurance companies, played a major role in the merging of the companies with CUNA Mutual in 1983.

many broken ties during the 1970s, and he was invited to credit union meetings previously off limits to CUNA Mutual leaders. Respect for CUNA Mutual grew, and even once-hostile political opponents acknowledged the society's contributions to the movement.

Relations became so good that, when Wegner resigned as CUNA managing director in 1979, the executive committee began exploring an "amalgamation" with CUNA Mutual. Some CUNA directors asked Curry whether he would be interested in heading such an organization. Though honored, Curry declined. The amalgamation talks were eventually dropped.

In the meantime, CUNA and CUNA Mutual became neighbors again. In 1980, CUNA, which had been considering moving to Washington, D.C., moved into a new building on CUNA Mutual's Mineral Point Road site. Wegner played a major role in the historic move but resigned under fire—some charged that his vision was not matched by his administrative abilities—before the CUNA managing director's office was finished. The World Council of Credit Unions also moved into a new building on the thirty-acre site.

Known as the Credit Union Center, the complex was dedicated on May 31, 1980, almost thirty years to the day after President Truman dedicated Filene House. More than a thousand credit union leaders from around the world attended the ceremonies. Among the speakers was Louise McCarren Herring, the retired ma-

Courtesy CUNA Mutual Archives

Louise McCarren Herring, a delegate to the CUNA constituting convention at Estes Park, Colorado, in 1934, spoke at the dedication of the Credit Union Center on May 31, 1980.

Courtesy CUNA Mutual Audio-Visual Services

Serving the Community

As CUNA Mutual's assets have grown, so has its commitment to its community. The society has long been the leading corporate blood donor in the Dane County, Wisconsin chapter of the American Red Cross, as well as one of the leading area contributors to the United Way. Many CUNA Mutual employees regularly donate their time to numerous social service organizations and campaigns in the Madison area. Collecting food for the Thanksgiving Food Drive for local food shelves, from left, are CUNA Mutual employees Beth Hons, Lynette Sutter, Bernice Hamilton, and Lenny Hoffman.

In 1971, the society formed the CUNA Mutual Charitable Foundation to provide funds to social service organizations and agencies. In 1990, CUNA Mutual, along with CUNA and the World Council of Credit Unions, helped employees open a cooperative day-care center.

naging director of the Ohio Credit Union League whose youthful appearance had fooled Roy Bergengren on the train to Estes Park in 1934, and the Rev. Marion M. Ganey, a Jesuit priest who had built the credit union movement in the Fiji Islands. CUNA Mutual chairman Gerald J. Ring called the ceremonies "a new beginning" that "can only mean a stronger credit union movement in the years to come."

But as the 1980s began, the movement was weakened by the worst economic downturn since the depression of the 1930s. Unemployment and bankruptcies reached new highs. Runaway inflation and spiraling interest rates hurt credit unions even after the government dropped restrictions on the movement's long-standing 12-percent loan rate ceiling. As credit union growth stalled, so did CUNA Mutual. After reaching forty billion dollars in 1979, life insurance in force declined the next year.

Though a hiring freeze was instituted, the society struggled through the recession without layoffs. To stimulate sales, CUNA Mutual beefed up incentives for its field staff and began a cam-

paign to penetrate more of the country's two hundred largest credit unions. The society launched a marketing program with National Liberty Marketing, Inc., specializing in direct marketing of insurance, to provide life and health coverage. CUNA Mutual also started what became known as CUNA Mutual Financial Services Corporation, a company designed to work with leagues to build tailored brokerage operations.

These and other programs aided credit union growth but were not enough to quickly restart CUNA Mutual. Many believed the solution was to sell outside the credit union movement. The society had been considering offering credit disability and bond coverages to savings and loan institutions. A bank association had even asked to broker CUNA Mutual's bond to its members.

The move was tempting, especially since the leagues had not expressed opposition in the belief that any action that kept CUNA Mutual healthy was in their interest. At an annual forum, nearly two hundred CUNA Mutual managers, many of them young employees who had come to the society from outside the credit union movement, voted to support selling outside the movement. It seemed an opportunity for growth too inviting to pass up.

Robert L. Wermuth, executive vice president of CUNA Mutual.

Only two or three voted against the idea, among them Robert L. Wermuth, the longtime executive vice president of finance. The society had a powerful and unique relationship with the credit union movement, Wermuth believed, a connection that would pay dividends in the future. Credit unions would not be stalled forever; they would grow again. Breaking the society's exclusive bonds with the movement was a short-term solution.

Curry, who had not voted at the management forum, had told the CUNA Mutual managers he would take their overwhelming recommendation to the board. Although some directors had argued mightily against going outside the movement, a strong recommendation from Curry might sway the majority. But the closer the board meeting came, the more Curry came to believe the minority was right on this issue. He recommended against selling to institutions other than credit unions. The board agreed.

The economy eventually recovered. In 1983, the CUNA Mutual Insurance Group had its best year ever, reaching $46.6 billion of insurance in force.

The Credit Union Center, home of CUNA, CUNA Mutual, and the World Council of Credit Unions.

Children stood outside St. Michael's Parish Credit Union in Nevesi, Fiji. The credit union, the first in the Fiji Islands, was founded in the early 1950s.

CHAPTER SEVEN

Beyond the Horizon

The world is my country, all mankind are my brethren, and to do good is my religion.

— Opening speech by C.W. Hudson
at 1956 CUNA National Convention,
paraphrased from Thomas Paine

On July 25, 1898, four centuries after Christopher Columbus discovered a beautiful island that Spanish settlers later named Puerto Rico, American forces invaded the island towards the end of the Spanish-American War. Three thousand troops, among them a twenty-year-old soldier and poet named Carl Sandburg, landed on the beach at Guanica, a one-street town lined with palm and coconut trees, and overwhelmed Spanish defenders. Within two weeks, the fighting was over, and Spain later ceded Puerto Rico to the United States.

Luis Munoz Marin, the son of a prominent Puerto Rican, was born the year of the U.S. invasion. As a child, he saw the Americans build dams, hospitals, schools, and roads in his country. Munoz Marin also saw American sugar companies take nearly all the profits from the best plantations and mills. A land once penniless but content became, in the words of Munoz Marin, "a land of beggars and millionaires, of flattering statistics and distressing realities."

Seeking solutions to these problems, Munoz Marin, a popular poet and journalist, turned to politics. As head of the insular Puerto Rican Senate, he was one of the leading architects of Operation Bootstrap, an ambitious program to improve living conditions on the island. Large farms were bought by the government and redistributed to farm workers, educational programs reduced the numbers of Puerto Ricans who could not read or write, and thousands of slum dwellings were razed and replaced by modern housing.

Munoz Marin became one of the island's most powerful and beloved leaders. In 1948, after the U.S. Congress voted to allow Puerto Rico to elect its own governor, Munoz Marin was swept into office by a tide of youthful supporters, among them Carlos M. Matos, an agricultural extension agent.

The time was ripe for cooperative ventures. Believing that the cooperative methods developed at St. Francis Xavier University in Antigonish, Nova Scotia, could be applied to Puerto Rico as well, the University of Puerto Rico arranged for the Rev. Joseph A. MacDonald, a St. Francis Xavier instructor, to teach a summer course for the Puerto Rican extension service.

Matos signed up for the course, but he was not particularly enthusiastic. He chose a seat where he thought he could sleep. But Father MacDonald's speech, which centered on credit unions, opened Matos's eyes. Inspired by the message, he helped set up a credit union among extension service employees; then he was asked to concentrate on organizing rural credit unions.

Most of the organizing meetings were held at night and during weekends to accommodate the farmers. Four or five times a week, Matos and his wife, Connie, packed their baby son in a small hammock, tied it in the back seat of their Ford, and set out for meetings in remote farm dwellings, many with no electricity. In time, Matos's young son attended so many credit union meetings that he could recite the Rochdale principles, a set of English cooperative tenets that had guided the pioneers of the credit union movement. Matos earned a master's degree in agricultural economics at Cornell University in New York and became Puerto Rico's inspector of cooperatives and credit unions. Interested in the work of the Credit Union National Association, he attended the dedication of Filene House in Madison in 1950. When Matos returned to Puerto Rico, he helped set up a credit union league that affiliated with CUNA.

CUNA Mutual had been providing Loan Protection and Life Savings coverage for Puerto Rican credit unions since 1947. When the Puerto Rican league was formed, twenty-five credit unions carried CUNA Mutual insurance. Matos was an inspiring, energetic leader, and he became a strong advocate for the benefits of CUNA Mutual insurance. Since CUNA Mutual was not registered in Puerto Rico and Matos was not a licensed insurance agent for the society, his promotional efforts got him into some trouble with the Puerto Rican insurance commission. CUNA Mutual was soon registered in Puerto Rico, and Ernesto Rosario, a fellow worker of Matos, was named its agent.

As the credit union movement grew in the Caribbean, CUNA Mutual representatives made several trips to the areas. Orch Edgerton traveled to Puerto Rico in 1953 and also stopped at Jamaica, the second country outside the United States (after Canada) to receive CUNA Mutual services. Tom Benson visited Puerto Rico two years later and, on the way back, inspected credit unions in the Dominican Republic organized

under the authority of its dictator, Rafael Leonidas Trujillo Molina. After Benson's return, CUNA Mutual canceled all coverage in the Dominican Republic because it did not pay CUNA dues.

William Tenney visited Puerto Rico, but did most of his communicating through long, detailed letters explaining what Matos and other credit union leaders wanted to know about rates, loan policies, and bonding. Hank Timme also was closely involved in early international development.

Charles Eikel traveled to Puerto Rico in 1954 on a trip during which Matos encountered his high principles and forceful style. Not long before Eikel's visit, one member of a credit union organized by Matos was told by his doctor he had leprosy. Doubting the diagnosis, the member wanted to go to the Mayo Clinic in Minnesota. He needed a thousand dollars for expenses. When the credit

Courtesy CUNA Mutual Archives

Carlos M. Matos, above, became involved with credit unions as an agricultural extension agent in Puerto Rico. In 1962, he became the first director of CUNA Mutual's new International Department.

Courtesy CUNA and Affiliates Archives

Credit union leaders visit a Brazilian credit union.

Courtesy CUNA Mutual Archives

The Rev. Marion M. Ganey, left, played a major role in the international credit union movement, bringing credit unions to British Honduras (now Belize) and the Fiji Islands. Ganey visited with Thomas B. Benson, who made several international trips for CUNA Mutual in the 1950s.

concentrated on training prospective credit union organizers, many of them Catholic priests and nuns. Provided with a little money for promotional materials and having been taught accounting and bookkeeping, these pioneers fueled the rapid development of the international credit union movement in the late 1950s.

One of the most outstanding was the Reverend Marion Ganey, a Jesuit from Illinois. Sent to British Honduras (now known as Belize), he found an old mimeographed book on credit union theory and organized the first Caribbean credit unions in the village of Punta Gorda. But credit union growth in surrounding villages was slow until a hurricane destroyed 80 percent of Punta Gorda. The villagers' credit union experience enabled them to set up a disaster relief fund and quickly rebuild their homes. Word of the credit union spread quickly throughout British Honduras, and the movement soon flourished.

Ganey's work impressed the island's British governor. When the governor was reassigned to the Fiji Islands, he asked church officials to send Ganey there to organize credit unions. Development was slow at first. Exploited for years by outsiders, the villagers mistrusted newcomers. But after Ganey convinced villagers in Togalevu to start the Bergengren Credit Union in 1953, the Fijians quickly saw its benefits. In ten years, the islands had more than 250 credit unions with 32,000 members and more than a million dollars in assets.

Usury was common in the Fiji Islands. A plantation laborer who depended on his bicycle to get to work could, without much trouble, get a five-dollar loan to replace a broken chain, then pay back six dollars the following week. To outsiders, such an interest rate did not seem unreasonable until they learned that the average Fiji worker made less than three dollars per week.

Though the average credit union loan in Fiji was small—often just a few dollars—it was not insignificant. Credit union loans helped fishermen to buy nets and boats and farmers to replace forked sticks with plows and bullocks. To Fijians, credit union loans meant the chance to get medical care, an education, or even something as simple as a lamp or sewing machine.

To Fijians as to the citizens of other develop-

union asked whether CUNA Mutual's Loan Protection contract would cover a loan for the trip, Matos, assuming the man was already ill, said no.

When Eikel learned of the incident, he informed Matos with characteristic firmness that it was not Matos's job to act on behalf of the CUNA Mutual claims department. The claims staff decided the claim would be valid, and the credit union granted the loan. At the Mayo Clinic, the man learned he did not have leprosy. Matos gained new respect for CUNA Mutual.

Matos soon went to work for CUNA. The national association had been talking to the U.S. government about overseas credit union development and had recently become part of the government's CARE program to provide food packages for underdeveloped countries. Roy Bergengren was especially interested in international credit unions. A year before his death, he convinced the CUNA directors to establish a world extension department. Olaf Spetland was named director and Matos, assistant director.

With meager funds, the CUNA department

ing countries, the credit union meant at least some economic freedom. Often, the votes members cast for credit union officers constituted their first experience with democracy. Credit unions often helped Fijian women, traditionally forced into subservience, to take a more active role in the affairs of their families and communities.

Fijians did not take credit unions for granted.

When Ganey arrived by boat or horseback to organize a credit union, villagers transformed the event into a celebration complete with roast pig, dancing, ceremonial drinks, and treasured gifts like whale teeth.

When organizing a Fijian credit union, Ganey spoke in terms the seafaring villagers understood well. "We are traveling together to an island called Economic Security," he said.

A member of the Police Department Credit Union in Suva, Fiji Islands, made a savings deposit.

"Today you will elect your captain and chart your own course."

The rules of the journey were simple, Ganey said, but they were crucial to success in all credit unions: "Save regularly, borrow wisely, and repay promptly."

CUNA Mutual had been serving Fijian credit unions since 1953, when Ganey wrote Eikel to inquire about getting insurance and bonding coverage. Several years later, the Fiji Credit Union League opened a training school, called the Roy F. Bergengren School of Credit Unions, in a borrowed parish hall. CUNA Mutual later funded the school building and made annual contributions to its operation. Students from all over the Pacific—Australia, New Zealand, Tonga, Samoa, and the Solomon Islands—attended the school.

As credit unions exploded in Fiji, the movement also expanded into South and Central America, the Far East, and Ireland. By 1962, CUNA Mutual provided Loan Protection and Life Savings coverage by mail only, to twenty countries. Coverage totaled twenty-five million dollars. Areas with the highest coverage included Puerto Rico, Jamaica, the Dominican Republic,

Trinidad, the Panama Canal Zone, and Peru.

Matos left CUNA in 1962 but wanted to continue working in international development. He contacted Benson. Together they developed a plan for the CUNA Mutual International Department, approved by the board in 1962. Matos was the department's first director.

The department's goal was to improve overseas service and coverage. At the time, the three thousand credit unions outside the United States and Canada were projected to increase fivefold in the next decade. If CUNA Mutual coverage grew at the same rate, the society would not be able to handle overseas business by mail. The international department also was to work in cooperation with other credit union organizations.

One of Matos's most important early jobs was qualifying CUNA Mutual in various countries. In countries without mutual insurance laws, like Jamaica, Fiji, and Western Samoa, CUNA Mutual began offering its services before being registered. But some countries forbade the society from offering Loan Protection and Life Savings unless legally qualified. Qualifying was often difficult. Government officials were suspicious even when native credit union organizations vouched for the society. When CUNA Mutual tried to qualify in Colombia in 1964, attorneys grilled Matos about the society's contracts for four long days and took several months more to approve the simple policies. Colombia was the first country outside North America in which CUNA Mutual was licensed.

Qualifying in Australia was even more difficult. The credit union movement there was young but vigorous, often operating out of homes and garages. One of its most dedicated leaders was Stanley F. Arneil, an accountant and trade union advocate who had spent more than three years as a Japanese prisoner in Burma. Six feet, six inches tall, he weighed only ninety-six pounds when the war ended. Arneil, an emotional and zealous speaker, used his connections with the Australian Broadcasting Commission to deliver speeches about credit unions over television.

In just a few years, Australia had 215 credit unions, 47,000 members, and nine million dollars in assets. While CUMIS had little trouble

George McCready, a director of the New South Wales Credit Union League in Australia, got acquainted with Joey, a kangaroo from Madison's Henry Vilas Zoo, during a trip to CUNA Mutual. The photo of McCready and the kangaroo was cut out and superimposed over a picture of the home office lawn for the July 1967 *CUNA Mutual Newsletter.*

registering in 1965, the Australian government delayed approval of CUNA Mutual until 1969. In just a few months, 1,200 credit unions were covered by Loan Protection and Life Savings insurance. A year later, Arneil was named vice president and general manager of Australian operations for CUNA Mutual and CUMIS; a branch office eventually opened there.

Operating in countries without credit union laws sometimes called for creative methods of premium collection. CUNA Mutual began providing Loan Protection and Life Savings insurance to Irish credit unions in 1960, six years before Ireland passed a credit union law. Insurance was sold by mail to Irish credit unions, and the premiums were sent to CUNA Mutual through Nora Herlihy, the founder of the Irish credit union movement, who served the society as an unpaid agent. On at least one occasion, an Irish priest traveling to an international credit union conference in Madison brought in his

---

SERVING THE MOVEMENT

To the citizens of developing countries, the credit union meant greater economic freedom. Often, the votes members cast for credit union officers constituted their first experience with democracy. CUNA Mutual helped protect these credit unions, and played a major role in the movement's international development.

---

pockets several month's worth of CUNA Mutual premiums, amounting to thousands of dollars.

By 1963, Ireland had more than 600 credit unions, 12,000 members, and $500,000 in assets. CUNA Mutual provided a mortgage loan for the Irish League of Credit Unions' own building. CUNA Mutual also helped promote the Irish movement through seminars, policyowner programs, and credit union schools.

In 1969, CUNA Mutual and the Irish league

considered a plan whereby the league would act as CUNA Mutual's agent. The Irish were tough negotiators, and Charles Eikel balked at their demands for a share of the revenue generated from insurance sales in their country. Eikel preferred to see the money go to the policyowner credit unions. Neither side would budge.

"What do you want?" Eikel asked at one point. "My blood?"

The groups eventually compromised. Irish credit unions got 65 percent of the dividends generated by CUNA Mutual sales in Ireland. The Irish league received 5 percent of the dividends (a share that would soon rise to 20 percent, plus 5 percent of investment income).

After the negotiations, Irish officials set a glass of tomato juice in front of Eikel.

"Here's your blood back," they said.

Later that night, the negotiations were forgotten as Irish credit union officials treated Eikel and the other CUNA Mutual representatives to an unforgettable night of Irish songs, toasts, and fellowship.

Besides signing agent agreements with overseas leagues, CUNA Mutual began establishing its own representatives in strategic locations during the 1960s; the first were in Colombia, Trinidad, and the Netherlands Antilles.

While hiring one representative, Matos received a call from a priest who knew the candidate. He said the man had fallen behind on his loan payments and moved to another city. Matos investigated and learned that the man's father had died several years before, leaving him as the principal financial supporter of his family. He had put two brothers through medical school and was deeply in debt.

Matos discussed the situation with CUNA Mutual's executive vice president, Hank Timme, whom he often consulted on international business. Neither man knew whether to hire the man until Timme remembered Tom Doig.

"What would Tom have done?" Timme wondered. The answer was obvious: He would have paid the man's loan and hired him.

Courtesy CUNA Mutual Archives

Stanley F. Arneil, above, helped build the Australian credit union movement and was later named vice president and general manager of CUNA Mutual and CUMIS operations there.

CUNA Mutual and the Credit Union League of Ireland signed an agreement in 1969 granting the league a share of dividends generated by insurance sales in Ireland. Seated, from left, are Daniel A. Norrison, vice president of the Irish League, and Charles F. Eikel, Jr. Standing, from left, are Phil Ryan, managing director of the League; Robert L. Wermuth, vice president of finance, and Robert L. Curry, general counsel.

Courtesy CUNA Mutual Archives

MILESTONES

1965 First Policyowners' Representatives Program adapted to international members held in April on the island of Montserrat for Caribbean areas.

1965 CUNA International formed.

1970 World Council of Credit Unions replaced CUNA International as governing body of world's credit unions.

1971 CUNA Mutual and CUMIS signed an agreement February 19 with Latin American Confederation of Credit Unions (COLAC) in Bogota, Colombia, to provide technical assistance to the Latin American federations.

1974 Construction began on building in Bogota, Colombia, to house offices of CUNA Mutual, CUMIS and UCONAL, the Colombian league.

Matos and Timme did not go quite so far, but they did employ the young man. He turned out to be an excellent worker and eventually repaid his credit union loan.

By 1968, the society was serving credit unions in thirty-five countries, including Ireland and Great Britain, Lesotho in southern Africa, Hong Kong, and New Zealand. Insurance coverage tripled between 1962 and 1968, reaching ninety million dollars.

Serving the insurance needs of such diverse areas presented several challenges to CUNA Mutual's international department. Promotional materials had to be translated. Premiums were paid and dividends returned in local currencies, from pounds to guldens to balboas. Fluctuations in the value of foreign currencies and runaway inflation made it difficult to state accurately the value of CUNA Mutual assets worldwide or to measure growth.

A letter mailed from Madison might reach the capital city of a country in a few days but require several weeks longer to reach its final destination in some remote village. In Bougainville, part of Papua New Guinea in the Solomon Islands, officials traveling to some remote credit unions had to drive several hours on muddy, hole-ridden roads, ford several streams, park next to a gorge, then walk for another hour. When officials arrived, people were called to the meeting with a conch shell used as a horn.

Solving the governmental and logistical problems of overseas credit unions required constant legal advice. The CUNA Mutual international department was next door to the society's legal offices, and Matos conferred nearly every day with Robert Curry, then general counsel.

One of the most intriguing legal challenges was in Mexico. Because the country had no credit union law, CUNA Mutual could not qualify and was forbidden to write coverage for Mexican credit unions. Marion Gregory was unable to convince legislators to enact a credit union law during a trip to Mexico in 1955. Mexican credit union leaders had no more luck than Gregory.

The Mexican government's reluctance to enact a credit union law stemmed in part from its perception of credit unions as a church movement; though the government granted credit unions de facto recognition because of the Catholic church's overwhelming prestige in Mexico, it also desired to keep church and state matters separate. Thus while Mexican credit unions did not need a law to operate, outside credit union organizations like CUNA Mutual did.

The government also believed many Mexican credit unions had no need for insurance. Started in 1951 by Catholic priests to serve the poorest of the poor, the Mexican movement was initially heavy on philosophy and light on economics. Credit unions operated more like informal clubs. The average credit union had only thirty members, savings were small, bookkeeping was often neglected, and payment of treasurers was prohibited.

Matos had visited Mexico in the late 1950s, and his most vivid memory was the ancient station wagon driven by local credit union officials. The wagon was packed with four men, including Matos, plus a sizable load of papers, materials, and luggage. The inner tube of one tire was bulging at the side, and the wagon had one spare with no inner tube. Miraculously, the tire held up for a long round trip, a symbol, Matos would later recall, of the austerity and resolve of the Mexican movement's leadership.

Conditions gradually changed. With organizational and financial help from CUNA, CUNA

Mutual, and other credit union organizations, Mexican credit unions were transformed into true economic enterprises while retaining strong philosophical roots. Tiny credit unions were consolidated to provide better service. Managers were hired. Loans and savings increased; so did the need for Loan Protection and Life Savings insurance, which made the government's reluctance to qualify CUNA Mutual all the more frustrating.

To solve the problem, Curry suggested a contract eliminating all references to insurance. Loan Protection and Life Savings were described as "benefits." Curry contacted a Mexican lawyer to confirm the legality of the contract. The lawyer contacted a judge, who issued a legal opinion that the contract was permissible under Mexico's extensive cooperative laws. The contracts, called "quota share agreements," allowed the local credit union league to act as the insurer, with

African credit union leaders attended a World Council of Credit Unions conference.

Courtesy World Council of Credit Unions, Inc.

CUNA Mutual reinsuring or coinsuring between 80 and 100 percent of the total.

Between 1970 and 1981, membership in Mexican credit unions grew from 20,000 to 135,000. Assets increased from 23 million to almost 2 billion pesos, the equivalent of $79.3 million dollars. Eighty percent of Mexico's credit unions were protected by Loan Protection and Life Savings insurance.

While the quota share agreement helped CUNA Mutual to offer services in more countries, the society's relations with some foreign confederations became strained as its international coverage grew. Renewed national pride and the desire for self-determination accounted for much of their displeasure.

Some foreign confederations had also sought changes in the governing structure of CUNA International, as CUNA was known after organizing overseas credit unions in the 1950s and 1960s and integrating them into its organizational structure. Because the vast majority of the world's credit union members and assets were American, some foreign representatives felt their problems and concerns received less attention during CUNA International meetings than issues important to the United States.

To ensure greater representation to all credit unions, CUNA International was reorganized in 1970. Distinct regional federations were formed, representing Canada, the Caribbean, Australia, Africa, Asia, Latin America, and the United States, as well as freestanding leagues in Fiji, Great Britain, Ireland, and New Zealand. These organizations formed the World Council of Credit Unions.

As international credit unions wanted increased representation, many also desired more control of the movement's insurance operations in their countries. Charles Eikel warned of the anticolonial perceptions inherent in CUNA Mutual's overseas operations.

"When we enter the realm of the global village," he said, "our pride, success, and affluency become our burden, much like the rich man who sought to purchase rather than to earn friendships, and who, when called upon to give, did so with an air of self-righteous charity to the detriment of both the borrower and the lender."

Yet CUNA Mutual was reluctant to turn over control of its insurance operations. The organization had acquired its insurance expertise over several decades. Some leaders, including Eikel and Matos, feared local organizations might get into trouble without similar experience and resources.

But others, allowing that CUNA Mutual could provide the most efficient services, cautioned that efficiency was not the only point. The main intent of the credit union movement was to help people control their economic destiny. Many foreign nationals did not want an American company, no matter how beneficent, always looking over their shoulders.

Curry saw growing evidence of anti-American feeling during his travels abroad in the 1960s. While CUNA Mutual sent representatives to credit union meetings in other countries only when invited, some local officials invariably criticized the society's control of their country's insurance operations.

Relations were similarly tense during a meeting between CUNA Mutual officials and representatives of the Latin American Confederation of Credit Unions (COLAC) in Bogota, Colombia. During a lunch break, one of the COLAC officials, a former policeman from Guatemala, suddenly produced a deck of cards. He invited the Americans, Curry included, to join in a game of Spanish blackjack.

The Americans knew nothing about the game except that the rules seemed to change with every hand. They lost big and the COLAC officials shook with laughter. The game broke the ice between the groups, and they shared lunch and dinner and cards the next few days. Few American and Latin American credit union officials had ever really socialized before.

Out of the Bogota meeting, CUNA Mutual and COLAC negotiated a "bill of rights" governing CUNA Mutual's operations in Latin America. CUNA Mutual recognized the rights of credit union federations to hold controlling interests in the insurance organizations serving credit unions in their countries, if they desired it. The society also agreed to provide technical assistance in the gradual transfer of majority control to such organizations.

This localization policy was eventually applied to all CUNA Mutual's overseas operations.

Typically, overseas league departments or affiliated cooperative companies issued insurance directly to credit unions in their countries. CUNA Mutual initially reinsured 90 to 100 percent of the league's operations. Gradually, as the local organizations became more stable, they assumed more risk and CUNA Mutual's reinsurance share decreased.

Most national credit union leagues have allowed CUNA Mutual to retain at least a 25-percent reinsurance share in their insurance operations. Although some countries, like Ecuador, Ireland, Trinidad and Tobago, Colombia, and Jamaica, assumed total control of their insurance operations, most also signed contracts with CUNA Mutual that covered all losses beyond a specified amount.

By 1990, CUNA Mutual provided Loan Protection, Life Savings, CUMIS bond, group term coverage and hospital indemnity insurance to credit union members in nearly sixty countries. Coverage totaled nearly three billion dollars. The international department had twenty-seven employees in Madison, many of them multilingual.

More than a hundred additional employees represented CUNA Mutual worldwide, including branch offices in Australia, Jamaica, and Trinidad, and regional offices in Colombia and Hong Kong. Representatives were based in Great Britain, Indonesia, Kenya, Korea, the Netherlands Antilles, Panama, Peru, Taiwan, and Thailand.

CUNA Mutual continued to work closely with the World Council of Credit Unions, serving as an associate member of the council. Its employees participated in educational seminars and provided training in risk management, insurance, and auditing to credit unions around the world. CUNA Mutual provided financial aid to various World Council projects and was a major contributor to Initiatives for Growth, a World Council program targeting specific areas of opportunity for credit union growth.

One of the most promising regions for credit union growth was Eastern Europe, where country after country turned toward democracy in the late 1980s. In 1989, government representatives from Poland met with credit union leaders in Washington, D.C., about bringing the

Courtesy CUNA Mutual Audio-Visual Services

CUNA Mutual chief executive officer Richard M. Heins, right, talked with Lech Walesa in Walesa's office in Gdansk, Poland, after signing an agreement in October 1990 to bring Loan Protection and Life Savings insurance to Polish credit unions.

movement to their country. Hungary, Czechoslovakia, Bulgaria, and several Soviet republics also contacted credit union officials.

CUNA Mutual's Polish-born economist Jacek Cianciara traveled to Poland to study the government's interest in credit unions. He reported on his return that there were great opportunities for credit union growth in Poland, where people so distrusted state financial institutions that an estimated five to ten billion dollars in hard currency was stashed in mattresses and cookie jars.

To learn about how credit unions operated in a free market economy, a team from the Polish Ministry of Finance and Solidarity Union visited Madison in early 1990. During its visit, the team talked with CUNA Mutual about forming a joint company to provide insurance to the Polish credit union movement as it developed. The Poles brought as a gift an autographed copy of Lech Walesa's autobiography, believed to be the only one then in the United States.

CUNA Mutual continued to work closely with the Polish government. In 1991, the Polish parliament passed an amendment to its Trade Union Act to allow the formation of credit unions. It was the first such legislation in Eastern Europe.

"Because we had a credit union, our children have a future."

Paula Gonzalez, Credit Union Member.
"We were poor, migrant field workers. And I knew the only thing that could take my children out of poverty was education."

Elodia Elizondo, Weslaco Catholic Federal Credit Union.
"Paula insisted that her five kids go to parochial school. But she needed loans for tuition. The banks wouldn't help because she couldn't pay regularly."

Paula: *"For twenty years I kept on borrowing from the credit union. As soon as one loan was paid, I'd go back for another."*

Elodia: "She really struggled. Sometimes she'd have to skip a payment. But we always trusted her to pay. That's the credit union difference."

Paula: *"I'm so proud. My dream has come true. My René and Raul are attorneys. Anna is a registered nurse. Hernan is a social services director. Magdalena is an import specialist for U.S. Customs. And the first step in our success was the credit union."*

Credit union members like Paula Gonzalez are protected with insurance from the CUNA Mutual Insurance Group.

CUNA MUTUAL INSURANCE GROUP
We take care of our own

When banks denied a loan to Paula Gonzalez, above center, a farm worker of modest means, she borrowed parochial school tuition from Weslaco Catholic Federal Credit Union. Two sons became attorneys, another a county social services director.

One daughter is an industrial nurse, another works for U.S. Customs. The story of Paula Gonzalez is one of several CUNA Mutual advertisements showing how credit unions are unique financial institutions.

CHAPTER EIGHT

Embracing the Future

CUNA Mutual has never been hesitant to blaze new trails. It has been swift to adjust, flexible in its methods, and inflexible in its guiding principles and philosophy.

—Richard M. Heins

*R*obert Curry retired in October 1988 after fifteen years at the helm of CUNA Mutual. During his career, the society achieved unprecedented growth. Assets climbed from $186 million to nearly $1.5 billion, and life insurance in force increased from $21 billion to $76 billion. More important, Curry inspired a new spirit of understanding and cooperation among credit union organizations around the world. Curry's respect for others, his willingness to consider all opinions, and his determination to close wide personal chasms earned him the admiration of the entire credit union movement.

Curry was succeeded as chief executive officer by Richard M. Heins, CUNA Mutual's chief operating officer. The son of an accountant, Heins grew up in a small town in southwestern Wisconsin. As a teenager, he nearly lost his right leg in a hunting accident. Unable to participate in sports, he turned his energies to high school forensics, winning a state championship in oratory. He later competed on the debate team at the University of Wisconsin, where he earned his degree in business administration and accounting in 1949.

After graduating from the university, while a summer trainee with the Wisconsin insurance commissioner, Heins was approached about a job in CUNA Mutual's controller's department. The commissioner counseled Heins not to take the job. "I wouldn't get too excited about that socialist outfit," the commissioner said. "They run a pretty good insurance company, but instead of building a balance sheet, they give away all their assets and dividends to their members."

Though Heins did not take the CUNA Mutual job, his experience with the state insurance department predisposed him to a career in in-surance. Yes, insurance was foremost a business, but its profit motive was attached to a socially desirable objective: the prevention of loss. He earned master's and doctor's degrees in business administration, focusing on insurance, and taught at the University of California at Los Angeles (UCLA). Heins returned to the University of Wisconsin to finish his law degree, joined the faculty, and began consulting for CUNA Mutual in 1956.

Over the next three decades, Heins had an influential hand in numerous corporate developments, from select risk rating to CUMIS. He worked with almost every department of CUNA Mutual, especially field operations. While continuing to teach part time at the university, he ran CMCI, oversaw the investment department and headed its planning division. Heins also worked closely with CUNA, lecturing at the CUNA Schools for Credit Union Personnel in Madison and Los Angeles, assisting its Overseas Insurance Committee, and helping organize CUNA Mortgage Corporation, the mortgage banking company of the credit union movement.

In 1986, when Curry announced he would retire in two years, Heins became chief operating officer. One of Heins's most significant contributions in that position was realigning the organizational structure of the CUNA Mutual Insurance Group. The society had always managed and reviewed its operations along company lines. Since several of its individual companies offered the same products, the approach encouraged duplication and overlap; three companies with the same products meant three separate administrations where one would suffice. Managers examining financial reports also found it difficult to track the overall performance of specific lines, and CUNA Mutual's sales representatives sometimes had trouble knowing which company to contact when they had questions about specific products.

Heins realigned CUNA Mutual's management structure into strategic business units, each responsible for specific lines of business, from individual health and life to corporate property and casualty. The approach streamlined decision-making, enhanced accountability, improved communication with the field, and encouraged each business unit to think more creatively about ways to improve its service.

Heins had other changes in mind when he took over as CEO in October 1988. Deregulation was transforming the financial world. Companies that had once competed in different financial worlds now occupied the same marketplace, selling the same products to the same consumers. Retail corporations purchased insurance companies, credit card companies acquired brokerage houses, insurance companies purchased banks, and banks wanted to sell insurance. These new alliances, aided by technological advances, often met consumers' financial needs at a lower cost and with greater convenience than the institutions that had traditionally satisfied them.

The new arrangements, along with growing pressures on the credit unions' bottom-line performance, sorely tested member loyalty. Clearly, CUNA Mutual could no longer succeed simply by offering the best insurance contract. Only by providing new services, many of them beyond insurance, to help credit unions beat their financial competitors could CUNA Mutual meet its own competition.

CUNA Mutual's comfortable financial position made the need for change all the more critical, Heins believed. The more success, the greater the chance for failure. Too many successful business organizations became too content, believing that their markets would always stay the same. Instead of embracing and responding to change, they avoided it. Heins had occasionally encountered the same reactions from CUNA Mutual managers charged with implementing his innovative proposals. "Why don't you make him manage his ideas?" they had complained to Eikel and Curry.

Courtesy CUNA Mutual Audio-Visual Services

Richard M. Heins

*President and Chief Executive Officer
CUNA Mutual Insurance Society
1988–*

The need for change in the late 1980s also was complicated by the nature of the change required. Deregulation had not simply modified the marketplace; it had created a fundamentally different environment. Companies could not compete simply by becoming more efficient or by offering modified versions of the same products. Instead, they must look at their markets in completely fresh and original ways, building new structures and cultivating new alliances.

To move forward, Heins knew CUNA Mutual must first examine its past. To transform itself, a company must possess a strong culture—a mission, a vision, and shared values—and a strategic plan to drive that culture.

A mission told the company why it existed and what purpose it served. During Heins's tenure, CUNA Mutual developed a formal statement that reinforced and built on the society's original mission. Its primary tenet was to "promote the credit union concept as the practical approach to the financial well-being of people." CUNA Mutual was not in the insurance business, it was in the credit union business. The reason it sold insurance was to help credit unions and the unified credit union system succeed. All its efforts, its products, and services went toward that end.

CUNA Mutual had an advantage over competitors because it already had a comprehensive support system in place. The society supplemented its insurance coverages with a variety of programs such as advertising assistance, risk management programs, equipment leasing, marketing consulting services, and training courses to help credit union employees become more sensitive to the financial needs of their members—all to help credit unions prosper. CUNA Mutual's Policyowners' Program continued to keep the society and its policyowners mutually knowledgeable about each other's needs, and insurance seminars helped policyowner credit unions get the most out of CUNA Mutual's services.

CUNA Mutual's vision was to build on this support system so that the company would become the source of all insurance and related financial services for credit unions and credit union members the world over.

But keeping CUNA Mutual's long-range vision in sight was sometimes difficult when every day presented short-term pressures. Heins believed the solution was shared values. If every society employee clearly understood and believed in what the society was trying to accomplish, how they treated policyowners and each other, CUNA Mutual would succeed. Like cells of the body, each guided by a genetic code, they would almost automatically make the right decisions, encouraging greater delegation throughout the company.

In the late 1980s, CUNA Mutual asked its employees to define their values. Why do you work here? What does this company do that excites you? Why do you stay here? What does this company do that fulfills your personal values? Are we living up to your values? From the responses to these and other questions, CUNA Mutual developed several strategies for successful transformation.

Excellent service was at the top of the list. To sharpen its focus on customers, the society instituted special training. Employees gathered in small groups to share ideas on improving service and identify the organizational barriers that kept them from accomplishing those service goals. Because improving service is not a finite goal, but an ever-improving process, service action teams composed of employees in each department were formed to constantly examine and improve service procedures.

The results of team action were often sudden and dramatic. A claims service procedure that normally required sixty-four steps was reduced to eleven. The average time needed to settle coordinated credit disability and credit life claims dropped from ten days to three. Telephones were answered more quickly and questions settled more promptly.

To pinpoint policyowner needs, CUNA Mutual surveyed credit unions across the country. By inviting honest criticism of its performance, the society gained a clearer understanding of what was needed to improve service and strengthened its reputation for listening.

These efforts were complemented by the Marketplace Internship Program. CUNA Mutual managers spent two weeks each in credit unions across the country, learning every aspect of credit union operation and philosophy by helping the staff. Most important, after dealing hands-on with the problems encountered daily by credit unions, CUNA Mutual managers learned more about their role in helping credit unions succeed.

By inviting policyowners to help the society design what they wanted and needed, CUNA Mutual was transformed. No longer was the society driven by members; it was led by them. CUNA Mutual's commitment to service received favorable reviews both in national publications like the *Wall Street Journal* and in the credit union movement. In just two years, the society's penetration of the two hundred largest credit unions in the country—a priority market—grew from 34 to 54 percent.

CUNA Mutual enhanced its service strategy with technological systems designed to work in harmony with policyowner needs. Experts estimated that the wise use of microcomputers could reduce the cost of credit union operation by 30 percent or more. Given increasingly narrower margins and increased competition, technology would not just provide a competitive advantage; it was necessary for survival.

In 1988, CUNA Mutual Insurance Group introduced the MutuaLink® products, software programs which automated credit unions' lending processes and connected their personal computers with CUNA Mutual's mainframe. Credit union employees filing claims, making loans, or asking questions just pushed a few buttons, and the appropriate information appeared on their personal computer screens. They keyed in pertinent information, pushed a few more buttons, and loan documents were completed or insurance information was sent to CUNA Mutual. By bringing the society and its policyowners within a few keystrokes of each other, MutuaLink products cut expenses, reduced paperwork, quickened response, and improved service.

The Model Management System, which evolved from the Financial Planning System of the 1970s, helped credit unions plan by examining historical trends and testing new developments. Model Management helped many financially troubled credit unions achieve dramatic reversals.

Another requisite to successful transformation, Heins believed, was diversifying CUNA Mutual's products and services. The overwhelming majority of the society's business came from group life and health insurance and property and casualty coverages. What would happen if those lines lost popularity or competition cut the society's market share?

One of the most critical sources of new revenue was individual life insurance. The number of credit unions was declining, while individual

Courtesy CUNA Mutual Audio-Visual Services

MutuaLink software connected computers at credit unions around the country to CUNA Mutual's mainframe, cutting expenses, quickening responses, and improving service. Visitors to the first MutuaLink demonstration, at the 1988 CUNA national convention in Orlando, received a button with their picture on it. Charles Eikel III is pictured at right.

membership was growing steadily, to sixty million. By serving credit union members through individual insurance products, CUNA Mutual could continue to grow.

The society had recognized the need for a stronger individual life insurance program since the 1930s, but it made little progress selling by mail. In 1963, Charles Eikel hired Harry Manzer, a well-known Madison general agent, to build CUNA Mutual's individual life program. Manzer was hugely successful, building nineteen agencies covering the United States and Canada. In 1966, the third year of the program, CUNA Mutual sold nearly $69 million of individual life insurance, more than doubling its sales of the previous year.

But Manzer and his agents were too successful. The premiums associated with life insurance

During a break in a conference at Harvard Business School, CUNA Mutual's Richard M. Heins, left, and Irving R. Burling, CEO of Century Companies of America, came up with an idea to combine their companies' strengths to better serve credit union members.

contracts typically do not meet administration costs for several years, and CUNA Mutual's individual life policies sold so well they began to cut seriously into surplus. Manzer and his agents were advised to slow down sales until CUNA Mutual built more assets. The society also closed down several agencies and individual life sales slowed to a trickle.

Over the next twenty years, CUNA Mutual tried several methods to boost individual life sales without exhausting surplus, including direct response and joint ventures. In 1986, the society introduced a franchise system called PLAN AMERICA®, using credit unions as a distribution point for individual life and health products. CUNA Mutual sponsored financial planning seminars through individual credit unions, which invited members. Nothing was sold at the seminars, but interested members were invited to individual meetings with insurance agents afterwards.

In November 1986 Heins attended an advanced management program at Harvard Business School in Cambridge, Massachusetts. Sitting next to him was Irving Burling, CEO of the Century Companies of Waverly, Iowa, whom Heins knew casually. The seminar speaker was talking about change. The companies that would survive and grow, he said, must have long-term strategies. They must be willing not merely to reform themselves, they must transform themselves.

Heins and Burling met during a break.

"You know, this guy is hitting the nail right on the head," Heins said. "I don't think most of us are going to survive unless we can develop a good long-range strategy. I don't know how you people are doing, but we've got to move into a whole new world. We have the market. Our members know us and we know them. But if we're going to make any progress in individual life, we need a much better system for marketing and selling to them."

"We've got just the opposite problem," Burling said. "We have a career agency system. Our people are very good, but I don't think we're going to survive unless we do something about our distribution costs. What we need is a sponsored market so we can cut the time and energy we spend looking for prospects."

Light bulbs went off simultaneously above the men's heads: It sounded like a perfect match. Over lunch, Heins and Burling discussed the possibility of their companies working together, with Century Life's sales staff selling to and servicing credit union members in a relationship with CUNA Mutual. Negotiations continued for several months, Heins believing it was essential that CUNA Mutual have ultimate control of the products distributed to credit union members.

Century Life had been started more than a hundred years earlier by pastors of the Iowa Synod of the German Lutheran Church. At the time, many churches preached against insurance, believing that its use indicated lack of trust in God. But pastors saw too many families wiped out when the breadwinner died. They began to defend insurance from the pulpit, quoting 1 Timothy 5:8: "He who provideth not for his own is worse than an infidel."

To provide for parishioners—and discourage them from joining secret lodges offering insurance benefits—several German Lutheran pastors founded the Mutual Aid Society of the German Lutheran Synod of Iowa and Other States in 1879. The charter was written in German. Lutheran Mutual grew steadily during the next century, reaching a billion dollars of insurance in force in 1965 and three billion in 1978.

Burling, whose diverse pursuits while growing up in rural Minnesota included working for an undertaker and playing saxophone in a dance band, became an actuary with Lutheran Brotherhood, a fraternal insurance society in Minneapolis. He became CEO of Lutheran Mutual in 1976. Several years later, the organization changed its name to Century Life of America to signify its broader scope. Together with its subsidiaries, it was known as the Century Companies of America. By 1987, it had $1.4 billion in assets.

While Century Life was financially strong, Burling was concerned about its future. A consultant told him Century Life was a "typical" mutual insurance company. The assessment bothered Burling, since experts were saying that

the typical mutual company would struggle as heightened competition tested traditional agency loyalties and smaller profit margins failed to meet the costs of agency distribution.

Instead of acknowledging this fundamental change, many insurance companies were choosing to ignore the problem altogether, preferring to live off the profits of old business and hoping the situation would somehow reverse itself. Burling knew it would not.

Rather than dip into surplus, Burling tried to trim expenses. The task was difficult, for Century Life was already one of the leanest insurance operations in the industry. The company was downsized three times before Burling told the Century Life board of directors that he could do no more.

Burling believed an affiliation with CUNA Mutual was the best answer to Century Life's potential long-term problems. But convincing the Century Life board of the soundness of the plan was not easy. Why should Century Life affiliate with another company? Mergers occurred when one company was financially threatened, with debt or hostile takeovers. Century Life was financially healthy, rated A+ by the A. M. Best Company. CUNA Mutual was just as strong. What was the point? What would an affiliation mean to Century Life's employees? What would happen to their jobs?

The CUNA Mutual directors were even more concerned about the talks. A few years earlier, they had voted not to sell to groups outside the credit union movement. Now they were talking about an even closer relationship—a marriage, really—with a company that had nothing to do with the credit union movement. Would the leagues feel threatened by the prospect of opening their members to an outside sales force? What would the policyowners say?

What the credit union movement thought was just as important to the CUNA Mutual directors in the 1980s as it had been in 1935. Credit union involvement was still a requisite for CUNA Mutual directors. Most managed credit unions. Others were volunteers. Many served on CUNA committees, and most were active in their state leagues.

Unlike the directors of most insurance companies—who were usually employed in outside

MILESTONES

1988 Richard M. Heins named chief executive officer of CUNA Mutual.

Marketplace Internship Program initiated to give CUNA Mutual management employees experience working in credit unions.

MutuaLink® Lending System introduced.

1989 Permanent affiliation agreement signed on December 1 with Century Companies of America, Waverly, Iowa, to market individual life and annuity products to credit union members.

CUMIS Life Insurance, Inc. purchased Members Life Insurance Company of Texas.

Rosemarie Shultz elected first woman chair of CUNA Mutual board.

"Operations Grassroots" program initiated by CUNA with financial support from CUNA Mutual.

1990 CUNA Mutual board approved permanent affiliation of CUNA Mutual with Century Companies of America.

An Unchanging Commitment

The Policyowners' Program was established to provide credit union leaders with a two-way communication channel with their insurance societies. For more than thirty years, CUNA Mutual policyowners have traveled annually to Madison for an intense week of discussion and education. The program continues to provide CUNA Mutual with valuable input on the opinions, needs, and desires of its policyowners, while offering helpful information about products, services, and programs.

In connection with the 1991 Policyowners' Program, CUNA Mutual developed a videotape program called *Credit Unions on Trial*. Hosted by attorney F. Lee Bailey, right, the program offers unique perspectives on the campaign to rewrite credit union laws and the response of the credit union movement.

Courtesy CUNA Mutual Audio-Visual Services

businesses and regarded their board positions as a secondary interest—CUNA Mutual's directors were also its customers. The insurance society they served also served them. As a result, few boards knew as much about their organizations as the CUNA Mutual board. They brought to their positions a clear understanding of the society's market, for it was their market.

The directors added to their knowledge by representing CUNA Mutual at credit union meetings around the country. Each director was assigned to regularly attend important league meetings in three or four states. The intent was far more than political or ceremonial. As with CUNA Mutual's Policyowners' Program, the goal was enhanced communication. Besides giving speeches and reports, these directors discussed, participated, listened, and learned what their peers wanted and needed from CUNA Mutual.

These conversations often led to new policies and products. When the board learned that a competitor was offering credit unions a system that would connect their personal computers to its mainframe, CUNA Mutual decided to develop and introduce the MutuaLink products. Little information about competitive products escaped the society's directors, and their credit union experience enabled them to offer

helpful advice to staff in developing more effective alternatives.

At one time, the board had been so involved in the daily operations of CUNA Mutual that it reviewed every line of the budget and approved all insurance contracts before they were issued to credit unions. As CUNA Mutual grew, it became neither possible nor advisable to exert such control. During the 1970s the board assumed more of a supervisory role, establishing the overall policies of the society, representing the concerns of the credit union movement, and monitoring results.

Yet the board's unique role as watchdog and customer often led it to assume a more intimate role in the management of CUNA Mutual than did the boards of most other companies. As in most credit union organizations, the line between staff and board responsibility was broad enough that self-discipline was essential. A director who ventured too far into staff territory was brought quickly into line, sometimes through a prayer meeting.

The board's tradition of self-discipline and its commitment to communication with staff were generally effective guides to conduct. Thus board involvement was an asset, not a liability. Director Robert Kratt once accompanied Robert Curry to a credit union long alienated from the organized movement, and he helped convince the credit union to reaffiliate with CUNA and purchase CUNA Mutual coverages. Board and management became less like boss and employee, and more like a team.

During the 1970s and 1980s, CUNA Mutual's chairpersons brought different styles and strengths to the board. Some, like Kratt and James C. Barbre of Georgia, traveled widely, promoting the society's products at every opportunity. Others, like R.C. Robertson of Arizona and Franklin D. Miroff of Connecticut, stressed the evolving needs of the credit union member. Fred L. Crump of Kansas led quietly and consistently. A. Leonard Tune of Ontario contributed dynamic leadership and high integrity.

Gerald J. Ring of Wisconsin asked the hard questions and made sure the board considered all sides of the issue. Humio Okimoto insisted that the board carefully consider the human consequences of its actions, and ensured that its decisions be consistent with credit union philosophy. P. G. Gooch of Texas pushed for greater involvement of the entire board, not just the executive committee. Rosemarie M. Shultz of Washington, the first woman chairperson in CUNA Mutual's history, emphasized the importance of communication, both among the directors and with other credit union organizations.

Besides a commitment to credit union idealism, these and other directors shared a willingness to debate any issue. Honest dissent was encouraged. The directors had a motto: If you have a question or disagree with something, bring it up immediately; if your opinion is not heard, it's your fault for not making a louder noise. The old prayer meetings were rare, but directors still worked out problems and misunderstandings privately. Few boards were so willing to listen and challenge.

While the CUNA Mutual board initially challenged the idea of an affiliation with Century Life, it also listened. Heins and Burling were proposing a permanent affiliation, not a merger. Neither organization would lose its identity. No money would be exchanged. Though the affiliation would allow each organization to combine its resources to better serve individual credit union members, the plan would not affect other

CUNA Mutual services. Most important, the society would continue to sell its products only to credit union members. After extensive study and thorough discussion, the board backed the plan.

CUNA Mutual and Century Life tested the waters in 1987 with a pilot joint venture, patterned somewhat after CUNA Mutual's first PLAN AMERICA program. The PLAN AMERICA representatives, recruited and trained by Century Life managers, worked through credit unions. Credit union coordinators set up appointments for the representatives, saving much of the time usually spent looking for prospects.

By working through local credit unions, CUNA Mutual and Century Life hoped to eliminate much of the preliminary work that made agency methods so inefficient. Most insurance agents spent almost 80 percent of their time prospecting for clients and just 20 percent selling. It was the aim of the PLAN AMERICA program to reverse those figures.

Through this method, CUNA Mutual also

SERVING THE MOVEMENT

Through the new PLAN AMERICA program, CUNA Mutual and Century Life aimed for greater prospecting and service efficiencies. The goal was a better insurance deal for credit union members, more effective marketing channels for credit unions, and lower costs for CUNA Mutual and Century Life.

aimed to provide a better insurance deal to credit union members, more effective marketing channels to credit unions, and higher returns.

In July 1990, CUNA Mutual and Century Life signed a permanent affiliation agreement. Ninety percent of CUNA Mutual's policyowners approved the plan. Heins was named Deputy CEO of Century Life. Burling, who began splitting his time between Waverly and Madison, be-

"If I wasn't a Credit Union member, I wouldn't be a homeowner now."

Gina Brockel, Member, Capital Credit Union, Bismarck, N.D.
"I was paying too much rent, so I decided to buy a home. And I found one I could afford that was perfect.

"But my Realtor told me the bank had denied financing to the last seven people who had tried to buy the house. The bank felt the loan was too small, and didn't want to be bothered.

"So I talked to my Credit Union, and the people there were wonderful. They took me through all the steps, and found a way to give me the loan I needed. That's the Credit Union difference.

"Now, I'm paying even less than I was paying for rent, and I own my own home. That's a big deal to me, no matter what the bank says. Thank goodness for the Credit Union."

Credit Union members like Gina Brockel are protected with insurance from the CUNA Mutual Insurance Group.

"Our Credit Union is the financial foundation of our whole town."

Gene Gee, Mayor of Lefors, Texas and Member of Lefors Federal Credit Union.
"We talked to a lot of banks, but none of them would open a branch here in Lefors. We just weren't big enough for them to bother with.

"So Fred Blackwell and other town leaders decided to form a Credit Union. Now, people in Lefors have a place to go for savings accounts, home and auto loans, and more.

"The Credit Union has helped me and lots of other people in Lefors. It even helped us finance our ambulance. Our Credit Union's been a real lifesaver in lots of ways!"

Credit Union members like Gene Gee are protected with insurance from the CUNA Mutual Insurance Group.

"Without the Credit Union, I'd be sleeping on the floor."

Ray Hammond, Credit Union Member.
"When I joined the credit union, I didn't have any money saved. Didn't have any credit. But my bed had broken and I needed a new one."

Jenny Jervis, Cincinnati Central Credit Union.
"There are lots of people like Ray, who have a job, but haven't established credit. Sometimes it's hard for them."

Ray: "The bank said I was poor. They wouldn't even talk to me.

Jenny: "We worked with Ray to set up a budget. Then arranged a payroll deduction plan with his employer. That's the credit union difference."

Ray: "I got the bed, and that's fine. But I tell you what my credit union did for me . . . I feel like I can do things. I feel like I'm important here."

Credit Union members, like Ray Hammond, are protected with insurance from the CUNA Mutual Insurance Group.

"Fifteen years ago, my Credit Union said yes. Today, I say thank you."

George Malishewsky, Restaurant Owner.
"When I came here from the Ukraine, I was told that the American way to start a business was to get a loan from the bank. I guess nobody told the bank."

Roman Mycyk, President, Selfreliance Ukrainian Federal Credit Union.
"George didn't have the assets to qualify for a conventional bank loan. But he had some good ideas. So we helped him work out a business plan. And loaned him $5000 to get started. That's the credit union difference."

George: "My carpet business made money. I saved all I could, went back to the Credit Union and started another company."

Roman: "We've helped George get into the construction business, and woodworking, and making foreign car parts. Plus a brass bed company and a thriving restaurant, Galáns. I think maybe George is a conglomerate now."

George: "There's no bank in this town that can recognize a big idea if you have to say it in Ukrainian. As long as I'm in business, I'll do business with my Credit Union. This, by me, this is the American way."

George Malishewsky and millions of other Credit Union members are protected with insurance from the CUNA Mutual Insurance Group.

CUNA MUTUAL INSURANCE GROUP
WE TAKE CARE OF OUR OWN.

CUNA MUTUAL INSURANCE GROUP
WE TAKE CARE OF OUR OWN.

I stamp days are over."

Gorman, O.U.R. Federal Credit Union.
y joined up, she was on food stamps; just
o earn a living by making beautiful things
and selling them at the local vendors'

Nancy Barry, Credit Union Member.
I used up my savings and had no credit. But
y work was really starting to sell and I
eeded money for materials."

: "Since that first loan, we've kept working
y, showing her all the basics of good
anagement. That's the credit union

Nancy: "They understand me. There's
a real personal relationship. But
other places still won't acknowledge me as a valid person, even
though I've established myself."

n: "Nancy's sales have
an tripled in three years.
e's a proven success and
over the country."

Nancy: "Without their
help, I couldn't have
done it. They're great."
Union members
ancy Barry are
ted with insurance
he CUNA Mutual
ance Group.

CUNA MUTUAL INSURANCE GROUP
We take care of our own.

"My Credit Union not only saved my house, but my good name."

Desretta McAllister-Harper, Library and Information Sciences Educator, North Carolina Central
University, and Member of Self-Help Credit Union.
   "While I was in Jamaica on a Fulbright teaching assignment, I allowed an accountant to become a signatory on
my bank accounts. Her job was to pay my mortgage, my
bills and maintain my checking account while I was gone.
   "When I came back, I found out that not only had the
accountant misused my money, but the bank was ready
to foreclose on my house and none of my bills
had been paid for nearly a year! And to
make matters worse, no banks would
even think about lending me
money. Then I went to the
Credit Union. A wonderful
loan officer not only re-
financed my house...at a
lower monthly payment,
but helped me clear up
my bills. If it wasn't for
my Credit Union, I
don't know where I'd
be today."
   Credit Union
members like
Desretta McAllister-
Harper are protected
with insurance from
the CUNA Mutual
Insurance Group.

"It took all we had to buy this farm. Takes even more to keep it."

Dave Lollis, Central Appalachian People's Federal Credit Union.
"You look at our membership and you see an average income of maybe
$8000 a year."
   Jimmy and Ina Taylor, Credit Union members.
   "We raise tobacco, goats, some sorghum — even use Belgian horses to pull the plow.
      And we both have outside jobs."
Dave: "The finance companies here can charge people 36%. And the banks
just aren't interested."
   Ina: "The Credit Union made me a loan for an '81 Bonneville.
   I need a car to get to work, but the banks wouldn't lend
   on anything older than an '83."
Dave: "The average amount of our loans isn't too big. But they
come at crisis points."
   Jimmy: "When our cash crop check didn't come on time,
   the credit union helped us hold on. That's the credit union difference.
   There's nobody else we could go to and get help like that."
Credit Union members like Jimmy and Ina Taylor are protected with
insurance from the CUNA Mutual Insurance Group.

CUNA MUTUAL INSURANCE GROUP
WE TAKE CARE OF OUR OWN.

Telling a Unique Story

Credit union people are unique because the credit union movement is unique. For years, CUNA Mutual has told that story to regulators, legislators, and the general public through its corporate advertising campaigns. Recent campaigns have centered on how credit unions are different from other financial institutions.

CUNA Mutual's recent corporate advertising campaign, part of Operation Grassroots, has featured testimonials from members who were helped by their credit unions when other financial institutions declined. The ads have appeared in a wide variety of national magazines, such as *People, Sports Illustrated, Family Circle,* and *U.S. News and World Report.* CUNA Mutual has also advertised on network television news programs.

CUNA Mutual started the Marketplace Internship Program in 1989. For two weeks, CUNA Mutual managers work at credit unions around the country, learning about credit union needs by assisting the local staffs. Chris Granger, right, of the Southfield, Michigan office interned at Bell Tel Federal Credit Union.

came Deputy CEO of CUNA Mutual.

To fulfill some of the purposes of affiliation, CUDIS Insurance Society was renamed CUMIS Life Insurance, Inc.; it was to market and sell individual life insurance and annuity products. The organizations' individual insurance administration was consolidated in Waverly, group administration in Madison. The companies also combined their legal and investment departments. The CUNA Mutual board added five Century Life directors—Burling, James A. Halls, Omer K. Reed, Donald F. Roby, and Neil A. Springer—expanding its number to twenty, and six CUNA Mutual directors joined the Century Life board of eleven.

Leaders from both companies called the permanent affiliation one of the most significant events in their histories. The move created an alliance that in 1990 had $3.5 billion in as-

sets, $84 billion in life insurance in force, and returned more than $1 billion to policyowners in benefits, $800 million of that total by CUNA Mutual. Their combined strength created new possibilities of security and service, and laid the groundwork for a solid future.

Several decades earlier, people like Roy Bergengren and Tom Doig had challenged the belief that common people could not manage their own money, and the credit union movement was born. In 1990, by searching for new methods and alliances to respond to a changing financial world, CUNA Mutual had solidified its commitment and capacity to serve the credit union movement.

Still a Unique Vision

In 1988, there were almost sixteen thousand credit unions in the United States, with sixty million members and nearly two hundred billion dollars in assets. Many financial experts were touting credit unions, which typically outpaid banks and savings and loan institutions on savings and offered lower rates on mortgage and auto loans.

But success has bred hostility. In the late 1980s, the American Banking Association urged its members to lobby Congress to revoke the tax-exempt status of credit unions, especially those with ten million dollars or more in assets, and to absorb credit unions into the same agency that regulates banks.

In response to the ABA campaign, CUNA and other credit union organizations launched Operation Grassroots, a national effort by all levels of the movement to prevent other financial institutions from interfering with credit union laws. CUNA Mutual has supported Operation Grassroots with major financial contributions and advertising.

Some credit union leaders believe the campaign against credit unions is a golden opportunity to strengthen the movement. Opponents used to attack credit unions because they were different; now they claim credit unions are too similar to banks. Roy Bergengren worried about the day that the credit union movement would become too respectable, too comfortable. The current campaign provides credit unions the chance to further differentiate themselves from banks and other private financial institutions, to reconsider their roots, purposes, and principles.

"Credit unions have won the support of many industries and organizations in which they serve, and in legislative halls throughout this country and Canada, because of their appeal as human institutions," Charles Eikel said two decades ago. "We can lose much of this support if our membership and the general public begins to think of us as just another financial institution.

"I think we must begin by looking at the operations of our own credit unions to make certain they are really operating as credit unions," he explained. "Then we've got to start getting the powerful human story of credit union purpose, service, and accomplishment across to our members and anybody who will listen. This may sound like old-time religion, but I think it's precisely the remedy we need today."

Remembering that credit unions exist solely for the benefit of their members has never been more important. During the early years of the credit union movement, commitment and philosophy often outweighed financial expertise. Today, as many new employees enter the movement from other financial organizations, they bring with them essential financial training and skills. But if credit unions wish to maintain member trust, they must maintain the cultural philosophy and member service that distinguishes a movement from an industry.

CUNA Mutual has contributed mightily to that effort. Edward Filene believed the Golden Rule was an effective business strategy; the society he helped bring into existence with a twenty-five-thousand-dollar loan has proved it. CUNA Mutual has not only served the credit union movement, it has also been an active participant in shaping the history of the movement.

At a time when few credit union members could afford credit life insurance, CUNA Mutual pioneered Loan Protection and Life Savings. Besides protecting millions of families from the devastating consequences of death, the products played a significant role in convincing prospec-

"We've got to get the powerful human story of credit union purpose, service, and accomplishment across to our members and anybody who will listen. This may sound like old-time religion, but it's precisely the remedy we need today."

tive members to join credit unions. As such, Loan Protection and Life Savings played an essential role in aiding the development of the credit union movement.

As the needs of credit unions and credit union members expanded, CUNA Mutual broadened its arsenal of products, including credit disability insurance and a wide variety of individual life contracts. CUMIS was created to meet the movement's property and casualty needs, and its bond coverages have earned nearly universal acceptance by credit unions.

CUNA Mutual has done much more for the

The CUNA Mutual board in 1990. (1) Rosemarie M. Shultz, Tacoma, Washington; (2) Richard M. Heins, Madison, Wisconsin; (3) W. F. Broxterman, Diamond Bar, California; (4) Ralph B. Canterbury, Coraopolis, Pennsylvania; (5) Robert T. Lynch, Riverview, Michigan; (6) James C. Barbre, Alpharetta, Georgia; (7) Irving R. Burling, Waverly, Iowa; (8) Donald F. Roby, Des Moines, Iowa; (9) Neil A. Springer, Wheaton, Illinois; (10) E. Odell Smith, Mt. Juliet, Tennessee; (11) Franklin D. Miroff, Meriden, Connecticut; (12) Gerald J. Ring, Madison, Wisconsin; (13) Robert L. Curry, Madison, Wisconsin, director emeritus; (14) Larry T. Wilson, Raleigh, North Carolina; (15) Humio Okimoto, Kihei, Maui, Hawaii; (16) R. C. Robertson, Phoenix, Arizona; (17) James A. Halls, Minneapolis, Minnesota; (18) Omer K. Reed, Paradise Valley, Arizona; (19) Clyde N. Choate, Coppell, Texas; (20) Joseph N. Cugini, Westerly, Rhode Island; and (21) Robert A. Kratt, Davenport, Iowa.

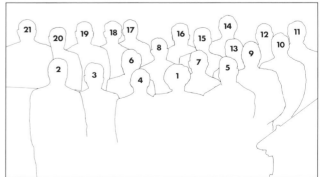

Courtesy CUNA Mutual Archives

credit union movement than sell insurance. The society has succeeded because it was committed to the success of the credit union movement; CUNA Mutual can be understood only by understanding its unique and intimate relationship to the movement. CUNA Mutual was the first insurance company organized to serve credit unions and their members exclusively.

That unchanging commitment helps explain the comprehensive services the society provides to credit unions beyond insurance and financial products: the Policyowners' Representatives program, technology-based programs, NARCUP, risk management services, its marketing relationships with state leagues, and its financial support of CUNA and the World Council of Credit Unions.

CUNA Mutual's commitment to credit unions makes clear why the society returns a higher percentage of every premium dollar to policyowners through claims and dividends than its competitors. When America went to war in the Persian Gulf in 1991, CUNA Mutual continued a policy established in World War II, being ready to pay any military claims and not including war-related losses in credit union experience. CUNA Mutual has done all these things because it is part of the credit union family.

Like all families, the credit union movement has had quarrels. But lessons of the past have been used to forge the unity of the present. Unity is essential, for no family can withstand attacks from outsiders without it. Thanks to directors and employees from both organizations, CUNA and CUNA Mutual have strengthened a mutually respectful and beneficial relationship neither can succeed without.

As its relationship with other credit union organizations has changed, so has CUNA Mutual. From its stark, second-story room in Raiffeisen House, the society has grown to fill an expansive headquarters equipped with the latest technology. Once staffed only by Earl Rentfro, CUNA Mutual and its subsidiaries now have four thousand employees around the world. Unsure of how to pay its first claim—for forty dollars—in 1935, CUNA Mutual now pays millions of dollars in claims every day. Once licensed only in Wisconsin, the society today serves credit unions in sixty countries.

But these are external changes and achievements, less important than the internal commitment that has produced them. CUNA Mutual has demonstrated its dedication to the credit union movement in new ways through new methods over the years, but its mission has not changed. That is a tribute to the policyowners, directors, employees, league personnel, credit union managers, and volunteers who built and served CUNA Mutual.

It is a tribute to the society's leaders as well. Edward Filene provided financial and moral support. Roy Bergengren gave energy and vision. Tom Doig gave the society its soul and compassion. Charles Hyland contributed enthusiasm. Employees like Earl Rentfro, Orch Edgerton, Elaine Richgels, and Tom Benson provided quiet skill and consistency. Charles Eikel gave passion and principle. Robert Curry brought a commitment to reconciliation and a determination to see the society grow. Richard Heins encouraged transformation and new alliances to ensure that CUNA Mutual continues to serve the credit union movement effectively for many years to come.

The dedicated directors who led, and continue to lead, CUNA Mutual have given their time, insights, and commitment. Credit union people first and foremost, the directors assure that the society remains true to its original mission and the movement that created it, even as they search for new ways to serve.

More than a half century after CUNA Mutual was founded, the debt still dies with the debtor. Because of the credit union movement, CUNA Mutual's purpose still lives.

Appendix

Appendix Contents

Articles of Incorporation
CUNA Mutual Insurance Society

ARTICLE I
Business to be Undertaken

Section 1. The undersigned do hereby associate themselves for the purpose of forming a mutual insurance association under Chapter 206 and such provisions of Chapter 180 relating to associations under the general law as set forth in subsection 9 of section 206.02 of the Wisconsin Statutes of 1933 and acts amendatory and supplementary thereto, the purpose of which association shall be to transact the business of: (a) writing insurance upon the lives and health of persons, and every assurance pertaining thereto, and to grant, purchase and dispose of annuities and endowments; (b) writing insurance against loss or damage by death by accident, and upon the health of persons.

ARTICLE II
Name and Location

Section 1. The name of such association shall be CUNA Mutual Society and its home office and principal place of business shall be in the city of Madison, County of Dane, Wisconsin.

ARTICLE III
Plan

Section 1. The Society shall be non-stock and no stock shall ever be sold or issued. The plan of operation of this Society shall be that of a mutual insurance association, but for the purpose of providing sufficient funds to defray the necessary expenses incident to organization and to provide the guaranty fund as security for the payment of losses, the Society may issue surplus fund notes in accordance with section 206.02 subsection (3) (a) of the Wisconsin Statutes of 1933 and may pay interest on such notes at the rate of not exceeding eight (8%) percent per annum, as in said section provided.

ARTICLE IV
Membership

Section 1. Membership in this Society shall be limited to bona fide policy holders in the Society. Each policy holder whose insurance shall be in force, and shall have been in force at least one year prior thereto, shall have one vote at all general elections, regardless of the number of policies or the amount of insurance carried.

ARTICLE V
Mode of Exercising Corporate Powers

Section 1. The Board of Directors shall consist of ten (10) persons, to be chosen by ballot from the members of the Society. Any policy holder entitled to vote at any election shall be qualified for election to the Board of Directors at any such election.

Section 2. Notice shall be given as provided by law fixing the time and place for the first meeting of the members for the election of directors, who shall serve until their successors are duly elected and qualified.

Section 3. The Board of Directors shall divide itself into four classes, two of which classes shall consist of two directors each, and two classes to consist of three directors. The term of the first class shall expire at the first annual general election held hereafter; the term of the second class shall expire at the second annual general election held hereafter; the term of the third class shall expire at the third annual general election held hereafter; and the term of the fourth class shall expire at the fourth annual general election held hereafter. At each general election of the Society the number of directors equal to the class then expiring shall be elected and shall hold office for four years and until their successors are elected, but any director shall be eligible for re-election. Any vacancy occurring during the interim between the annual general election shall be filled by the Board of Directors and the person so elected shall serve until the next general election.

Section 4. The Board of Directors shall have power to enact rules and regulations for the government of the Society and the conduct of its affairs, not inconsistent with the charter and the laws of the State, and such rules and regulations may be amended or repealed by the directors at any regular meeting of the Board; provided, however, the members at any legal general election may amend or repeal any such rules and regulations by a two-thirds majority of those voting.

Section 5. The Board of Directors shall have general control of the business affairs of the Society, adopt rates and applications, policies and all other forms; provide for inspection of risks; classify hazards and enact rules and instructions governing the acceptance of risks; elect all officers and committees, fix the salaries and compensation of the officers, and when not otherwise provided for, to define their duties.

Section 6. The Board of Directors shall possess and exercise all other powers usually vested in the directors and trustees of insurance associations, which are consistent with the provisions of this chapter and with the laws of the state, and may accept any additional powers and privileges which any like insurance association may be authorized by the legislature of the State of Wisconsin to exercise.

ARTICLE VI
General Officers

Section 1. The general officers of the Society shall be a president, two vice-presidents, a secretary and a treasurer, who shall be elected by and from the Board of Directors, together with an assistant general manager who shall be chosen by the first vice-president from the policyholders.

ARTICLE VII
Duties of Officers

Section 1. The president shall be chairman of the Board of Directors and of the Executive Committee; he shall preside at all meetings of the Society, the Board of Directors, and the Executive Committee, and shall present an annual report to the members at their annual meeting. He shall perform such other duties as shall be assigned to him from time to time.

Section 2. The first vice-president shall be general manager of the Society, and shall perform all duties usually incident to his office subject to the Board of Directors and to the Executive Committee in the interim between directors' meetings. He shall sign policies, sign, endorse and accept checks, notes and drafts on behalf of the Society subject to such limitations as the Board of Directors may impose, provided, however, that no note, acceptance or other bill payable and no contract under seal shall be signed by him in behalf of the Society unless authorized by the vote of the Board of Directors, or be issued until countersigned in approval thereof by the secretary. He shall collect, receive and turn over to the treasurer all monies, funds and securities of the Society. He shall pay all expenses, losses and debts of the Society by draft on the treasurer. All checks shall be countersigned by the secretary. The general manager shall have determination of all matters of personnel.

Section 3. The second vice-president shall, in the event of the absence or disability of the first vice-president, perform the duties of said officer.

Section 4. The secretary shall keep a record of the votes and of the other proceedings of all general elections of the Society and of all meetings of the Board of Directors; shall record all policies issued and all authorized assignments, transfers and cancellations thereof; and keep such other books and records as the Board of Directors may require. He shall have the custody of the corporate seal and affix the same to all instruments required to be sealed, and shall perform such other duties as are required of him by the laws of the State, the Board of Directors and the by-laws of the Society. His books of account and records shall, at all reasonable times, be open to the inspection of the members of the Society. He shall furnish to the directors, whenever required by them, such statements and abstracts of his records as are necessary for a full exhibit of the financial condition of the Society.

Section 5. The treasurer shall receive from the first vice-president and general manager and safely keep all monies, funds and securities of the Society. He shall honor all drafts of the first vice-president and general manager for losses, expenses and debts of the Society; keep an accurate account of all monies received and disbursed and render such accounts, statements and inventories of monies received and disbursed, as shall be required by the Board of Directors. He shall have no authority to dispose of any securities of the Society or to borrow money in its behalf until expressly authorized to do so by the vote of the directors.

Section 6. The assistant general manager shall perform such duties of active management of the Society as may be delegated to him from time to time by the first vice-president and general manager.

Section 7. The Board of Directors may pro-vide for the appointment of such additional sub-ordinate officers as they may deem for the best interests of the Society. Whenever the Board of Directors may so order, the duties of any two officers of their choosing may be combined and assigned to one person. The said officers shall perform such additional or different duties as shall from time to time be imposed or required by the Board of Directors, or as may be prescribed from time to time by the by-laws.

ARTICLE VIII
The Executive Committee

Section 1. The officers shall constitute the Executive Committee, which said committee shall exercise between meetings of the Board of Directors such of the functions of said board as may be delegated to said committee by said Board of Directors.

ARTICLE IX
Fiscal Year

Section 1. The fiscal year of this Society shall coincide with the calendar year.

ARTICLE X
Amendments

Section 1. These articles may be amended by a vote of three-fourths of the members voting at a regular or special meeting after the proposed amendment has been filed with the secretary of the Society and with the Commissioner of Insurance, and a copy thereof, with notice of the time and place of meeting, has been mailed to each member at least thirty days prior to such meeting.

Original By-Laws
CUNA Mutual Insurance Society

ARTICLE I
Purposes and Operating Principles

Section 1. This Society organized in accordance with the provisions of a mutual law (and therefore not for profit) operates for the primary purpose of serving credit union members with life insurance on principles consistent with credit union operating practices.

Section 2. It is the purpose of this Society to issue term policies on the lives of credit union borrowers as protection against the possible death of the borrower before payment in full of his loan and it is the further purpose of this Society in this regard to provide such insurance at the lowest possible cost consistent with the accumulation of surplus as aforesaid.

ARTICLE II
Method of Operation

Section 1. This Society shall operate directly through credit unions in the matter of loan protection insurance as previously referred to.

Section 2. Every effort shall be made consistent with the insurance laws of the State of Wisconsin to establish and maintain a unity of interest and direction by and between this Society and the Credit Union National Association.

Section 3. The books of account and all papers relating to a proper understanding of the affairs of this Society at any given time shall be open to the inspection of such agency as may be designated from time to time by the Board of Directors of the Credit Union National Association.

ARTICLE III
Meetings of the Board of Directors

Section 1. Stated meetings of the Board of Directors of this Society shall be held each year on the second Tuesday of May and on the second Tuesday of each and every third month thereafter on such day of the month, such hour of the day and at such place as the Board of Directors may determine at least three weeks prior to such meetings, except that all such meetings shall be held within the State of Wisconsin.

Section 2. The February meeting of the Board of Directors shall be designated as the annual meeting and shall be held immediately following the annual general election. At such annual meeting the directors shall elect the officers of the Society and appoint the standing committee hereinafter designated and transact such business as pertains to the annual meeting of the board.

Section 3. Special meetings of the Board of Directors may be called by any three of the directors or by the president or first vice-president, by giving reasonable written notice thereof to all of the directors.

ARTICLE IV
Finance Committee

Section 1. The Board of Directors shall elect from their own number a Finance Committee of three members.

Section 2. Two members of the Finance Committee shall constitute a quorum.

Section 3. The Finance Committee shall have the following duties, which they shall exercise under the general direction of the Board of Directors: (a) have general oversight over the financial affairs of the association; (b) make loans and investments of the funds of the company consistent with the provisions of the laws of the State of Wisconsin pertaining thereto; (c) make such collection or call of said loans from time to time as the best interests of the association may require and invest and re-invest the same; (d) act upon and determine the substitution of new and other securities in place of those held by the Society.

Section 4. The Finance Committee shall make a complete report at each meeting of the Board of Directors of the then condition of the investments of the Society and shall, upon request of any three directors at any time, make a complete report to said directors of the then condition of the investments of the Society.

Section 5. The Finance Committee shall make no loan or investment of funds of the Society in any way or manner, directly or indirectly, in such fashion as to affect in any way or promote the interests of any director or employee of this Society.

Section 6. The Finance Committee shall perform such other duties as may be entrusted to it from time to time by the Board of Directors.

ARTICLE V
Audits

Section 1. The books and accounts of this Society shall be audited at least annually by a certified public accountant to be selected by the Board of Directors at its annual meeting each year for the ensuing year. On the request of any three members of the board at any time a special audit shall be made of the affairs of the Society in the way and manner above provided.

ARTICLE VI
General Elections

Section 1. The annual meeting, also known as the general election of the Society for the purpose of electing directors and for the transaction of the general business of the Society, shall be held at Madison, Wisconsin, on the second Tuesday of February of each year from 10:00 A.M. to 4:00 P.M.

Section 2. Special meetings of said Society may be called by the president or the vice president and general manager or by the secretary in the way and manner hereinafter provided, upon request in writing by a majority of the Board of Directors. The business of special meetings shall be limited to the business described in the call.

Section 3. The general election and all special meetings of the Society shall be conducted in accordance with Chapter 206 of the Wisconsin Statutes of 1933. Nine members shall constitute a quorum. Any annual meeting or special meeting at which no quorum is present may be adjourned to a future time consistent with the provisions relative to notice of meetings contained in the law of Wisconsin pertaining thereto and these by-laws.

Section 4. At least two weeks before the annual meetings, also known as the general election, and at least seven days before any special meeting, the secretary shall cause a written or printed notice thereof to be sent to every person entitled to vote at said meeting. Every person entitled to vote shall be notified in similar fashion of the date of any adjourned meeting at least five days prior to said adjourned meeting. Such other notice shall be given as may be required by the laws of Wisconsin pertaining to notice of meetings.

ARTICLE VII
Bonds

Section 1. All officers and employees of the Society handling cash or securities of the Society shall give a faithful performance surety bond in such sums as the Board of Directors may from time to time determine and require and as shall be approved by the Insurance Commissioner of the State of Wisconsin. All bond premiums shall be paid for by the Society.

ARTICLE VIII
Inspection

Section 1. Each and every member of the Society shall be allowed during the business hours of any day to make such examination as he may see fit of the books, papers and general transactions of the Society, on application to the secretary.

ARTICLE IX
Dissolution

Section 1. This Society may be dissolved in the way and manner provided in the laws of the State of Wisconsin pertaining thereto. If at any time this Society shall be dissolved or shall cease to do the business of insurance, in that case whatever shall remain of its reserve fund and surplus reserves, after payment of all losses sustained and all losses which may be sustained after such dissolution and prior to the distribution herein after referred to on policies then in force and after the payment of all debts and liabilities of the Society, shall be divided and distributed to the policy holders of the Society at the time of such dissolution or ceasing to transact the business of insurance in the way and manner outlined in the insurance laws of the State of Wisconsin pertaining thereto. All interest of policy holders in reserve and surplus funds shall cease upon their withdrawal from the Society, except as otherwise provided by law.

ARTICLE X
Amendments

Section 1. These by-laws may be amended, altered or repealed in any manner not inconsistent with the Insurance law by a majority vote of the directors at any meeting lawfully convened, but no motion or resolution amending, altering or repealing any by-laws shall be adopted at a meeting of the directors held on the same day upon which it is offered.

The CUNA Mutual Insurance Group

Mission

To promote the credit union concept as the practical approach to the financial well-being of people, to pursue quality and innovation in insurance and finance-related products and excellence in service, to provide service directed to building and supporting the credit union system, to provide a dynamic organization of employee growth and public respect while maintaining the highest ethical standards.

Companies

The CUNA Mutual Insurance Group is a unique economic democracy serving only credit unions and credit union members. In the United States, the CUNA Mutual Insurance Group consists of CUNA Mutual Insurance Society and eight subsidiary companies that provide insurance programs consistent with CUNA Mutual's high standards for value and quality.

The companies include:

CUNA Mutual Insurance Society. Writer of all basic forms of life and health insurance and the world's leading provider of credit life insurance.

CUNA Mutual Investment Corporation. Wholly-owned subsidiary of CUNA Mutual Insurance Society that holds all of the stock in the following companies:

CUMIS Insurance Society, Inc. Provider of property, casualty and fidelity coverages.

CUMIS Life Insurance, Inc. Established as a credit insurance writer, now a reinsurer and direct writer of individual life insurance in affiliation with Century Life of America.

CMCI Corporation. An insurance broker that also provides financial and management services to credit unions.

League Life Insurance Company. Provider of credit insurance products and group life coverages to credit unions and their members in Michigan and other selected states.

League General Insurance Company. The property and casualty affiliate of League Life.

CBS Holding Company, Inc. A holding company which wholly owns the stock of CUNA Brokerage Services, Inc.

Members Life Insurance Company. Purchased by CUMIS Life Insurance, Inc. in 1989, the company underwrites life insurance coverages for credit union members primarily in Texas.

Permanent Affiliation

Century Life of America. In 1990, Century Life of America, an individual life insurance company, and CUNA Mutual joined in a permanent affiliation, utilizing the strengths of the companies to provide policyowners with a strong, diversified portfolio of individual life insurance coverages and services.

Board of Directors: 1935–1991
CUNA Mutual Insurance Society

Name	State/Province	Term
Edward A. Filene	Massachusetts	May 20, 1935–September 26, 1937
Roy F. Bergengren	Massachusetts	May 20, 1935–May 9, 1941
Thomas W. Doig	Minnesota	May 20, 1935–November 21, 1939
Earl Rentfro	Wisconsin	May 20, 1935–September 3, 1939
Charles G. Hyland	Wisconsin	May 20, 1935–September 3, 1939
Claude E. Clarke	Ohio	May 20, 1935–December 7, 1940
Claude R. Orchard	District of Columbia	May 20, 1935–August 14, 1938
Hubert M. Rhodes	District of Columbia	May 20, 1935–May 17, 1939
Edward L. Shanney	Massachusetts	May 20,1935–May 14, 1948
John L. Moore	California	May 20, 1935–May 11, 1956
Joseph S. DeRamus	Illinois	November 11, 1937–May 10, 1962
Moses C. Davis	Georgia	August 14, 1938–August 9, 1957
Gurden P. Farr	Michigan	May 17, 1939–May 15, 1943
		November 11, 1944–May 17, 1958
George F. Feller	Minnesota	September 3, 1939–May 10, 1947
William W. Pratt	Pennsylvania	September 3, 1939–May 9, 1968
William Reid	New York	November 21, 1939–May 1, 1967
Robert L. Conrod	Texas	December 7, 1940–February 10, 1945
Hugh G. Stout	Oregon	September 5, 1941–May 10, 1942
Harry C. Lash	Iowa	May 10, 1942–May 14, 1954
F. L. Andrews	Florida	May 15, 1943–November 11, 1944
Harold Moses	Louisiana	February 10, 1945–July 12, 1959
Thomas M. Molloy	Saskatchewan, Canada	May 10, 1947–May 12, 1950
Leonard W. Mitchell	Ontario, Canada	May 14, 1948–May 16, 1952
J. W. Burns	British Columbia, Canada	May 12, 1950–March 1, 1951
J. D. N. MacDonald	Nova Scotia, Canada	March 1, 1951–May 9, 1968
W. A. Dunkin	Missouri	May 16, 1952–May 11, 1956
		August 9, 1957–May 9, 1958
A. P. Quinton	Ontario, Canada	May 14, 1954–June 4, 1966
C. Frank Pratt	California	May 11, 1956–May 9, 1968
W. G. Lonergan	Washington	May 11, 1956–May 9, 1968
C. E. Burdick	Texas	May 9, 1958–May 12, 1966
Edwin W. Eich	Wisconsin	August 8, 1958–June 5, 1963
Paul D. Deaton	Ohio	August 14, 1959–May 16, 1978
Bill P. Williams	Illinois	May 10, 1962–May 12, 1966
William H. Scogin	Alabama	June 29, 1963–August 5, 1972

Name	State/Province	Term
P. G. Gooch	Texas	May 12, 1966–November 30, 1987
Robert A. Kratt	Iowa	May 12, 1966–present
George A. Swales	Alberta, Canada	August 11, 1966–May 6, 1972
Charles W. Jones, Jr.	South Carolina	August 10, 1967–May 16, 1978
Fred L. Crump	Kansas	May 9, 1968–May 31, 1986
Ray D. Hagen	Utah	May 9, 1968–December 1, 1970
Gerald J. Ring	Wisconsin	May 9, 1968–present
A. Leonard Tune	Ontario, Canada	May 9, 1968–July 9, 1978
Sydney B. Wexler	New York	August 7, 1968–May 4, 1976
Clyde P. Dwyer	Colorado	August 7, 1968–May 25, 1982
Al J. Day	Florida	August 7, 1968–July 15, 1970
Lee L. Sell	Pennsylvania	November 6, 1968–May 25, 1982
Wendell F. Walker	California	November 6, 1968–May 4, 1976
C. F. Eikel, Jr.	Wisconsin	July 15, 1970–May 4, 1976
R. C. Robertson	Arizona	May 17, 1971–present
Robert L. Curry	Wisconsin	May 6, 1972–October 4, 1988
Humio Okimoto	Hawaii	May 4, 1973–present
Harold W. Price	California	May 4, 1976–May 25, 1982
James P. Kirsch	Virginia	May 4, 1976–May 8, 1984
James C. Barbre	Georgia	May 4, 1976–present
Rosemarie M. Shultz	Washington	May 16, 1978–present
Franklin D. Miroff	Connecticut	May 16, 1978–July 3, 1991
Harold Korman	New York	May 27, 1980–May 31, 1986
W. F. Broxterman	California	May 25, 1982–present
Ralph B. Canterbury	Pennsylvania	May 25, 1982–present
E. Odell Smith	Tennessee	May 25, 1982–present
Robert T. Lynch	Michigan	May 8, 1984–present
Joseph N. Cugini	Rhode Island	May 31, 1986–present
Larry T. Wilson	North Carolina	May 31, 1986–present
Richard M. Heins	Wisconsin	May 14, 1988–present
Clyde N. Choate	Texas	October 4, 1988–present
Neil A. Springer	Illinois (Century)	July 20, 1990–present
James A. Halls	Minnesota (Century)	July 20, 1990–present
Omer K. Reed	Arizona (Century)	July 20, 1990–present
Donald F. Roby	Iowa (Century)	July 20, 1990–present
Irving R. Burling	Iowa (Century)	July 20, 1990–present

Principal Officers of the Board: 1935–1991 CUNA Mutual Insurance Society

President of the Board	Term
Edward A. Filene	May 20, 1935–October 5, 1935
Claude E. Clarke	October 5, 1935–May 18, 1939
John L. Moore	May 18, 1939–May 15, 1943
Edward L. Shanney	May 15, 1943–May 12, 1946
Joseph S. DeRamus	May 12, 1946–May 13, 1949
Moses C. Davis	May 13, 1949–May 11, 1951
William Reid	May 11, 1951–May 8, 1953
Harry C. Lash	May 8, 1953–May 14, 1954
William W. Pratt	May 14, 1954–May 13, 1955
Gurden P. Farr	May 13, 1955–May 10, 1957
Harold Moses	May 10, 1957–May 8, 1959
J. D. N. MacDonald	May 8, 1959–May 10, 1961
William W. Pratt	May 10, 1961–May 10, 1962
C. Frank Pratt	May 10, 1962–May 7, 1964

Chairman of the Board (position retitled)	Term
W. G. Lonergan	May 7, 1964–May 12, 1966
A. P. Quinton	May 12, 1966–August 11, 1966
Paul D. Deaton	August 11, 1966–May 7, 1969
William H. Scogin	May 7, 1969–May 17, 1971
Robert A. Kratt	May 17, 1971–May 8, 1973
P. G. Gooch	May 8, 1973–May 27, 1975
A. Leonard Tune	May 27, 1975–May 10, 1977
Fred L. Crump	May 10, 1977–May 15, 1979
Gerald J. Ring	May 15, 1979–May 5, 1981
Humio Okimoto	May 5, 1981–May 16, 1983
R. C. Robertson	May 16, 1983–May 20, 1985
Franklin D. Miroff	May 20, 1985–May 9, 1987
James C. Barbre	May 9, 1987–May 7, 1989
Rosemarie M. Shultz	May 7, 1989–June 15, 1991
W. F. Broxterman	June 15, 1991–present

Ex Officio Directors

	Term
H. G. Wegner, Managing Director, CUNA	August 6, 1974–February 24, 1979
J. R. Williams, President, CUNA	May 12, 1979–January 15, 1987
J. L. H. Lanctot, President, The CUMIS Group Limited of Canada	May 27, 1980–January 1, 1990
Ralph S. Swoboda, President, CUNA	May 9, 1987–present
George W. Berquist, President, The CUMIS Group Limited of Canada	February 2, 1990–November 16, 1990
Neil A. Springer (Century)	May 7, 1989–July 20, 1990
James A. Halls (Century)	May 7, 1989–July 20, 1990
Donald F. Roby (Century)	May 7, 1989–July 20, 1990
Irving R. Burling (Century)	May 7, 1989–July 20, 1990
J. Lawrence Purdy, President, The CUMIS Group Limited of Canada	December 7, 1990–present

Honorary Director

	Term
Charles F. Eikel, Jr.	May 4, 1976–May 25, 1988

Director Emeritus

	Term
Robert L. Curry	October 3, 1988–present

Financial Summary: 1935–1990
CUNA Mutual Insurance Society

The following numbers are the combined figures for CUNA Mutual Insurance Society, CUMIS Insurance Society, Inc., CUMIS Life Insurance, Inc., CUNA Mutual Investment Corporation, CMCI Corporation, League Life Insurance Company and League General Insurance Company. Eliminations were made to the assets totals for the net worth of the subsidiaries for the years 1960 through 1990. In addition, for the years 1985 and 1990 eliminations were made to the insurance-in-force totals for the reinsurance assumed by League Life from CUNA Mutual Insurance Society. No other eliminations were made.

Year	Assets	Life Insurance in Force	Premiums	Claims	Dividends
1935	$ 36,503	$ 2,050,449	$ 11,750	$ 1,653	$ 0
1940	446,216	83,497,533	610,586	379,130	52,267
1945	945,126	89,147,297	733,769	519,350	316,426
1950	4,398,858	606,033,099	4,645,615	2,584,773	714,463
1955	15,033,348	2,352,086,858	16,953,750	10,606,301	3,247,344
1960	36,118,878	5,765,256,091	44,147,367	31,104,822	7,914,603
1965	58,546,315	9,728,269,502	73,966,194	52,999,804	10,011,188
1970	99,922,069	15,600,000,000	119,965,165	91,367,444	11,300,000
1975	228,909,014	25,156,861,000	262,575,510	163,371,847	12,457,090
1980	599,689,377	35,112,376,000	375,123,084	266,285,020	18,155,000
1985	1,130,736,776	64,439,932,664	713,947,416	475,668,849	26,020,000
1990	1,843,644,324	75,627,946,799	1,101,536,791	739,058,541	14,583,000

Employee Growth: 1935–1991
CUNA Mutual Insurance Society

Year	Number of Employees
1935	2
1940	26
1945	21
1950	41
1955	107
1960	237
1965	428
1970	796
1975	1,380
1980	2,243
1985	2,600
1991	3,641

The Worldwide Credit Union Movement

The CUNA Mutual Insurance Group operates in 58 international areas, including:

Antigua	Ireland	Singapore
Australia	Jamaica	Solomon Islands
Bahamas	Japan	Saint Kitts
Barbados	Korea	Saint Lucia
Belize	Lesotho	Saint Vincent
Bermuda	Liberia	South Africa
Colombia	Malawi	Sri Lanka
Dominica	Mauritius	Surinam
Dominican Republic	Mexico	Taiwan, Rep. of China
Ecuador	Montserrat	Thailand
El Salvador	Netherlands Antilles	Togo
Fiji	New Zealand	Tonga
Grand Cayman	Nigeria	Trinidad & Tobago
Great Britain	Overseas Military Bases	U.S. Trust Territories
Grenada	Panama	Venezuela
Guatemala	Paraguay	Virgin Islands
Guyana	Peru	Western Samoa
Honduras	Puerto Rico	Zambia
Hong Kong	Seychelles	
Indonesia	Sierra Leone	

Estes Park Delegates and Family Members (photo on pages 18,19)

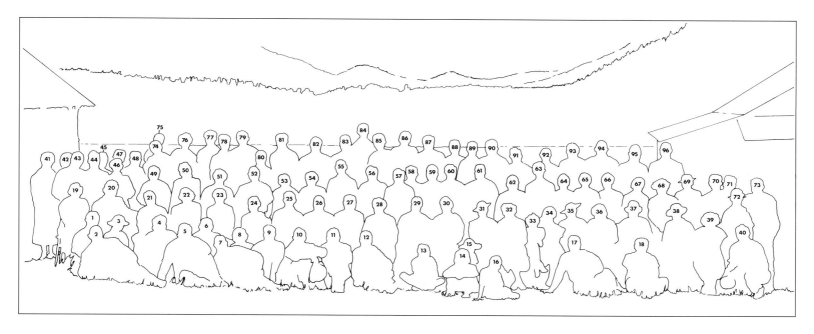

A list identifying the participants at the Estes Park conference in 1934 was included in a box of Roy F. Bergengren's material given to CUNA Mutual by his wife, Gladys. Pictured are: (1) John L. Howard, Colorado; (2) C. T. Bergeron, Texas, (3) Mrs. Howard, Colorado; (4) Andrew J. Percival, Illinois; (5) E. H. Berry, Tennessee; (6) Presley D. Holmes, Illinois; (7) Clyde C. Parker, Alabama; (8) unidentified, (9) Paul A. Boberg, Washington; (10) Mr. Hutchins, Iowa; (11) Brice Martin, Illinois; (12) John L. Moore, California; (13) Jean O'Shaughnessy, Illinois; (14) Prescilla Holmes, Illinois; (15) unidentified, (16) Presley D. Holmes, Jr., Illinois; (17) Joseph Campana, Massachusetts; (18) Sidney Stahl, New York; (19) Effie Eldridge, District of Columbia; (20) Ralph G. Long, Illinois; (21) Mrs. Percival, Illinois; (22) Mildred R. Holmes, Illinois; (23) Mrs. Long, Illinois; (24) Miss Winchester, New York; (25) Claude R. Orchard, Nebraska; (26) Edward A. Filene, Massachusetts; (27) Roy F. Bergengren, Massachusetts; (28) Mrs. Seibert, Kentucky; (29) Mrs. Donahoe, Massachusetts; (30) Mrs. Ingram, Arkansas; (31) Mrs. Pitts, Texas; (32) Mrs. Hutchins, Iowa; (33) unidentified; (34) Claudia Bergeron, Texas; (35) Bess Rentfro, Missouri; (36) Beulah Doig, Minnesota; (37) Gladys Bergengren, Massachusetts; (38) Anna Read, Washington; (39) Lois Doig; (40) Thomas W. Doig, Minnesota; (41) Mabelle Orchard, Nebraska; (42) Agnes C. Gartland, Massachusetts; (43) Clifford O. Skorstad, Minnesota; (44) Emil V. Riley, California; (45) Mr. Winchester, New York; (46) Mrs. Hutchins, Iowa; (47) Harold P. Winchester, New York; (48) Leo Kaminsky, Indiana; (49) Dora Maxwell, New York; (50) unidentified; (51) Mrs. Wanner, Illinois; (52) A. J. Clauter, Illinois; (53) Mrs. Clauter, Illinois; (54) Mrs. Howell, Michigan; (55) Garfield Seibert, Kentucky; (56) Claude E. Clarke, Ohio; (57) Charles F. Donahoe, Massachusetts; (58) Harold L. Loughrey, Minnesota; (59) Earl Rentfro, Missouri; (60) the Rev. J. M. Campbell, Iowa; (61) T. J. O'Shaughnessy, Illinois; (62) Sol Cohen, Illinois; (63) Clyde M. Knodell, Illinois; (64) Mrs. Brainard, Illinois; (65) Mrs. McKeag, Illinois; (66) Miss McKeag, Illinois; (67) Clarissa Kerr, unidentified; (68) Dorothy Bergengren, Massachusetts; (69) Mrs. Pinkney, Missouri; (70) William E. McKibben, Iowa; (71) Bertram B. Fowler, unidentified; (72) Mr. Pitts, Texas; (73) Harry F. Ingram, Arkansas; (74) Louise McCarren, Ohio; (75) James O'Shaughnessy; (76) Mrs. Martin, Illinois; (77) Ben Hillebrandt, Jr., Missouri; (78) Arthur Clauter, Illinois; (79) Ben Hillebrandt, Missouri; (80) Mr. Clauter, Illinois; (81) Jerome K. Eldridge, District of Columbia; (82) J. Clarence Howell, Michigan; (83) E. G. Hampton, Wisconsin; (84) Hubert M. Rhodes, North Carolina; (85) Charles G. Hyland, Wisconsin; (86) Joseph S. DeRamus, Illinois; (87) R. H. Pitts, Texas; (88) Leslie A. Pinkney, Missouri; (89) Arthur L. Wanner, Illinois; (90) A. Neal Hutchins, Iowa; (91) Anton Westergaard, Iowa; (92) Mr. Hill, unidentified; (93) Nial L. Brainard, Illinois; (94) Louis G. Weiler, New York; (95) Albert F. Dodd, Colorado; and (96) Frank D. McKeag, Illinois.

Index

146; Brazil, 145; Canada, 27, 39, 40, 68; C. F. Eikel on, 101, 167; children and, 120; competition, 125, 133-34; conventions, 18-20; cooperative movement and, 85-86; CUNA affiliates, 59; educational aspects, 6, 11; embezzlement, 135; employers and, 10-11; Fiji, 142, 146, 147-48; fraud, 135, 136; Georgia, 11, 12; Hawaii, 48; Illinois, 13, 30-31; interest, 32; international development, 145-53; Ireland, 149; Jamaica, 148; law and legislation, 4, 6, 8, 14, 16-17, 32-33, 150-51, 153; liability, 109-11, 114; Massachusetts, 10; membership, 17, 33; Mexico, 152; Michigan, 85, 107-8, 137-38; Minnesota, 11, 26; Missouri, x; national associations, 17-20; New Hampshire, 6; New York, 11, 87; nonprofit tax status, 67-68; North America, 4; number of, 17, 166; Ohio, 18; Oregon, 107-8; organizers and organizing, 11-14, 60-62; personal property risks, 109-10; Poland, 152-53; President Truman on, 63; Puerto Rico, 144-46, 148; race bias and, 60-61; R. F. Bergengren on, 51; risk management, 135; R. L. Curry on, 122; security, 136; Texas, 6; thrift and, 33; T. W. Doig on, 57; unions and, 60; volunteers and, 11; Wisconsin, 12-13, 15, 47

Cress, J., 15

Crump, Fred L., 125, 163

CUDIS Insurance Society (*See also* CUMIS Life Insurance, Inc.), 127, 134; LOANLINER, 134; renamed, 166

Cugini, Joseph N., 168

CUMIS Insurance Society, 134, 167; and CUNA Mutual, 124-24, 150; Australian registration, 148-49; bond coverage, 114; C. F. Eikel, Jr. and, 109-14; charter,

112; CUMIS Comprehensive Security Policy, 113; Financial Records Policy, 114; 578 Full Discovery Bond, 121, 127; growth, 121; homeowners' insurance, 113; incorporation, 103; in Ireland, 149; joint board meetings, CUNA Mutual, 124; loss ratios, 115; name, 113; organization, 109-14; Package of Protection, 116, 121; Risk Management Program, 135-36; sales staff, 113; stock issue, 113, 115; Travel Accident insurance, 136

CUMIS Life Insurance, Inc., 166; incorporation, 137; premiums, 113-14; purchases Members Life Insurance Company (TX), 161

CUNA Brokerage Services, 135

CUNA Credit Union (Madison, WI), 131

CUNA/CUNA Mutual/CUMIS Insurance Study Committee, 114-16

CUNADATA: CUNA Mutual and, 133

CUNA International: and World Council of Credit Unions, 152

CUNA Mutual Charitable Foundation, 139

CUNA Mutual-CUMIS Services, Ltd. (Canada), 127

CUNA Mutual Financial Services Corporation, 135, 139

CUNA Mutual Insurance Group, 127, 134; organizational structure, 154, 156-57, 164-65

CUNA Mutual Insurance Society (*See also* CUNA Mutual Insurance Group): accountants, 35; advertising, 29, 59-62, 66, 68-69, 70-71, 87, 89; agency system, 112; and Century Life, 160-62, 166; and COLAC, 152-53; and cooperative movement, 86, 107-8; and Credit Union League of Colombia, 152; and Credit Union League of Ireland, 150; and

credit union movement, 30, 33, 102-3, 106, 137; and CUMIS, 124-25, 150; and CUNA, 27-31, 38-39, 42-46, 48-49; 58-59, 76, 78-82, 84-86, 90-92, 94, 97-99, 102, 104-6, 110-16, 122-28, 138; and CUNADATA, 133; and CUNA Supply, 88, 94, 102; and Latin American Confederation of Credit Unions (COLAC), 152; and Solidarity, 152-53; and Wisconsin Insurance Department, 43; and World Council of Credit Unions, 152-53; annual meetings, 90-91; area meetings, 48-49; assets, 166; audits, 38; Australian coverage, 149; board of directors, 27, 83-84, 124, 168; Business Development Consulting Service, 136; business practices, problems of, 38-39; California, offices, 120; Canadian offices, 46, 49, 51, 116, 120; cartoons, 106; C. F. Eikel and, 59-64, 79-84, 90, 94, 96, 98-99, 102-6, 109, 111, 116-19, 121-32, 136, 145-49, 152, 159; C. G. Hyland and, 27-28, 34-37, 59; children and, 120-21; claims (*See also* War claims *under this topic*), 29, 38-39, 50, 146, 169; C. M. Matos and, 144-46, 148-51; community involvement, 139; competition, 59, 102-3, 107-8, 119; computers, 113, 159; contracts, 39; co-operative day care center, 139; coverage, 66, 69, 112, 149, 153; credit disability coverage, 33, 131-32, 134, 167; credit life insurance, 32-33, 38; Credit Union Center, 100, 138-39, 140-41; credit unions and, 120, 167, 169; *Credit Unions on Trial* (videotape), 162; CUNA Mutual Newsletter, 148; customer service, 75, 158-59; deregulation and, 157-63; Dialogue meetings, 132; directors, 85, 161-63, 168; E. A. Filene and, 27-29; E. Rentfro and, 27-29, 33-38, 43-44, 48; elections, 94-95;